TROUT LOCHS OF SCOTLAND

Also available from Collins Willow

THE ART OF SEA TROUT FISHING
Charles McLaren

COARSE FISHING IN IRELAND
Hugh Gough

COLLINS NEW ENCYCLOPEDIA OF FISHING IN BRITAIN AND IRELAND
Edited by Michael Pichard

CONRAD VOSS BARK ON FLYFISHING
Conrad Voss Bark

THE DEEPENING POOL - THE CHRONICLE OF A COMPULSIVE ANGLER
Chris Yates

FISH TALES - A COLLECTION OF TRUE ANGLING STORIES
Billee Chapman Pincher

FISHING THE DRY FLY
Dermot Wilson

THE FLYTIER'S MANUAL
Mike Dawes

JOHN GODDARD'S WATERSIDE GUIDE
John Goddard

MR CRABTREE GOES FISHING
Bernard Venables

THE NEW ILLUSTRATED DICTIONARY OF TROUT FLIES
John Roberts

RIVER TROUT FLYFISHING
Peter Lapsley

SALMON AND SEA-TROUT FISHERIES OF SCOTLAND
Crawford Little

TROUT FROM STILLWATERS
Peter Lapsley

TROUT AND SALMON LOUGHS OF IRELAND
Peter O'Reilly

TROUT LOCHS OF SCOTLAND

Bruce Sandison

CollinsWillow
An Imprint of HarperCollins*Publishers*

First published in Great Britain in 1983 by
Allen and Unwin

Revised third edition published in 1992 by
CollinsWillow
an imprint of HarperCollins*Publishers*
London

Reprinted 1994

**A CIP catalogue record for this book is
available from the British Library**

ISBN 0 00 218414 1

Typeset by axis design
Printed and bound in Hong Kong

Contents

Introduction to the Third Edition

I would like to thank the friends and fellow fishermen who have helped me to revise and update this new edition of Trout Lochs of Scotland. Without their unfailing patience, courtesy and consideration, producing this book would have been impossible. For errors, omissions and other sins of the text, I beg their forgiveness; but I have tried to be as accurate as possible and I very much hope that this book will help all anglers to discover the wonderful joy that is brown trout fishing in Scotland.

Much has happened since I wrote the first edition that has been detrimental to our favourite sport, and to the landscape of my beloved Scotland. Factory-tree-farming for tax-avoidance purposes has devastated thousands of acres of once open moorland, particularly in the magnificent Flow Country of Caithness and Sutherland; and a new threat now faces this area – commercial peat extraction, for barbecue charcoal and horticultural use. Monoculture, blanket afforestation, and commercial peat extraction are potent threats to our environment, and to the quality of game fishing in Scotland. Tree-farming exacerbates the problems of acid rain and causes flash-flooding which can destroy fish spawning grounds; forestry ploughing deposits silt in lochs and rivers, smothering plant life upon which insects, and ultimately fish, depend for food. Commercial peat extraction totally destroys the ecology of whole areas.

In my opinion, as anglers our duty is clear: we must oppose any further environmentally damaging attacks upon the Scottish landscape. I urge you to express your concern by writing to the Scottish Secretary, New St Andrews House, Edinburgh, asking for a total ban on any further tree planting in the Flow Country, and for an end to commercial peat extraction. You might also care to write to the Director of Planning, Highland Regional Council, Glenurquhart Road, Inverness, who supports commercial peat extraction, begging him and his colleagues to think again.

I wish you nothing but well in all your fishing efforts. Scottish wild brown trout are an asset beyond compare, a priceless jewel in Scotland's crown. Come and see for yourself; walk and fish amidst our magnificent mountains and glens, where for company you will have otter, golden eagle, greenshank and curlew – and your own free spirit. Tight lines when you do, and best wishes from the far north.

Bruce Sandison
Hysbackie
Tongue
31 March 1992

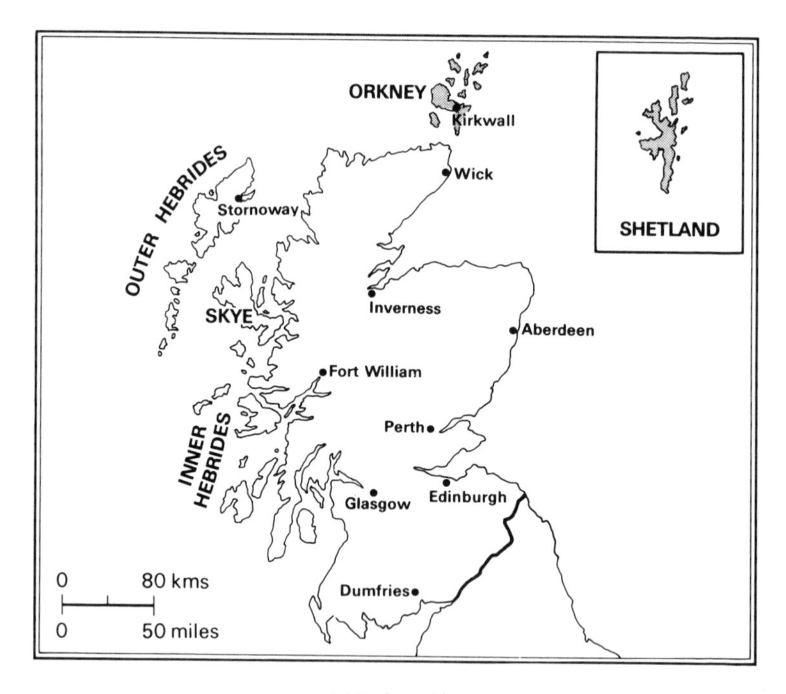

1 Northern Isles

1 Northern Isles

The Northern Isles are magnificent. Whether you arrive by sea or by air you will experience an immediate sense of 'being away from it all'. Gentle isles, full of 'sweet airs that give delight and hurt not '; shining white sands, washed by endless, green, foam-fringed waves; moorlands where you may walk all day without meeting another soul; ancient monuments, such as Skara Brae and Mousa Broch; outstanding wildlife – Arctic skua, hen harrier, snowy owl, black-throated, red-throated and great northern divers, otters and seals – and much more. The islands cast a magic spell, drawing visitors back, year after year. The hardest part, always, is leaving. Fishing and boats are readily available for visiting anglers on Orkney from a number of locations. On Shetland, boats may be hired from the angling association by contacting the Tourist Office in Commercial Street, or Andrew Miller, Club Secretary, The Shetland Anglers' Association, 3 Gladstone Terrace, Lerwick, tel: Lerwick (0595) 3727. Fishing on Orkney and Shetland is, theoretically, free. However, in practice, the superlative quality of sport is maintained by the hard work of the angling clubs. Become a member. By doing so, you will be supporting their efforts and helping to preserve this priceless asset for the pleasure and enjoyment of future generations.

THE LOCHS OF UNST

LOCH OF SNARRAVOE 1/570016

Permission: J. Hunter, The Garage, Baltasound, Unst.
Tel: Baltasound (095781) 306

This is the best loch on Unst and is easily accessible, being near to the road at Belmont. The loch has been stocked with Loch Leven trout in the past and these fish have evolved into beautifully marked, golden trout which fight hard. Bank fishing only, but fish come to the margins to feed, particularly in the evenings. The average weight is 12oz, but trout of up to 4lb 8oz have been taken. Sea trout arrive in August. Use Black Pennell, Kingfisher Butcher and Silver Butcher.

LOCH OF STOURHOULL 1/578028

Permission: Not required

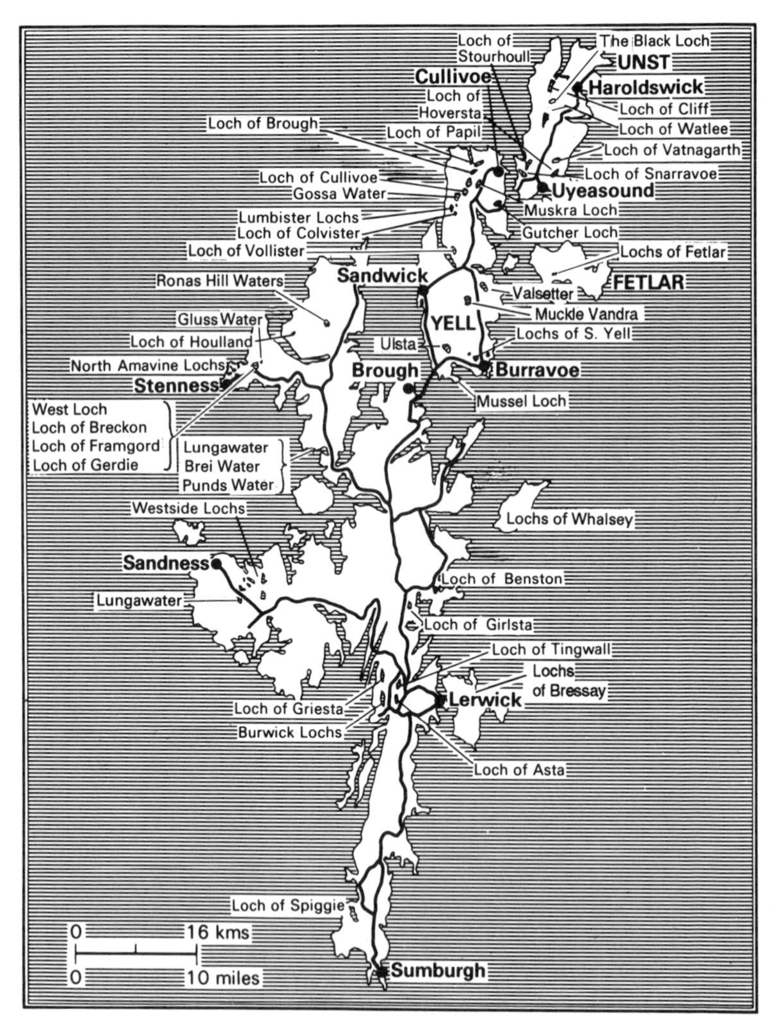

2 Shetland

Take the first left from the pier at Belmont on the A968 and then a short walk south. Stourhoull is a dour loch with a reputation for holding large trout. Fish of up to 3lb 8oz have been caught and, like Snarravoe, Stourhoull has in the past been stocked with Loch Leven trout. Use similar patterns of fly.

1 Fishing a North Unst loch

LOCH OF VATNAGARTH 1/609028
LOCH OF HOVERSTA 1/608026

Permission: Not required

These lochs lie to the north of Mainland near Uyeasound and the A968. Hoversta is the largest and contains the best trout – fish of up to 2lb 8oz – although the average weight is 12oz. The fish are hard to catch so do not expect large baskets. Vatnagarth also holds excellent trout, just as hard to catch, but this loch becomes weedy as the season advances. The margins are soft, making wading dangerous. Stay on the bank and offer them Greenwell's Glory, Grouse & Claret, and various Butchers.

LOCH OF CLIFF 1/600120

Permission: Not required
Boat: Tel: Baltasound (095781) 322/224

This is the largest loch on Unst and the most frequently fished. Approach it from the B9086. Loch of Cliff is peaty, with trout averaging 10oz, and the best fishing areas are down the east and west shores. Sea trout arrive in September and are most often caught at the south end. The loch becomes weedy from July onwards. Flies to use include Greenwell's Glory, Grouse & Claret, Teal Blue & Silver,

Wickham's Fancy and Butchers. Baskets of 10–15 trout are taken frequently and the heaviest fish recorded weighed 10lb. A good loch in a dramatic setting.

LOCH OF WATLEE 1/595055

Permission: Not required

Watlee lies 3 miles south from Loch of Cliff and is linked to it by a feeder stream. Access is from a good track leading out from the A968 at the southern end. Watlee is also peaty, with fish averaging 10oz, but trout of up to 4lb have been taken. Best flies include Black Pennell and Butchers. Watlee is a lovely loch to fish, complete with little island and classic 'fishy' headland on the west shore.

THE BLACK LOCH 1/598064

Permission: Not required

A small, peaty loch to the north of Loch of Watlee (above) in the valley of the Burn of Caldback. The Black Loch is dour, but from time to time produces some really large trout. They may be few and far between, but it is always worth walking over for a cast if things are quiet on Watlee. Concentrate your efforts at the south end. Do not attempt to wade.

HELLIERS WATER 1/610047

Permission: Not required

This water lies to the east of the A968, and is approached along a good track, followed by a half-hour's walk. It has a glorious setting on the moorlands by Burral Knowe and Vord Hill.

THE LOCH OF GARTH 1/545006

Permission: Not required

Because there are no fish in it.

KIRK LOCH 1/532050

Permission: Not required

Since the second edition of this book, Kirk Loch has been stocked and it still contains a few very good fish of up to 5lb. But be warned: they are very difficult to catch.

LOCHS OF NORTH YELL

LOCH OF PAPIL 1/541042

Permission: Not required – but a subscription to the Yell Anglers' Association should be paid to David Nisbet, The Secretary, Yell Anglers' Association, Altona, Mid Yell.
Tel: Mid Yell (0957) 2037

Papil lies to the east of Greenbank, north from Cullivoe on the B9803, on the cliffs between Papil Bay and Bay of Brough. Trout average 6oz, fight hard and rise well to the fly. Although the loch is weedy at times, there is an area along the north shore which always remains clear. Bank fishing only and take care – there is a bad hole at the north end by the stony beach. Use standard pattern loch flies.

LOCH OF BROUGH 1/530030

Permission: Not required – but a subscription to the Yell Anglers' Association should be paid to David Nisbet, The Secretary, Yell Anglers' Association, Altona, Mid Yell.
Tel: Mid Yell (0957) 2037

Approach from the stony road west from Cullivoe. This loch provides the water supply for North Yell and the building of the dam has not helped the fishing. Nevertheless, reasonable baskets may be taken and trout average 8–12oz, with the occasional fish of 2–3lb. Bank fishing only. Beware of the soft margins and do not attempt to wade.

LOCH OF CULLIVOE 1/534023

Permission: Not required – but a subscription to the Yell Anglers' Association should be paid to David Nisbet, The Secretary, Yell Anglers' Association, Altona, Mid Yell.
Tel: Mid Yell (0957) 2037

Park at the Loch of Brough (above), west from Cullivoe, and walk south-west over the moor. Cullivoe is the best loch in the area and contains good trout averaging 8–10oz with the odd fish of up to 2lb. Bank fishing only and wading requires great care. There are large, hidden boulders, just below the surface, particularly in the north-west corner. Use standard pattern loch flies.

MUSKRA LOCH 1/522021

Permission: Not required – but a subscription to the Yell Anglers' Association should be paid to David Nisbet, The Secretary, Yell

Anglers' Association, Altona, Mid Yell.
Tel: Mid Yell (0957) 2037

This is a small loch to the south of Cullivoe and Brough with a dour reputation, but it is easily accessible and can often produce excellent results. Certainly worth a few casts and look out for large fish. Use standard pattern loch flies.

GOSSA WATER 1/49000

Permission: Not required – but a subscription to the Yell Anglers' Association should be paid to David Nisbet, The Secretary, Yell Anglers' Association, Altona, Mid Yell.
Tel: Mid Yell (0957) 2037

The largest loch on Yell, to the west of the A968, it is best approached by following up the Burn of Gossawater from the road. Occasionally fish of up to 3lb have been caught, but the average weight is in the order of 6–8oz. Depending upon water levels in the burn, sea trout may be caught from September onwards. Use standard pattern loch flies.

LOCH OF COLVISTER 1/500970

Permission: Not required – but a subscription to the Yell Anglers' Association should be paid to David Nisbet, The Secretary, Yell Anglers' Association, Altona, Mid Yell.
Tel: Mid Yell (0957) 2037

To the west of the A968, north from Camb, approached from Colvister village by following up the outlet burn from the road. A dour loch, not much fished, with trout averaging three to the pound. There are some larger fish, so have a cast on your way over the moor – there is much better to come.

LOCHS OF LUMBISTER 1/485965

Permission: Not required – but a subscription to the Yell Anglers' Association should be paid to David Nisbet, The Secretary, Yell Anglers' Association, Altona, Mid Yell.
Tel: Mid Yell (0957) 2037

A wonderful series of six lochs, lying 2 miles west from the A968. Approach from Loch of Colvister (above). Trout average 6–8oz, with the occasional larger fish, and all the lochs offer excellent sport. Local angler Ian Nisbet tells me that the main loch is the most beautiful in Yell, with sandy bays and delightful small islands. He says, 'Fish caught are a bonus.'

LOCH OF GUTCHER 1/548993

Permission: Not required – but a subscription to the Yell Anglers' Association should be paid to David Nisbet, The Secretary, Yell Anglers' Association, Altona, Mid Yell.
Tel: Mid Yell (0957) 2037

A small loch at the end of the A968, close to the ferry terminal to Unst. Good trout averaging 8oz with easy bank fishing. From August to October there can be great sport with sea trout. Perfect for an evening cast, and with wonderful views to Fetlar and Unst. Use standard pattern loch flies.

LOCHS OF MID YELL

LOCH OF VOLLISTER 1/478943

Permission: Not required – but a subscription to the Yell Anglers' Association should be paid to David Nisbet, The Secretary, Yell Anglers' Association, Altona, Mid Yell.
Tel: Mid Yell (0957) 2037

Vollister is an RSPB reserve and anglers should take great care to avoid disturbing nesting birds. The loch lies on the north shore of Whale Firth and is a stiff walk out from Windhouse on the A968. Good-quality trout averaging 12oz, with fish of up to 2lb, are taken most seasons. Utterly superb setting.

HOULLS WATER 1/455953
VIRCH WATER 1/452938
CRO WATER 1/450937

Permission: Not required – but a subscription to the Yell Anglers' Association should be paid to David Nisbet, The Secretary, Yell Anglers' Association, Altona, Mid Yell.
Tel: Mid Yell (0957) 2037

These lochs lie to the south of Whale Firth, guarded by The Herra, and are best approached from the minor road leading off the A968 just south of Windhouse at the head of the firth. Walk out from Efstigarth. You will find hard-fighting trout amidst some of the finest scenery in Scotland.

LUNGA WATER 1/460899
SAND WATER 1/465900
MILL LOCH 1/448902

LOCH OF BIRRIESGIRT 1/442910

Permission: Not required – but a subscription to the Yell Anglers' Association should be paid to David Nisbet, The Secretary, Yell Anglers' Association, Altona, Mid Yell.
Tel: Mid Yell (0957) 2037

All these waters offer good sport with small trout, and the odd larger fish, to keep your interest. They lie close to the village of West Sandwick and, apart from Birriesgirt, are easily accessible. Birriesgirt lies on the cliffs, north from Mill Loch, in a shallow valley between Burn Hill and The Head. Use standard pattern loch flies.

LOCH OF VALSETTER 2/534892

Permission: Not required – but a subscription to the Yell Anglers' Association should be paid to David Nisbet, The Secretary, Yell Anglers' Association, Altona, Mid Yell.
Tel: Mid Yell (0957) 2037

A large loch with a large population of trout which average three to the pound. Easily accessible by car and the ideal place for beginners. Approach from Mid Yell, round the Hill of Liussetter to North Westerhouse. Sea trout may be caught from August onwards. Bank fishing only, using standard pattern loch flies.

MUCKLE VANDRA WATER 2/486894

Permission: Not required – but a subscription to the Yell Anglers' Association should be paid to David Nisbet, The Secretary, Yell Anglers' Association, Altona, Mid Yell.
Tel: Mid Yell (0957) 2037

A long walk in from Mid Yell, but worth every step of the way. Approach from the school in the village and follow up the course of the Laxa Burn. After 1½ miles bear right, where the outlet stream from Muckle Vandra joins the Laxa.

LOCHS OF SOUTH YELL

LOCH OF KETTLESTER 2/513805
LOCH OF LITTLESTER 2/513797
LOCH OF NEAPABACK 2/525807

Permission: Not required – but a subscription to the Yell Anglers' Association should be paid to David Nisbet, The Secretary, Yell Anglers' Association, Altona, Mid Yell.
Tel: Mid Yell (0957) 2037

Boat on Littlester: J. C. Wilson, The Manor House, Yell.
Tel: Burravoe (095782) 233

Littlester is the most productive loch, although it can prove to be dour at times. Already this season (1991) trout of 5lb and 8lb 8oz have been caught. The best fishing area is round the south-west shore, towards the outlet burn. Kettlester, to the north of the village, has fish of 12oz and there are plenty of them. Neapaback also offers good sport, and all these lochs are easily accessible. Use standard pattern loch flies.

LOCH OF ULSTA 2/472812

Permission: Not required – but a subscription to the Yell Anglers' Association should be paid to David Nisbet, The Secretary, Yell Anglers' Association, Altona, Mid Yell.
Tel: Mid Yell (0957) 2037

The ideal place for beginners, Ulsta is close to the B9081, 2 miles from the ferry pier. It is full of small trout which average three to the pound and they rise readily to the standard pattern loch flies.

MUSSEL LOCH 2/472788

Permission: Not required – but a subscription to the Yell Anglers' Association should be paid to David Nisbet, The Secretary, Yell Anglers' Association, Altona, Mid Yell.
Tel: Mid Yell (0957) 2037

This loch is situated at the southern end of the island, above Wester Wick of Copister and the Sound of Brough. Follow the minor road that runs east from the pier, then turn south along the line of the Saidlas Burn. Trout average 12oz and are of splendid quality. Bank fishing only and, other than at the south-east end, very difficult wading.

LOCHS OF FETLAR

PAPIL WATER 2/605905
SKUTES WATER 2/623981
WINYADEPLA 2/640930
LOCH OF FUNZIE 2/655900

Permission: Not required

These are four excellent lochs on one of the most lovely of the Shetland islands. Papil is the most easily accessible and contains good trout of up to 2lb. Skutes is the public water supply and has fish of 8oz, along with some stocked rainbow trout. Funzie also contains 8-oz trout and lies close to the B9088 road. Winyadepla is the most remote water, involving a 2-mile hike over the moor to the Hill of Mongirsdale. The scenery is spectacular but you will have to work hard for a fish – Winyadepla is dour – although you may be rewarded with a trout of up to 3lb. Large stones make wading difficult, so take great care.

LOCHS OF WHALSAY

LOCH OF HUXTER 2/558623
LOCH OF LIVISTER 2/558631
LOCH OF ISBISTER 2/577643
LOCH OF VATSHOULL 2/571658
NUCKRO WATER 2/569635

Permission: Brian J. Polson, Whalsay Anglers' Association, Sheardaal, Huxter, Symbister, Whalsay.
Tel: Symbister (08066) 472

The Whalsay lochs offer visiting anglers excellent sport with superb-quality, hard-fighting trout, and in 1983 George Irvine took a trout of 9lb 4oz from Loch of Huxter, caught on a Black Pennell. All the lochs are easily accessible, and on Isbister trout average 12–14oz, with occasional fish of up to 3lb. The best fish in recent years weighed 4lb 10oz; Huxter trout average 10–12oz; Nuckro Water, a small, shallow loch with a rocky bottom, has fish which average 1lb and some considerably larger specimens.

LOCHS OF BRESSAY

LOCHS OF BEOSETTER 4/490437

Permission: Andrew Miller, The Shetland Anglers' Association, 3 Gladstone Terrace, Lerwick.
Tel: Lerwick (0595) 3729

A series of four interlinked lochs at the north of the island, west from Gunnista. In the past, the association has stocked these lochs, and West Beosetter, also known as Loch of Cruester, has the best reputation, with trout averaging 1lb and fish of 4lb occasionally being taken.

LOCH OF BROUGH 3/512408
LOCH OF SETTER 3/514418

Permission: Andrew Miller, The Shetland Anglers' Association, 3 Gladstone Terrace, Lerwick.
Tel: Lerwick (0595) 3729

Both lie to the west of Ander Hill lochs and may easily be fished during the course of a day. Brough has the larger fish, which average 10oz, and wading is comfortable. Setter trout average 8oz and wading is not recommended. Standard pattern loch flies do the damage.

LOCHS OF MAINLAND SHETLAND

LOCH OF HOULLAND 3/215792
LOCH OF GERDIE 3/206782
LOCH OF BRECKON 3/214779
LOCH OF FRAMGORD 3/209785

Permission: Andrew Miller, The Shetland Anglers' Association, 3 Gladstone Terrace, Lerwick.
Tel: Lerwick (0595) 3729

These lochs are situated in Esha Ness in north-west mainland and are the most consistently productive of all mainland waters. Houlland is a classic limestone loch which produces fish of up to 7lb and fishes best round the north and east shore. The other lochs are all capable of producing trout of up to 2lb, but as they are shallow they tend to be affected by weed as the season advances. Wading can be difficult and it is best to fish these waters early in the season.

GLUSS WATER 3/256814

Permission: Andrew Miller, The Shetland Anglers' Association, 3 Gladstone Terrace, Lerwick.
Tel: Lerwick (0595) 3729

Follow the B907 to Braewick and then turn north on the minor road. Park near the Giants Stones. Gluss Water lies at the end of the rough track in Scora Field. A dour water, but with the possibility of the odd trout of up to 3lb. The average weight is 12oz. Loch Ordie, Black Pennell and Butchers.

RONAS HILL LOCHS

SANDY WATER 3/305865
LOCH OF MANY CROOKS 3/314864
LOCH OF HADD 3/305865
SWABIE WATER 3/311854
TONGA WATER 2/333875
LANG CLODIE 1/312878

LITTLE LUNGA 1/320882
MUCKLE LUNGA 1/327884
BIRKA WATER 1/316875
ROER WATER 2/336863

Permission: Andrew Miller, The Shetland Anglers' Association, 3 Gladstone Terrace, Lerwick.
Tel: Lerwick (0595) 3729

Offering some of the finest fishing in Scotland, and situated in really stunning surroundings, the lochs around Ronas Hill have something for everyone. A veritable hill-walker's and angler's paradise. All the waters contain hard-fighting trout which vary in size from 8oz up to 3lb and more. My favourites are Little Lunga, Muckle Lunga and Birka Water, which has one of the most dramatic waterfalls that I have ever seen. Compass and map country, and everlasting, wonderful memories.

LUNGAWATER 3/319708
BREI WATER 3/318712
PUNDS WATER 3/325715

Permission: Andrew Miller, The Shetland Anglers' Association, 3 Gladstone Terrace, Lerwick.
Tel: Lerwick (0595) 3729

North from Klev on the A970 Hillswick road, turn left towards Mangaster. This series of lochs may be fished in circuit and you should allow a full day to do them justice. Don't wade. Wear stout walking shoes and fish from the shore.

LUNGA WATER 3/235525
THE SMA LOCHS 3/228524

Permission: Andrew Miller, The Shetland Anglers' Association, 3 Gladstone Terrace, Lerwick.
Tel: Lerwick (0595) 3729

A roadside loch which forms part of the public water supply. Trout average 10oz, although some 2-lb fish are caught. Avoid wading. To the south-west of Lunga Water, but approached from Walls via the track to the radio station, lie the Sma Lochs, three excellent little lochs, all containing good trout.

WEST SIDE LOCHS

CLINGSWATER 3/310558

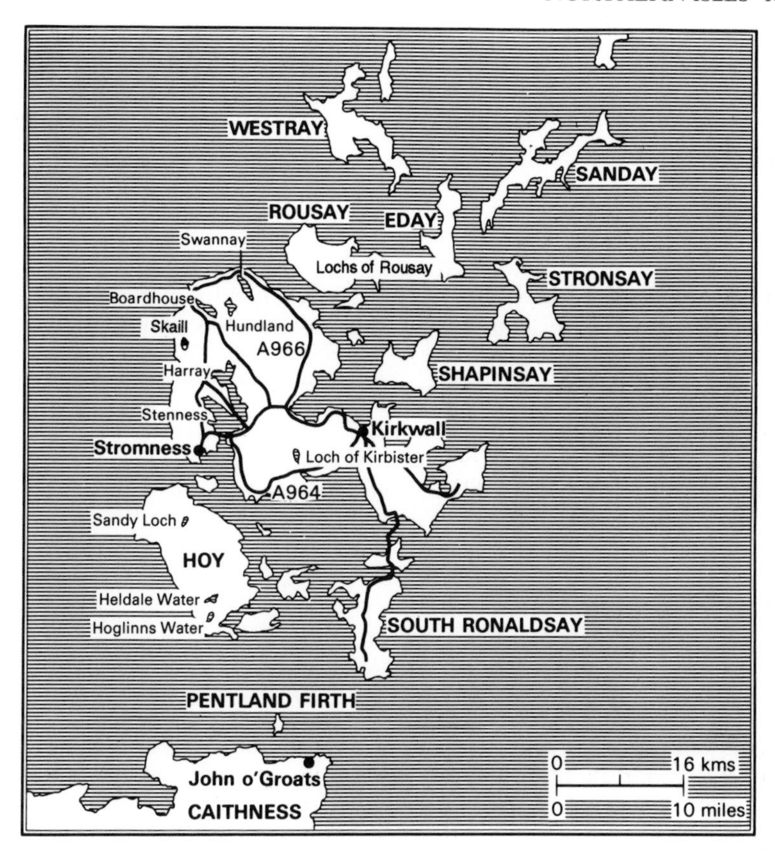

3 Orkney

MOUSA WATER 3/288443
LOCH OF GRUTING 3/294503
LOCH OF GRUNNAVOE 3/258493
LOCH OF HOLLORIN 3/276558
SULMA WATER 3/261551

Permission: Andrew Miller, The Shetland Anglers' Association, 3 Gladstone Terrace, Lerwick.
Tel: Lerwick (0595) 3729

Follow the A971 north-west from Lerwick until you run out of road. In the immediate vicinity there are more than 40 trout lochs, all offering good sport, with those noted above being but a small sample of the variety of excellent fishing available. Clingswater can produce fish of up to 1lb 8oz, Mousa, trout averaging 10oz, with others up to 2lb 8oz. Hollorin fish average 14oz, and sea trout visit Sulma from August onwards. Reserve at least a months's fishing – and you will still not have time for them all. Invicta, Black Zulu, Soldier Palmer and Loch Ordie produce results.

EAST SIDE LOCHS

LOCH OF SKELLISTER 3/460563

Permission: Andrew Miller, The Shetland Anglers' Association, 3 Gladstone Terrace, Lerwick.
Tel: Lerwick (0595) 3729

This loch lies to the west of the B9075 in South Nesting. Approach along a rough track from Newing. Apart from the northwest shore, where, with care, it is possible to wade, stay on the bank. This can be a dour, frustrating loch, but fish of over 4lb have been taken

LAXO WATER 3/445653

Permission: Andrew Miller, The Shetland Anglers' Association, 3 Gladstone Terrace, Lerwick.
Tel: Lerwick (0595) 3729

The ideal place for beginners, full of small, breakfast-sized trout which average 5–6oz. Nevertheless, they rise readily to the fly and give a good account of themselves. The real beauty of Laxo Water is, however, its remote setting, and this is a perfect place to spend a day 'away from it all'.

CENTRAL AND SOUTH MAINLAND LOCHS

LOCH OF GIRLSTA 3/435520

Permission: Andrew Miller, The Shetland Anglers' Association, 3 Gladstone Terrace, Lerwick.
Tel: Lerwick (0595) 3729

This loch is adjacent to the A970, 10 miles north from Lerwick. It is 1½ miles long by up to ¼ mile wide and can be a wild, windy, dangerous place, either afloat or when fishing from the bank. Take great care at all times, and avoid wading, particularly from the east shore, where you may be tempted out onto a dangerous sandbank. Also, look out for excellent sport. Girlsta has produced fish up to 12lb 8oz and the average weight is 1lb. A Loch Ordie is the best fly to tempt them.

LOCH OF BENSTON 3/462535

Permission: Andrew Miller, The Shetland Anglers' Association, 3 Gladstone Terrace, Lerwick.
Tel: Lerwick (0595) 3729

A glorious loch with great fish averaging over 1lb, and each season producing trout of up to 3lb. It is regularly stocked by the association and well managed. The best fishing area is along the shore near the church. Use Loch Ordie, Soldier Palmer and Black Pennell.

LOCH OF GRIESTA 4/408438
LOCH OF USTANESS 4/399434
BROO LOCH 4/399442
JAMIE CHEYNE'S LOCH 4/400428
MAGGIE BLACK'S LOCH 4/397424
LOCH OF GARTH 4/402423

Permission: Andrew Miller, The Shetland Anglers' Association, 3 Gladstone Terrace, Lerwick.
Tel: Lerwick (0595) 3729

Griesta is an excellent limestone loch to the west of the B9074, north of Scalloway. Trout average 12oz, but several heavier fish are taken each season. Permission also includes fishing on the series of lochs to the south of Griesta in the area of Setter Hill and the Hill of Burwick which contain trout averaging 8–10oz. Use standard pattern loch flies.

LOCH OF TINGWALL 4/414425
LOCH OF ASTA 4/413415

Permission: Andrew Miller, The Shetland Anglers' Association, 3 Gladstone Terrace, Lerwick.
Tel: Lerwick (0595) 3729

The most popular loch on Mainland, to the west of Lerwick, easily accessible and regularly stocked by the association. Trout average 10–14oz and a good day should produce a basket of up to 10 fish. The shallow southern bay fishes well, but the best drift is in the north bay, from the north-east corner, south-west across the loch – or the other way round, depending upon the wind. Bank fishing is most productive in the vicinity of the island, where the loch narrows, from either shore. Asta also contains brown trout of excellent quality and the east bank is the most productive fishing area. Both lochs are limestone waters. Use standard pattern loch flies.

LOCH OF SPIGGIE 4/373166

Permission: Andrew Miller, The Shetland Anglers' Association, 3 Gladstone Terrace, Lerwick.
Tel: Lerwick (0595) 3729

Spiggie, one of the largest lochs in Shetland, can be waded from shore to shore at the north end where the best bank fishing is a spot known as 'The Deep'. Chest waders are required to reach it. From the boat, the east and west shores are the most productive areas. A good basket should produce five or six trout averaging 12oz to 1lb, but fish of up to 6lb have been caught in recent years. An RSPB conservation area, it is a beautiful loch to fish, in spite of its proximity to Sumburgh Airport.

LOCHS OF ORKNEY

LOCH OF BOARDHOUSE 6/270260

Permission: Not required, but visitors should subscribe to the Orkney Trout Fishing Association. Contact: W. S. Sinclair, 27 John Street, Stromness, for details.

Boardhouse is a shallow loch which fishes well over its total area. No one place is substantially better than another, but my favourite fishing area is at the southern end, round the weed beds in the centre of the loch. Trout average 12oz and baskets of up to a dozen fish are taken frequently, with the occasional trout of 4lb being caught. Use standard pattern loch flies, but always have a Ke-He on the 'bob'.

LOCH OF HARRAY 6/300140

Permission: Not required, but visitors should subscribe to the Orkney Trout Fishing Association. Contact: W. S. Sinclair, 27 John Street, Stromness, for details.

Harray, the most popular Orkney loch, is 6 miles long by 1½ miles wide. Trout are of superb quality – silvery, hard-fighting and pink-fleshed. Although the average weight is 12oz, each season produces fish of 4lb and over; the heaviest fish taken from the loch, in 1964, weighed 17lb 8oz. Bank fishing can be as productive as boat fishing, especially in Kirk Bay by Tormiston Burn, where sea trout may be caught, but take great care when afloat: the loch is scattered with sudden skerries, rocky outcrops, just below the surface. Find them and fish in these areas, as well as along the margins, particularly in the vicinity of the burn mouths at Ballarat on the east bank and Bankhead at the north end. Below the Ring of Brodgar is also a favourite fishing area and, on the east shore, Holm Bay. Flies to use include Black Pennell, Ke-He, Wickham's Fancy, Greenwell's Glory, Soldier Palmer, Invicta and Butchers.

LOCH OF HUNDLAND 6/295260

Permission: Not required, but visitors should subscribe to the Orkney Trout Fishing Association. Contact: W. S. Sinclair, 27 John Street, Stromness, for details.

This small, shallow, peaty loch lies between Swannay and Boardhouse and has a reputation for being dour. It is stocked by the association and the best fishing areas are at the southern end, where the Burn of Hillside enters the loch. Trout average 12oz but fish of over 2lb are not uncommon. This is the loch to head for on bright, sunny days. Use standard pattern loch flies.

LOCH OF STENNESS 6/280130

Permission: Not required, but visitors should subscribe to the Orkney Trout Fishing Association. Contact: W. S. Sinclair, 27 John Street, Stromness, for details.

Stenness is the most scenic of the major Orkney lochs, dominated by the backdrop of the mountains of Hoy, overlooked by the Stenness Standing Stones and the Ring of Brodgar. The largest trout ever caught on Orkney came from this wonderful loch and weighed 29lb 8oz. The quality of trout is superlative, both in their fighting capabilities and in their appearance. But they are hard brutes to catch and blank days are frequent. However, the rewards for trying can be spectacular and fish of up to 7lb may be caught. The loch is connected directly to the sea, and consequently the water is brackish. Apart from brown trout and sea trout, turbot, garfish, mullet, saithe, lyth, herring and cod all visit the loch and are sometimes taken. But above all, Stenness is probably one of the most exciting trout lochs in Scotland. Bank fishing is excellent and all the standard pattern loch flies can produce results. Crossing the fingers helps as well.

LOCH OF SWANNAY 6/310280

Permission: Not required, but visitors should subscribe to the Orkney Trout Fishing Association. Contact: W. S. Sinclair, 27 John Street, Stromness, for details.

Swannay is my personal favourite and lies in the northern part of Mainland. It is a shallow loch, so high winds can churn up the bottom, making for difficult fishing conditions, but the quality of Swannay trout, and their fighting ability, more than compensate for such minor discomforts. Boat fishing is most productive and the best areas to fish are southwards from Dale Farm on the west shore and round the island of Muckle Holm. Nevertheless, bank fishing can be just as good, although great care must be taken when wading. Standard pattern loch flies do the damage, but always have on either a Black Pennell or a Black Zulu. Trout average in the order of 1lb and each season produces good numbers of fish of between 2 and 4lb.

LOCH OF KIRBISTER 6/370080

Permission: Not required, but visitors should subscribe to the Orkney Trout Fishing Association. Contact: W. S. Sinclair, 27 John Street, Stromness, for details.

Kirbister lies 5 miles west from Kirkwall, along the A964, and it is the ideal beginner's loch. Trout average 8oz, are very pretty, and fight well. No boats, but wading is comfortable, particularly in the vicinity of Breck along the north shore.

LOCH OF SKAILL 6/240180

Permission: Restricted access. Permission must be obtained from the Orkney Trout Fishing Association. Contact: W. S. Sinclair, 27 John Street, Stromness

Until fairly recently this loch was strictly preserved, but limited access is now available. In the past some enormous trout have been taken from this little loch, and it can still produce trout of superb quality. Park the family on the beach at Bay of Skaill and look out for action. Use standard pattern loch flies.

LOCH OF CLUMLY 6/255165

Permission: As for the other Orkney Lochs

Clumly is a small water, south from Loch of Skaill (above), close to the A967. Permission to approach the loch should be obtained before fishing from the local farmer, Queena Farm, just north of the crossroads by Hestwall. Fish of up to 2lb may be caught. Bank fishing, and the only fishing area is from the north shore.

LOCHS OF HOY

SANDY WATER 7/250914
HELDALE WATER 7/255923
HOGLINNS WATER 7/250914

Permission: Not required

Although the quality of fishing on these lochs may not match the sport to be had on Mainland, their magnificent setting is reason enough for visiting them. There are regular ferries from Mainland and all these waters have good fish of up to 5lb. Few anglers fish on Hoy – which is another good reason for giving them a try – and your efforts could produce 'one for the glass case'.

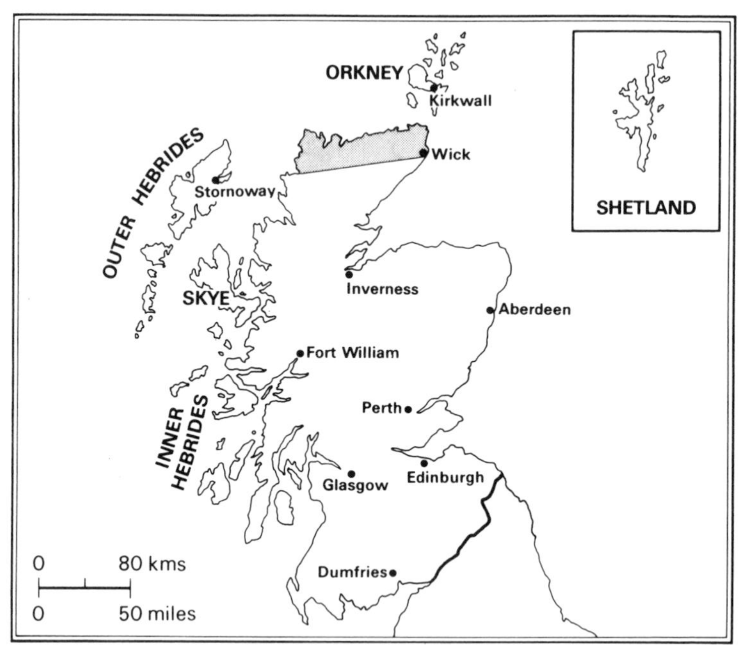

4 Caithness and North Sutherland

2 Caithness and North Sutherland

Few areas in Europe can match the diversity and quality of trout fishing in Caithness and North Sutherland. There is an endless array of wonderful lochs set amidst some of the most dramatic scenery in Scotland; from the gentle lowlands of Caithness to the rugged splendour of Ben Loyal, Ben Hope, Foinaven, Arkle and Ben Stack in the west, exciting fishing awaits. Loch Watten, in Caithness, is one of Scotland's finest fisheries; the Durness limestone lochs are utterly magnificent and beyond compare; the hundreds of hill lochs round Scourie are full of wild brown trout, all just waiting for your first, well-presented cast. It would take several lifetimes to do justice to all the fishing that the area has to offer. Don't waste another moment – pack your rod and head north – now !

LOCHS OF CAITHNESS

LOCH WATTEN 11/230560

Permission:
Hugo Ross, Tackle Shop, 16 Breadalbane Crescent, Wick.
Tel: Wick (0955) 4200
The Loch Watten Hotel, Watten.
Tel: Watten (095582) 232
David Gunn, Watten Lodge, Watten.
Tel: Watten (095582) 217
J. A. Barnetson, Lynegar Farm, Watten.
Tel: Watten (095582) 205
John Swanson, Aspen Bank, Banks Road, Watten.
Tel: Watten (095582) 326
Harpers Fly Fishing Services, Drill Hall, Sinclair Street, Thurso.
Tel: Thurso (0847) 63179
Facilities for Disabled Anglers: Contact G. Douglas, 53 Brownhill Road, Thurso.
Tel: Thurso (0847) 64216

Loch Watten is a shallow, marl loch, 3 miles long by up to 1/2 mile wide. Trout rise and are caught throughout, from the shallows to the middle, north, south, east and west. Fish with confidence, anywhere. My favourite drift is from Factor's Bay (at the Watten end), down the

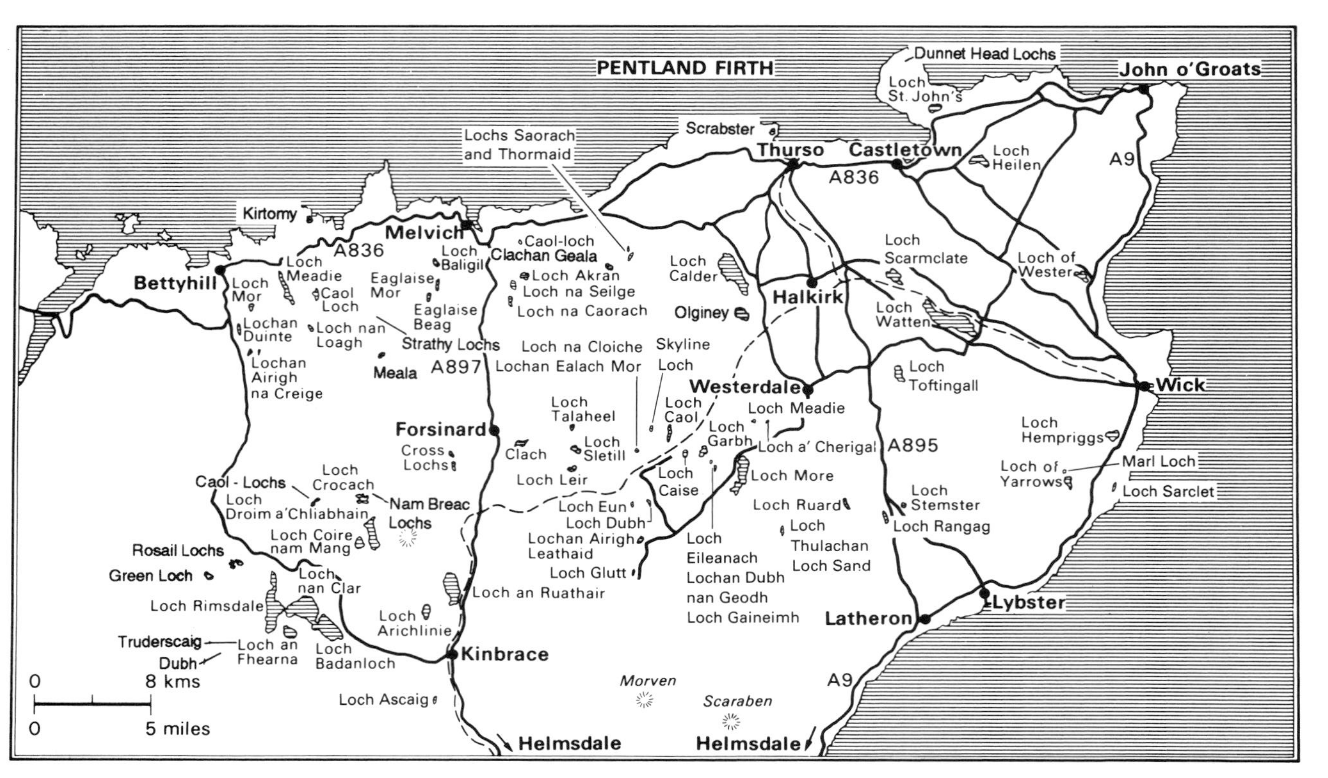

5 Caithness, Strath Halladale and Strathnaver

2 Hay time at Loch Watten

north shore, past the fence post and into Lynegar Bay with its small island. At the north end, fish in the vicinity of the red boat house near Oldhall, and in Shearer's Pool, where the burn runs in from Loch Scarmclate. Trout average 1lb with much heavier trout being caught – one of 4lb 8oz during 1990. A few salmon enter the loch from the Wick River, and in the past six years two have been landed. Try a Ke-He on the 'bob', Greenwell's Glory in the middle, and a Silver Butcher on the tail. Pack an outboard motor and a drogue and look out for sea trout–silver fish of the highest quality.

LOCH SCARMCLATE 12/200595

Permission: Harpers Fly Fishing Services, Drill Hall, Sinclair Street, Thurso.
Tel: Thurso (0847) 63179
Facilities for Disabled Anglers: Contact G. Douglas, 53 Brownhill Road, Thurso.
Tel: Thurso (0847) 64216

Also known locally as Stemster Loch, but not to be confused with Loch Stemster at Achavanich (see below). Scarmclate is joined to Watten (above) and acts as a nursery for its more famous neighbour. Access is from the A882 Wick–Thurso road, down a rough track, crossing the railway. Wading is dangerous and boat fishing is most productive on this shallow, sometimes weedy loch. Recently, the average weight of trout has improved and is now in the order of 12–14oz. Scarmclate trout fight just as well as Watten fish and this is a good place for beginners. Wonderful bird life is a bonus.

LOCH CALDER 11/070600

Permission: D. G. Mackay, Achaguie, Scotscalder, Halkirk.
Tel: Halkirk (084783) 650
Harpers Fly Fishing Services, Drill Hall, Sinclair Street, Thurso.
Tel: Thurso (0847) 63179
Facilities for Disabled Anglers: Contact G. Douglas, 53 Brownhill Road, Thurso.
Tel: Thurso (0847) 64216

Calder is the largest and deepest loch in Caithness, 120 feet deep at the north end, and is the water supply for the town of Thurso. It contains a multitude of small brown trout, Arctic char and some very large *ferox*. Trout of up to 7lb have been caught in recent years and fish of over 3lb are not uncommon. The margins, owing to water fluctuations, become soft and dangerous, so fish from a boat. Also, along the west shore, the water deepens quickly in several places. This loch can be very wild, so you need an outboard motor, to be safe, and a good drogue. Fish the shallow, western bays at the south end, then work up the west shore. Use standard pattern loch flies.

LOCH OLGINEY 11/090573

Permission: Harpers Fly Fishing Services, Drill Hall, Sinclair Street, Thurso.
Tel: Thurso (0847) 63179

Olginey lies to the south of Loch Calder, to the west of the B870, and is reputed to have been stocked many years ago with fish from Loch Heilen. This is a shallow loch which becomes cloudy in high winds. Wading is comfortable, with care, and trout average in the order of 10–12oz. Standard pattern loch flies work well.

LOCH ST JOHN'S 12/225720

Permission: The Northern Sands Hotel, Dunnet, Caithness.
Tel: Barrock (084785) 270
Facilities for Disabled Anglers: Contact G. Douglas, 53 Brownhill Road, Thurso.
Tel: Thurso (0847) 64216

One of the best-known lochs in Scotland, famed for the size and quality of its trout. The loch is efficiently managed by an excellent association, who have their own hatchery which stocks the loch using native species. Best drift is from the harbour directly north to the mouth of the spawning burn. There is a good mayfly hatch in late June, the best time to fish St John's.

DUNNET HEAD LOCHS

MANY LOCHS 12/200748
SANDERS LOCH 12/187748
BLACK LOCH 12/203745
SANDERS LOCH 12/210754
LONG LOCH 12/205760
LOCH OF EASTERHEAD 12/208763

Permission: Brough Tea Room, Dunnet, Caithness.

The Dunnet Head Fishing Club manages these delightful little lochs, visited as much for the beauty of their surroundings as for the quality of sport. They may also claim the distinction of being the most northerly trout lochs on mainland Britain and simply to be there is reward enough. Outstanding bird life, with a good possibility of meeting red-throated divers.

LOCH HEILEN 11/255685

Permission: Hamish Pottinger, Greenland Mains, Castletown.
Tel: Castletown (084782) 210
Harpers Fly Fishing Services, Drill Hall, Sinclair Street, Thurso.
Tel: Thurso (0847) 63179

My favourite Caithness loch, containing wonderful fish, but they are the very devil to catch. Blank days are frequent. Nevertheless, I keep going back because specimen trout of the highest quality frequent this shallow, weedy water. In recent years, a trout of 8lb 8oz was landed and fish of 3–4lb are taken regularly. Bank fishing is just as productive as fishing from the boat – the 8-lb 8-oz monster was hooked from the bank – and on balance I prefer bank fishing. Creep up on them silently on a warm June evening, fingers crossed. Use Loch Ordie, Black Pennell and Silver Butcher.

SCRABSTER LOCH 12/087704

Permission: Harpers Fly Fishing Services, Drill Hall, Sinclair Street, Thurso.
Tel: Thurso (0847) 63179

A small loch on Holburn Head, above Scrabster Harbour, stocked in recent years and now a popular venue for both local and visiting anglers because of its easy access. Bank fishing only. Trout average 12oz and may be taken anywhere along the shoreline.

LOCH OF TOFTINGALL 12/190520

Permission: Mrs Atkinson, c/o The Bradford & Bingley Building Society, Sinclair Street, Thurso.
Tel: Thurso (0847) 63291

This loch is close to Watten village, but is now surrounded by commercial forestry. Toftingall still holds good stocks of trout which average 10oz, and the odd larger fish is occasionally caught. In high winds this loch often became unfishable, since the bottom became churned up. Forestry has exacerbated the problem, with large quantities of silt apparently washed into the loch from forestry ploughing.

LOCH SAORACH 11/015606
LOCH THORMAID 11/010604

Permission: Mrs Atkinson, c/o The Bradford & Bingley Building Society, Sinclair Street, Thurso.
Tel: Thurso (0847) 63291

These lochs, which lie in the west of the county, have been much affected by commercial forestry, and are now easily approached from a hill road. The average weight of trout is 6oz and there seems to be, at present, plenty of them.

LOCH NAN CLACHAN GEALA 12/002585

Permission: Mrs Atkinson, c/o The Bradford & Bingley Building Society, Sinclair Street, Thurso.
Tel: Thurso (0847) 63291

This little loch lies beyond Saorach and Thormaid and is approached by the same forestry track from Broubster. Many years ago Clachan Geala was an outstanding fishery but over-fishing all but wiped out the stock. The loch has now been restocked with Strath Halladale trout and is well worth a visit.

LOCH RUARD 11/140430

Permission: Mrs Atkinson, c/o The Bradford & Bingley Building Society, Sinclair Street, Thurso.
Tel: Thurso (0847) 63291

Ruard lies to the west of the A895 Latheron–Thurso road, an easy 40-minute walk following a good track. At the farm buildings at Acheraskill (158423), keep to the north of the outlet burn – the south side is heavy going. Ruard trout average 8–10oz and fight hard. A reasonable day should produce a basket of 10–15 fish. A good boat is available at the loch, as well as a boat house, which makes it an ideal loch for a family outing. With great wildlife – otters, divers, wildcat, a wide variety of flowers, lichens and mosses – it is a perfect place to fish. Any of the standard pattern loch flies will produce results.

LOCH STEMSTER 11/188423

Permission: Mrs Atkinson, c/o The Bradford & Bingley Building Society, Sinclair Street, Thurso.
Tel: Thurso (0847) 63291

A small, circular loch to the north of Latheron, east from Achavanich. Boat and bank fishing for trout which average 8–10oz, with some larger fish as well. I prefer bank fishing and, particularly in high winds, this is the loch to choose. No matter how strong or from which direction the wind is blowing, Stemster always provides some shelter – and great sport. Easily accessible, and you can park by the water's edge. Use Soldier Palmer, Black Pennell, Silver Invicta and Ke-He.

LOCH RANGAG 12/178415

Permission: Mrs Atkinson, c/o The Bradford & Bingley Building Society, Sinclair Street, Thurso.
Tel: Thurso (0847) 63291

The loch lies immediately adjacent to the A895, with the remains of a broch on a small island on the east shore. It is absolutely full of little trout, making it the perfect loch for beginners, big or small. Success is guaranteed.

LOCHAN AIRIGH LEATHAID 11/990039

Permission: The Ulbster Arms Hotel, Halkirk.
Tel: Halkirk (084783) 206

A group of three classic hill lochs to the west of Dalganachan. Approach from Westerdale, then along the rough estate road. The walk up to the lochs can be tiring, but the effort is well worth while. Bank fishing only, but easy wading on the two larger lochs, where trout average in the order of 1lb. The smaller loch, dark and peaty, is also worth a cast, or two or three. There are some good fish waiting.

LOCH A'CHERIGAL 12/100489

Permission: The Ulbster Arms Hotel, Halkirk.
Tel: Halkirk (084783) 206

Approach from Westerdale and park near Strathmore Lodge by the Thurso River. A 10-minute walk north brings you to the loch. Although a'Cherigal can be dour, on its day sport can be fast and furious, with trout averaging 1lb. Boat fishing only, the best area being in the vicinity of the headland to the right of the mooring bay. Use standard pattern loch flies.

LOCH MEADIE 12/090480

Permission: The Ulbster Arms Hotel, Halkirk.
Tel: Halkirk (084783) 206

Another beginner's loch, easily accessible from the road out from Westerdale. There is a small, sandy beach at the south end, ideal for a picnic and the bucket-and-spade brigade, while you fish. All flies produce results on Meadie.

LOCH EILEANACH 12/070475
LOCHAN DUBH NAN GEODH 12/060477
LOCH GAINEIMH 12/050470

Permission: The Ulbster Arms Hotel, Halkirk.
Tel: Halkirk (084783) 206

These three lochs lie close to the new forestry road from Loch More to Altnabreac. Good baskets of wild brown trout which average 8–12oz, with the odd big fish being taken from time to time – Nan Geodh produced a trout of 4lb 12oz in 1986 – so concentrate, all the time. Boat fishing is best and standard pattern loch flies do the work.

LOCH GLUTT 11/993375

Permission: The Ulbster Arms Hotel, Halkirk.
Tel: Halkirk (084783) 206

An expert's loch, Glutt can drive the ordinary angler (me) mad with frustration. The water is gin-clear and few fish rise, but when they do they are likely to be in the order of 4lb. It is a long, rough drive, out from Westerdale, but Glutt is a 'must' for those of you who enjoy a challenge.

LOCH EUN 12/893426

Permission: The Ulbster Arms Hotel, Halkirk.
Tel: Halkirk (084783) 206

Eun is possibly the best of the Ulbster Arms trout lochs, containing superb-quality fish which average 1lb. Follow the estate road out past Loch Dubh (below) and then turn left at Altnabreac Station, to Cnoc Seasaimh. Eun is ½ mile further on. On its day, magnificent sport and well worth fishing. Use standard pattern loch flies.

LOCH DUBH 12/011411

Permission: The Ulbster Arms Hotel, Halkirk.
Tel: Halkirk (084783) 206

You pass Loch Dubh on the way to Eun (above), overlooked by gaunt Lochdubh Lodge. Trout average 8oz, but fish of 3lb have been taken.

LOCH THULACHAN 12/106414
LOCH SAND 12/098410

Permission: The Ulbster Arms Hotel, Halkirk.
Tel: Halkirk (084783) 206

Follow the road from Westerdale, out to Loch More, where there is a locked gate. Reduce your walk by making sure that you have taken the key. Drive on and park at 084443. From here a good track leads out to the lochs, where you will find a ruined shooting lodge by the shores of Thulachan. Fish average 8oz and rise readily to most patterns of fly. The scenery is magnificent and these two lochs offer some of the most enjoyable sport in Caithness.

LOCH BREAC 12/064377

Permission: The Factor, Dunbeath Estate, Dunbeath.
Tel: Dunbeath (05933) 308

One of the most lovely and most productive of all the Caithness lochs, protected by being in the heart of the wilderness and at the end of a long, long hike. Trout average 10oz, fight furiously, and there are a few much larger fish lurking in the depths. Bank fishing and wading are easy and I have taken fish all round the shore. Carrying them home is another matter. Use Black Pennell, Ke-He, Loch Ordie and Butchers. A very special place.

GARBH LOCH 11/037465

Permission: The Forsinard Hotel, Forsinard, Strath Halladale.
Tel: Forsinard (06417) 221
Mrs Atkinson, c/o The Bradford & Bingley Building Society, Sinclair Street, Thurso.
Tel: Thurso (0847) 63291

This loch used to be one of our favourites, but it has now been surrounded by forestry and the heather moorlands we loved have long since gone. Trout in Garbh average 8–10oz, although I once encountered an enormous fish which most certainly weighed over 4lb. Bank and boat fishing are equally productive and flies to try should include Black Pennell, Ke-He and Invicta.

LOCH CAISE 12/026466

Permission: The Forsinard Hotel, Forsinard, Strath Halladale.
Tel: Forsinard (06417) 221
Mrs Atkinson, c/o The Bradford & Bingley Building Society, Sinclair Street, Thurso.
Tel: Thurso (0847) 63291

The new forestry road from Loch More to Altnabreac touches the southern shoreline, and this little loch is packed with small, free-rising trout which grab anything. An ideal beginner's water.

SKYLINE LOCH 12/010480

Permission: The Forsinard Hotel, Forsinard, Strath Halladale.
Tel: Forsinard (06417) 221

This loch is now greatly affected by commercial forestry, but still, in my opinion, holds some of the best fighting trout in Caithness. Bank fishing, and no need to cast any distance, as good trout lie very close to the shore. We have never caught anything in Skyline less than 2lb – but we have lost a good few, much larger fish. Use Loch Ordie, Black Zulu and Silver Butcher.

CAOL LOCH 11/025485

Permission: The Forsinard Hotel, Forsinard, Strath Halladale.
Tel: Forsinard (06417) 221

Caol lies to the west of the railway line, near Altnabreac Station, and is also much changed by commercial forestry. There is a good little boat house, with boat and bank fishing producing equally good results. The north end has always been most kind to me and trout average 12oz. Wonderful views (until the trees grow) southwards to the Caithness mountains. Use standard pattern loch flies.

LOCH HEMPRIGGS 12/343470

Permission: Thrumster Garage, Thrumster, Wick.
Tel: (095585) 252

Hempriggs lies adjacent to the A9, 3 miles south from Wick. This is a shallow, peaty water, windy and exposed, but it can produce excellent sport with trout averaging 8–10oz. Bank fishing only, with the east shore being most convenient. Wading requires great care since there are underwater rocks waiting to topple the unready. Use standard pattern loch flies.

LOCH OF YARROWS 12/310440

Permission: Thrumster Garage, Thrumster, Wick.
Tel: (095585) 252

Yarrows is the water supply for Wick, and as such is a deep loch. But it is full of small trout averaging 6oz and huge baskets are frequently taken. Boat fishing only, since the margins are deep and although the trout may not be very large, the setting and surrounding scenery more than compensate.

MARL LOCH 12/302441

Permission: Thrumster Garage, Thrumster, Wick.
Tel: (095585) 252

Marl Loch was recently formed by damming an inlet burn to Loch of Yarrows, and then stocking it with Yarrows trout. Because of the excellent feeding available, these trout have thrived mightily and now average 1lb. Bank fishing only, and fish may be caught from anywhere round the shores.

LOCH SARCLET 12/344428

Permission: Thrumster Garage, Thrumster, Wick.
Tel: (095585) 252

Sarclet lies to the south of Wick, close to the cliffs of Gearty Head. This loch contains some very good fish of great quality which average 1lb. Trout of up to 6lb have been caught in the past and most seasons produce fish of 3lb. Bank fishing, particularly in the evenings, can bring spectacular results. Silver Invicta, Blue Zulu and Ke-He work well.

LOCH OF WAREHOUSE 12/300424

Permission: Thrumster Garage, Thrumster, Wick.
Tel: (095585) 252

A tiny loch in the hills above Loch of Yarrows, with utterly spectacular views out to Sutherland and over the Pentland Firth to Orkney. It is almost possible to cast across the loch from one shore to the other, and there are still a few good fish to be caught. Go there as much for the view as for the fishing, but do go.

LOCH WATENAN 12/319410

Permission: John Swanson, Aspen Bank, Banks Road, Watten.
Tel: Watten (095582) 326

One of my favourite Caithness lochs, close to the A9 near Ulbster and the famous Whaligoe Steps. Only the southern part of the loch is fishable, owing to enormous weed growth, but there are some really good trout waiting to be caught. The trout are dark and golden and fight furiously, and fish of over 4lb have been taken. Most of all, I enjoy Watenan because of the bird life. In the spring the air is so full of continuous birdsong that you can barely make yourself heard.

LOCH OF WESTER 12/325592

Permission: A. Dunnet, Auchorn Farm, Lyth.
Tel: Keiss (095583) 208

Wester lies close to the A9, north from Wick on the road to John

3 Loch Sletill - before afforestation

O'Groats. Its primary interest is as a sea-trout fishery, the only one in Caithness, and the brown trout tend to be small and white-fleshed. Sea trout arrive from September onwards and give great sport, along with the odd salmon. Boat and bank fishing are available.

LOCHS OF STRATH HALLADALE

LOCH SLETILL 11/958470

Permission: Forsinard Hotel, Forsinard, Strath Halladale.
Tel: Forsinard (06417) 221

Loch Sletill, one of the best lochs in the north, lies to the east of the A897 Helmsdale–Melvich road. Much of the surrounding area is afforested, and access to Sletill is by means of a forestry road, rather than by foot across the moor. Trout average 12oz, with the occasional fish of up to 3lb, and there are two boats available. Bank fishing can be just as productive as boat fishing, particularly in high winds, when the north shore is ideal and easy to wade. All standard patterns of flies work well.

LOCH LEIR 11/955458

Permission: Forsinard Hotel, Forsinard, Strath Halladale.
Tel: Forsinard (06417) 221

South of Sletill (above), also afforested, and approached by the same track, Leir contains smaller fish but they are splendid fighters and rise readily to the fly. There is a boat, and fish are taken all over the loch, but bank fishing is just as good. Wade eastwards from the mooring bay, past the headland, and look out for action. Use standard pattern loch flies.

LOCH TALAHEEL 11/955489

Permission: Forsinard Hotel, Forsinard, Strath Halladale.
Tel: Forsinard (06417) 221

This delightful loch is a 20-minute walk over the moor from Sletill and contains good stocks of trout which average 8–10oz. Fish of over 1lb are rare, but expect large baskets and good sport with hard-fighting trout.

LOCHAN EALACHMOR 11/967480
LOCHNA CLOICHE 11/975475
LOCHAN NAM BREAC 11/002478
CLAR LOCH 11/953443

Permission: Forsinard Hotel, Forsinard, Strath Halladale.
Tel: Forsinard (06417) 221

These lochs are now accessible by forestry roads and full of large numbers of bright little trout. Clar Loch, close to the railway line, still requires a not inconsiderable hike, but all these lochs are ideal for those who enjoy fishing in remote places. Any flies.

LOCHAN NAN CLACH GEALA 11/935495

Permission: Forsinard Hotel, Forsinard, Strath Halladale.
Tel: Forsinard (06417) 221

This is one of the most enigmatic lochs in Sutherland, capable of producing marvellous baskets of superb trout – in the recent past 10 trout weighing 21lb 8oz. And yet there are times when you would swear that there wasn't a single fish in the loch. Don't be deceived – there are, and in the adjacent loch to the west. But they rise infrequently and the trick in catching them is being in the right place at the right time. Keep trying. The west shore is my preferred area of the main loch and both lochs are small enough to be thoroughly explored in a day. Always have a Ke-He on your cast.

LOCH BAD A'BOTHAIN 10/918507

Permission: Forsinard Hotel, Forsinard, Strath Halladale.
Tel: Forsinard (06417) 221

Approach via the new forestry track which leaves the A897 1 mile north from Forsinain Farm road. Bad A'Bothain is surrounded by commercial forests and contains trout which average 8–10oz. It is easily accessible and ideal for a few casts after dinner. Use standard pattern loch flies.

LOCH NA SEILGE 11/920585-10/919586

Permission: Forsinard Hotel, Forsinard, Strath Halladale.
Tel: Forsinard (06417) 221

Now my favourite Strath Halladale loch, to the east of the Helmsdale–Melvich road, remote and beautiful and as yet unmarked by commercial forestry. Trout average 12oz and are plentiful, rising well to standard pattern loch flies. Boat fishing brings the best results, although good sport may also be had from the bank. Drift round the island in the south bay, and along the south shore. The large bay on the north shore also produces excellent sport. Lunch on the island. Watch the world go by.

LOCH NA CAORACH 10/913584

Permission: Forsinard Hotel, Forsinard, Strath Halladale.
Tel: Forsinard (06417) 221

The Melvich Hotel, Melvich.
Tel: Melvich (06413) 206

Another excellent loch, untouched by commercial forestry, a short walk from the Helmsdale–Melvich road near the north of the Strath. The north end is very shallow and most of the action takes place at the south end, particularly in the vicinity of the headland on the east shore. Fish from either boat or bank with complete confidence. Trout average 10oz, with a few larger fish to keep the interest alive. Standard patterns work well.

LOCH AKRAN 11/925605

Permission: Forsinard Hotel, Forsinard, Strath Halladale.
Tel: Forsinard (06417) 221
The Melvich Hotel, Melvich.
Tel: Melvich (06413) 206

Akran lies to the north of Caorach and Seilge (above) and is an ideal beginner's loch. The walk out is easy, and there is a sandy beach on the west shore for picnics. The loch is packed with little trout which average 6oz and provide great sport for newcomers to the 'gentle art'. Any flies take fish.

CAOL-LOCH 11/923615

Permission: Forsinard Hotel, Forsinard, Strath Halladale.
Tel: Forsinard (04617) 221

The loch lies just north of Akran and is similar in style and quality of fish, with the odd trout of up to 2lb. Tends to be more exposed, but is delightful to fish, with large baskets the rule rather than the exception. The south shore, by the promontory and small island, is the best area.

THE CROSS LOCHS 10/870465

Permission: Forsinard Hotel, Forsinard, Strath Halladale.
Tel: Forsinard (04617) 221

Accessibility via forestry tracks has not made Cross Lochs trout any easier to catch. The lochs lie west of the Helmsdale–Melvich road and have always had a dour reputation. There are a series of five waters, the most productive of which, generally speaking, are McNicholl's and Jubilee. Some huge trout have been caught, including specimens of up to 8lb, and hardly a season passes without trout of between 3 and 5lb being landed. Jubilee is gin-clear, with a marl bottom, while the others are dark-stained and peaty. Well worth your attention, and always fish with a Blue Zulu, which seems to fish rather better than most other patterns.

LOCH CROCACH 10/805437
LOCH GAINEIMH 10/798430

Permission: Forsinard Hotel, Forsinard, Strath Halladale.
Tel: Forsinard (04617) 221

Crocach was once one of the remotest, least fished lochs in Strath Halladale, but is now 'tamed' by forestry roads. It lies in the shadow of Ben Griam Beg and Beinn a' Mhadaidh in a splendid setting, and is scattered with tiny islands, full of nooks and fishy corners, and abounds with super little trout which average 8oz. Fish or not, Crocach is perfect, as is its tiny neighbour, Gaineimh, to the south, which might just surprise you.

LOCH NAM BREAC 10/826480
LOCH SAOBHAIDHE 10/800470
LOCH DUBH 10/817475
LOCH BADIREACH NA GOITHE 10/844510

Permission: Forsinard Hotel, Forsinard, Strath Halladale.
Tel: Forsinard (04617) 221

Another group of once remote, now easily accessible lochs, to the north of Crocach (above), full of bright little trout and a few larger fish. Great fun for beginners. All the standard pattern loch flies take fish – in large numbers.

LOCH NA H-EAGLAISE MOR 10/862600
LOCH NA H-EAGLAISE BEAG 10/855590

Permission: The Melvich Hotel, Melvich.
Tel: Melvich (06413) 206

A peat road leads out from the A836, west from Melvich. Park at the end of the track. The lochs lie 2 miles south, over the moor, which can be very wet and soggy, particularly after heavy rain.

Eaglaise Mor, the first loch, contains a good stock of trout averaging 8–10oz, with some larger fish of up to 2lb. Best fishing area is down the east shore, and in the top bay. Bank fishing is difficult and not very productive.

Eaglaise Beag lies ½ mile south from Eaglaise Mor and contains larger fish, with trout of up to 3lb. Close to the west shore, at the south end, are two patches of weed – a great fishing area, as is the vicinity of the feeder streams which enter from the west. Good bank fishing and easy wading. Use Ke-He, March Brown and Alexandra to tempt them out.

ACHRIDIGILL LOCH 10/858613

Permission: The Melvich Hotel, Melvich.
Tel: Melvich (06413) 206

You pass Achridigill on the way to and from the Eaglaises (above), and most anglers do, but it is always worth stopping for a cast. Full of small fish, but from time to time it produces some really large specimens. Easy to bank-fish, great fun, and the trout are not particularly fussy about what flies they grab.

LOCHAN NAN CLACH 10/862590
LOCHAN COULBACKIE 10/874614

Permission: The Melvich Hotel, Melvich.
Tel: Melvich (06413) 206

Nan Clach lies south of Eaglaise Mor and west from Eaglaise Beag. If things are not busy on the Eaglaises, walk over and have a cast. Fish average 14oz and expect to catch at least a brace.

Visit Coulbackie on your way home, as an alternative to Achridigill. Swing north-east from the mooring bay at Eaglaise Mor – Coulbackie is about 1 mile away.

LOCH EARACHA 10/899608

Permission: The Melvich Hotel, Melvich.
Tel: Melvich (06413) 206
Facilities for Disabled Anglers: Easily accessible roadside lochan.

Earacha lies adjacent to the A897 Melvich–Helmsdale road, in a loop of the Halladale River. The loch has plenty of small fish, and also fish of up to 2lb. Earacha is ideal for elderly or handicapped anglers, and most standard pattern loch flies will produce excellent results.

LOCH AN RUTHAIR 17/865370

Permission: The Head Keeper, Achentoul Estate, Kinbrace, Helmsdale.
Tel: Kinbrace (04313) 227

Ruthair is adjacent to the A987, midway between Melvich and Helmsdale. The loch is 1 mile long by up to ¾ mile wide, windswept and bleak. Rare! Trout average 8–10oz and there are plenty waiting to be caught. Fish at the northern end, where the feeder burn enters. The estate has a marvellous cottage for rent at Greamachary, by the Ben Griams and Meall a'Bhuirich.

LOCH CULAIDH 17/864390
LOCH LUCY 17/879395

Permission: The Head Keeper, Achentoul Estate, Kinbrace, Helmsdale. *Tel:* Kinbrace (04313) 227

Culaidh is to the north of the rough track which goes out to Greamachary Cottage and consists of one big loch and two smaller 'ponds'. Lucy is close to the railway and the A897, so can be somewhat overlooked. Both lochs, however, have good stocks of hard-fighting, readily rising, 8-oz trout.

LOCH ARICHLINIE 17/847350

Permission: The Head Keeper, Achentoul Estate, Kinbrace, Helmsdale. *Tel:* Kinbrace (04313) 227

The loch lies south-west from Ruathair, and has an average depth of 4–5 feet. It is full of 6-oz trout, and a 1-lb fish would be king. Good boat house and boat, excellent bank fishing and a perfect beginner's water where any flies are eagerly accepted. Park by Achentoul Farm and follow the track west.

4 Bruce Sandison and Breac by Caol-Loch Mor, in Badanloch

LOCHS OF BADANLOCH

LOCH COIRE NAM MANG 10/800405

Permission: Richard MacNicol, Badanloch, Helmsdale.
Tel: Kinbrace (04313) 232
The Garvault Hotel, Kinbrace, Helmsdale.
Tel: Kinbrace (04313) 224

This loch lies 1½ miles from the B871 Kinbrace–Syre road, near to the Garvault Hotel – the remotest hotel on mainland Britain. Both boat and bank fishing, but best results come from the first. Circular, averaging 12ft deep, Coire nam Mang contains trout averaging 10oz, with fish of over 3lb being taken most seasons, as well as Arctic char. Three feeder burns enter in the south-east corner and this is a favourite fishing area. Use standard pattern loch flies.

LOCH DRUIM A'CHLIABHAIN 10/810410

Permission: Richard MacNicol, Badanloch, Helmsdale.
Tel: Kinbrace (04313) 232
The Garvault Hotel, Kinbrace, Helmsdale.
Tel: Kinbrace (04313) 224

Joined by a stream to Coire nam Mang (above) and ½ mile further north, Chliabhain is more than 1½ miles long by up to ½ mile wide and contains trout of excellent quality which average 12oz. This loch has a reputation for holding really large fish and the west shore of the north bay is a good place to start looking for them. An outboard motor would be ideal on this often windy loch, but getting it up there is another matter. One of my friends solved the problem by strapping an outboard to a golf-caddying car when no-one was looking.

CAOL-LOCH BEG 10/779435
CAOL-LOCH MOR 10/782445
LOCHAN SGEIREACH 10/758432

Permission: Richard MacNicol, Badanloch, Helmsdale.
Tel: Kinbrace (04313) 232
The Garvault Hotel, Kinbrace, Helmsdale.
Tel: Kinbrace (04313) 224

A superb day out, walking and fishing. Start from the Garvault Hotel and walk north, keeping to the left of the Garbh-allt burn, and maintaining the high ground – above the bog. From the north shoulder of Beinn a' Mhadaidh, you can see the Caol-lochs ahead. From the north end of Caol-loch Mor, walk south-west for Sgeireach; thence, as best you can, round the west side of Mhadaidh, back to the hotel. It will take all day, but along the way you will catch some wonderful little trout and see an amazing array of wildflowers, plants, birds and animals. Utterly splendid.

LOCH NAM FAOILEAG 10/734408
LOCH MOLACH 10/724420
RHIFAIL LOCH 10/720425
PALM LOCH 10/710410
ROSAIL LOCH 10/710405

Permission: Richard MacNicol, Badanloch, Helmsdale.
Tel: Kinbrace (04313) 232
The Garvault Hotel, Kinbrace, Helmsdale.
Tel: Kinbrace (04313) 224

Another wonderful day out, just as splendid but not quite as taxing as the previous waters. Drive west from the Garvault Hotel and park near to where the Allt Lon a'Chuil burn crosses the road. Follow the burn north for ¾ mile and then angle right to reach nam Faoileag. North-west, back across the burn, takes you to Molach and Rhifail; due south, across the road, to Palm Loch. Follow the outlet burn from Palm Loch, east down to Rosail. These lochs contain 8-oz trout. The burn, a classic highland stream, holds fish of up to 2lb.

GREEN LOCH 16/720393
LOCHAN A'CHOIRE BHUIDHE 16/703387

Permission: Richard MacNicol, Badanloch, Helmsdale.
Tel: Kinbrace (04313) 232
The Garvault Hotel, Kinbrace, Helmsdale.
Tel: Kinbrace (04313) 224

From the same parking place as above, walk 100 yards west and you will find a track leading south. Follow this track until it crosses a small stream and then turn right up the stream for the Green Loch. Walk west from the Green Loch to reach a'Choire Bhuidhe. Both have good stocks of fine trout which average 6–8oz, as well as a few larger fish. Use standard pattern loch flies.

LOCH BADANLOCH 17/770340

Permission: Richard MacNicol, Badenloch, Helmsdale.
Tel: Kinbrace (04313) 232
The Garvault Hotel, Kinbrace, Helmsdale.
Tel: Kinbrace (04313) 224

South from the Garvault Hotel, averaging 17 feet deep, this is one of a chain of three, interlinked lochs, covering an area of 4½ miles long by up to 1 mile wide. Badanloch fishes best from a boat and the most productive area is in the narrows, between the island of Rubha Mor and the south shore. Dapping is good, and although the average weight of trout is only about 8oz, there are a few, much larger fish. The water level fluctuates during the season, but this does not seem to upset the trout. Boats are moored at the east end. An outboard motor is almost essential, and since none is available for hire, you will have to take your own. Use standard pattern loch flies, but Black Pennelll and Black Zulu should always be fished.

LOCH NAN CLAR 16/755355

Permission: Richard MacNicol, Badenloch, Helmsdale.
Tel: Kinbrace (04313) 232
The Garvault Hotel, Kinbrace, Helmsdale.
Tel: Kinbrace (04313) 224

A continuation, westwards, of Badanloch, and similar in character. Trout average 8oz, with a fish of 4lb 12oz being taken during 1991. Best fishing area is where the loch narrows, before joining Loch Rimsdale. Salmon are also sometimes caught here, so be ready. Boats are available. When using an outboard, take great care. The average depth of the loch is only 12 feet, and at the narrows no more than 4 feet. Use the same flies as for Badanloch (above).

LOCH RIMSDALE 16/740355
LOCH TRUDERSCAIG 16/710325
LOCHAN DUBH 16/720329

Permission: Richard MacNicol, Badenloch, Helmsdale.
Tel: Kinbrace (04313) 232
The Garvault Hotel, Kinbrace, Helmsdale.
Tel: Kinbrace (04313) 224

The last of the Badanloch waters, and the best, containing brown trout, Arctic char and the occasional salmon. Rimsdale lies north and south of its neighbours and is 3 miles long by ¾ mile wide. Boats are moored at the north-east corner with easy access from the B871 Kinbrace–Syre road. Dapping brings good results and baskets of up to 20 trout are taken frequently, as well as much larger specimens. A trout of 9lb 8oz was landed in June 1991. Use standard pattern loch flies, but always try a Kingfisher Butcher or a Dunkeld.

Truderscaig is joined to Rimsdale by the Allt an Loin Tharsuinn burn, and Lochan Dubh is to the east of Truderscaig.

LOCH AN FHEARNA 16/750335
LOCH NA GAINEIMH 17/767304

Permission: Richard MacNicol, Badenloch, Helmsdale.
Tel: Kinbrace (04313) 232
The Garvault Hotel, Kinbrace, Helmsdale.
Tel: Kinbrace (04313) 224

Both lochs lie to the south of the Badanloch waters and are approached from Badanloch Lodge by the road that runs along the south shore. Shallow waters, but with trout that fight very well and average 8oz, with the occasional much larger fish being taken most seasons. Boat fishing brings best results. Standard pattern loch flies and dapping work well.

LOCH ASCAIG 17/850255

Permission: Gamekeeper, Borrobol Estate, Kinbrace.
Tel: Kinbrace (04313) 252

A few miles north of Kildonan Lodge in the Strath of Kildonan, turn left down the Borrobol drive, which crosses the Helmsdale River. The gamekeeper's house is beyond the lodge, on the left. From here a good hill road runs westwards, out to Loch Ascaig. Ascaig is well managed, with a large, natural stock of wild brown trout averaging three to the pound; but recent improvements, including raising the water level and selective phosphating, have resulted in a pH of 7.8 and significant numbers of 1-lb and a few 3–4-lb trout being caught. Salmon from the Helmsdale River enter the loch via the Borrobol Burn during the autumn. Fly only, boat and bank fishing – and, better still, there are two excellent, self-catering cottages giving fishing rights on both the loch and the Borrobol Burn. An ideal place for a marvellous sporting and wildlife holiday. Book now.

LOCHS OF STRATHY AND BETTYHILL

LOCH MEALA 10/789569

Permission: Tom Weston, Kirtomy Leisure Ltd, Tigh na Sgoil, Kirtomy, Bettyhill.
Tel: Bettyhill (06412) 375

Turn south from the A836 at the signpost reading 'Strathy East/Strathy West'. A long, bumpy ride brings you to the end of a forestry track and then a short, easy walk from the parking place brings you to one of the best trout lochs in the area. The boat is tucked away in a small, neat mooring bay at 791567. The west shore is best, either from boat or bank, and trout average 10oz, with a few much heavier fish sometimes being taken. Try Loch Ordie, Greenwell's Glory and Black Pennell.

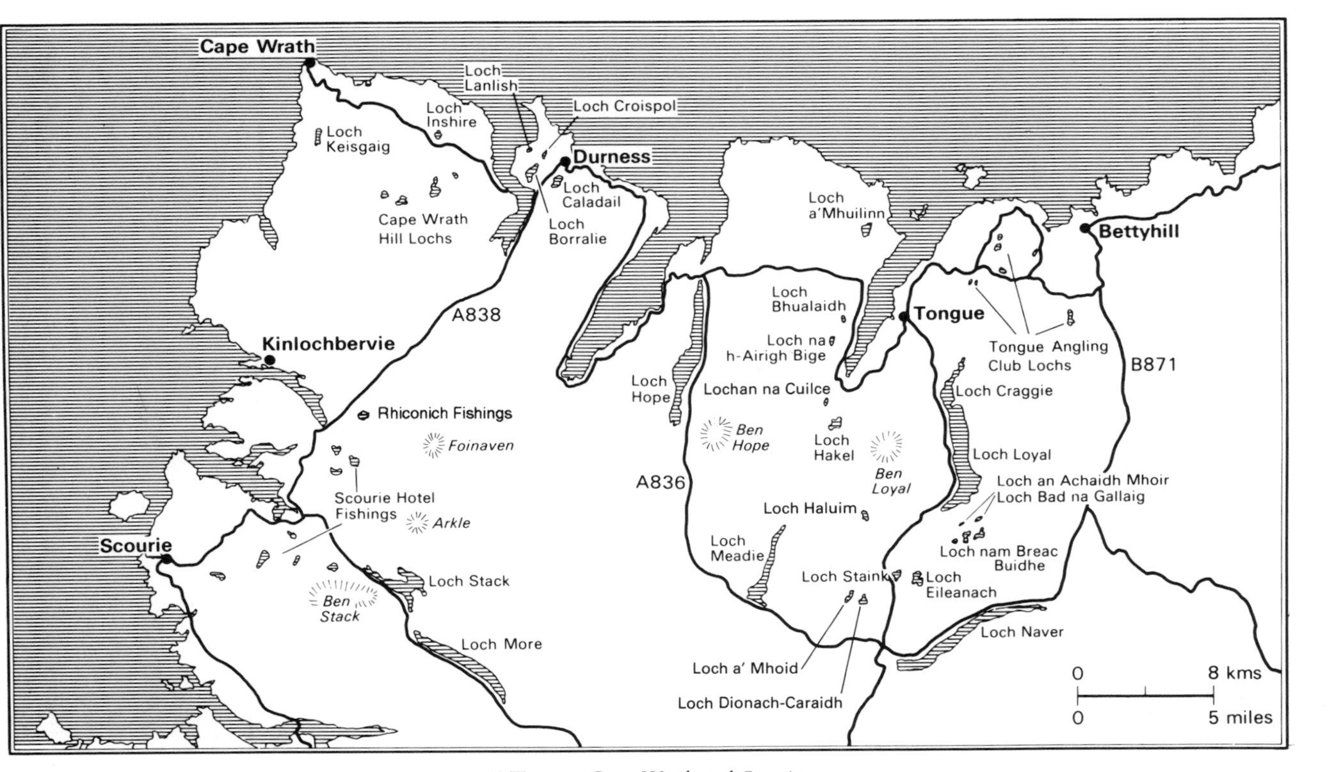

6 Tongue, Cape Wrath and Scourie

LOCH NA H-IMRICHE 10/767643
LOCHAN TIORMACHD 10/762648

Permission: Tom Weston, Kirtomy Leisure Ltd, Tigh na Sgoil, Kirtomy, Bettyhill.
Tel: Bettyhill (06412) 375

Two small lochs, rarely fished, but both holding excellent trout, particularly h-Imriche, where the average weight is around 12oz. Approach via the peat track from Kirtomy at 755642. Use standard pattern loch flies.

LOCH GAINEIMH 10/765610

Permission: Tom Weston, Kirtomy Leisure Ltd, Tigh na Sgoil, Kirtomy, Bettyhill.
Tel: Bettyhill (06412) 375

A fine moorland loch, and two adjacent small waters, all offering good sport with trout averaging 8–10oz. Easily accessible from the peat track which leaves the A836 at 750620 (take the same route for Loch Meadie, noted below). Most flies produce results.

LOCH EILENACH 10/790608

Permission: Tom Weston, Kirtomy Leisure Ltd, Tigh na Sgoil, Kirtomy, Bettyhill.
Tel: Bettyhill (06412) 375

Excellent sport with small, hard-fighting trout, and a few fish of up to 2lb. Three islands and bays and fishy corners make Eilenach one of the most attractive little lochs in the area and a delight to fish. Bank fishing only. Use standard pattern loch flies.

LOCH BUIDHE BEAG 10/773595
LOCH BUIDHE MOR 10/778584

Permission: Tom Weston, Kirtomy Leisure Ltd, Tigh na Sgoil, Kirtomy, Bettyhill.
Tel: Bettyhill (06412) 375

Two rarely fished lochs, forming the headwaters of the Armadale Burn, to the west of Strathy Forest and Beinn nam Bo. First-class fishing. Last season (1991) produced trout of over 4lb and the average is about 10oz. Bank fishing at present, but there are plans for boats. Use standard pattern loch flies.

CAOL-LOCH 10/843582
LOCH NAM BO UIDHRE 10/855570
CAOL-LOCH 10/850550

Permission: Tom Weston, Kirtomy Leisure Ltd, Tigh na Sgoil, Kirtomy, Bettyhill.
Tel: Bettyhill (06412) 375

These lochs are approached from the Strathy Forest track, and thence west and south-west over the moor. They are remote waters, offering sport with traditional highland wild brown trout of good quality, and a few larger fish, particularly in the northern Caol-loch. Privacy and absolute peace are guaranteed. Bank fishing only. Use standard pattern loch flies.

LOCH NAM BREAC BEAG 10/815606
LOCH NAM BREAC MOR 10/812602
LOCH A'CHRUGAN 10/826630

Permission: Tom Weston, Kirtomy Leisure Ltd, Tigh na Sgoil, Kirtomy, Bettyhill.
Tel: Bettyhill (06412) 375

These lochs are situated within the Strathy Forest and draining into the Strathy River, a useful spate salmon stream. Nam Breac Mor has the best fish, but all three lochs hold good stocks of small fish which average 8oz and give a good account of themselves. Any flies will produce results.

LOCH GAINMHICH 10/812650
LOCHAN EALACH 10/820651

Permission: Tom Weston, Kirtomy Leisure Ltd, Tigh na Sgoil, Kirtomy, Bettyhill.
Tel: Bettyhill (06412) 375

Adjacent to the A836 and consequently very public. Small fish which rise to any flies.

LOCH BALIGILL 10/855620

Permission: Tom Weston, Kirtomy Leisure Ltd, Tigh na Sgoil, Kirtomy, Bettyhill.
Tel: Bettyhill (06412) 375

The best loch in the area and capable of producing trout of considerable size – up to 8lb and more. A boat is available, but bank fishing can be just as productive, relatively speaking, because Baligill is a dour loch that can frequently drive anglers mad with frustration. However, on its day, it is one of the finest trout lochs in the north. Approach from the end of the track at 861632.

KIRTOMY LEISURE 10/744632

Kirtomy is 2 miles east of Bettyhill on the A836, beside the north coast of Sutherland. The sturdily constructed 19th-century school and schoolhouse have been comprehensively redeveloped by Kirtomy Leisure Ltd. It is noted here simply because it is one of the best furnished and most attractive small sporting lodges in the north. Well managed, offering stalking and shooting as well as salmon and trout fishing, it is an ideal centre for exploring the area – and for the removal of trout from their natural habitat.

LOCH MEADIE 10/753600

Permission: The Bettyhill Hotel, Bettyhill.
Tel: Bettyhill (06412) 202

This loch is 1½ miles long by 250 yards wide, and is easily accessible from a good track which leaves the A836 east of Bettyhill. At the time of writing, bank fishing only, but boats are planned for the future. Meadie is an exciting loch and even in windy conditions it is possible to find a sheltered corner. The south end holds the best fish. Offer them standard pattern loch flies.

LOCH MOR 10/720609

Permission: The Bettyhill Hotel, Bettyhill.
Tel: Bettyhill (06412) 202

A small loch, a few hundred yards to the south of the hotel. It contains excellent trout with an average weight of 12oz, but fish of over 2lb are also caught. Use standard pattern loch flies.

LOCH DUINTE 10/717584

Permission: The Bettyhill Hotel, Bettyhill.
Tel: Bettyhill (06412) 202

Instead of crossing the River Naver, continue south and you will find this little loch on your left, close to the road, after about 1 mile. It is well sheltered on windy days by the crags to the east, and well supplied with hard-fighting, little trout. At lunch time, visit the site of the pre-Clearances village, immediately adjacent to and overlooking the loch.

5 Concentration on Loch Meadie

CAOL LOCH

10/763597

Permission: The Bettyhill Hotel, Bettyhill.
Tel: Bettyhill (06412) 202

To the east of Loch Meadie, in the shadow of Creag Meadie, this remote and lovely little loch is about 700 yards long by 80 yards wide. It contains good wild brown trout which rise readily to standard pattern loch flies, cast from anywhere around the shore. The most productive area, however, is at the south end.

LOCH NA CLAIC
CAOL LOCH

10/766586
10/770570

Permission: The Bettyhill Hotel, Bettyhill.
Tel: Bettyhill (06412) 202

Na Claic is a small loch lying in the hills between Meadie and Caol Loch. It is rarely visited but well worth stopping off at for a few casts on your way south. Caol Loch is a considerable step further south and is one of the most remote of the Bettyhill waters, requiring a walk of about 4 miles. Approach from the A836 and follow the route south, past Loch Meadie. Trout average 8oz and rise readily to most patterns of fly.

LOCHAN AIRIGH NA CREIGE 10/730582

Permission: The Bettyhill Hotel, Bettyhill.
Tel: Bettyhill (06412) 202

Two lochs, joined by a tiny feeder stream, offering excellent sport in superb surroundings. The name means 'loch of the little rocky shieling'. Follow the track out from 715595 and use standard pattern loch flies.

LOCH NAN LAOG 10/770575
LOCH MOR NA CAORACH 10/758558

Permission: The Bettyhill Hotel, Bettyhill.
Tel: Bettyhill (06412) 202

A long, tiring walk, but well worth the effort. Start from 737547. Mor na Caorach has four principal satellite lochs, including Loch nan Laog, which means 'loch of the deer calf' and all these waters contain excellent, well-shaped trout. Mor na Caorach has the best fish, reputed to be up to 4lb, while the others are more modestly supplied with trout which average 8–10oz. Once visited, never forgotten.

ALTNAHARRA AND TONGUE LOCHS

LOCH MEADIE 16/495400

Permission: Paul Panchaud, The Altnaharra Hotel, Altnaharra.
Tel: Altnaharra (054981) 222

A long, narrow loch, adjacent to the tortuous road from Altnaharra to Loch Hope, packed with small trout which average 6oz. But last June, John Meldrum, a local gillie, took a fish of 4lb 8oz and in 1990 a salmon was caught. Therefore, treat every rise with respect – you never know your luck. One of the most beautiful lochs in Scotland, with wonderful, tree-clad islands, round which, particularly at the south end, is a favourite fishing area; as are the narrows, northwards, and the far north end.

LOCH STAINK 10/580406

Permission: Paul Panchaud, The Altnaharra Hotel, Altnaharra.
Tel: Altnaharra (054981) 222

Adjacent to the A836 Altnaharra–Tongue road, easily accessible and full of small, 6–8-oz trout. Boat and bank fishing, and large baskets.

LOCH NAM BREAC BUIDHE 10/617434

Permission: Paul Panchaud, The Altnaharra Hotel, Altnaharra.
Tel: Altnaharra (054981) 222

Six miles north from Altnaharra on the road to Tongue. Park ½ mile south of Inchinloch at 596438 and follow the deer fence of the north side of the forestry plantation. Where the fence turns, the loch is a few hundred yards east. There is a boat, and trout rise and are caught all over the loch. Excellent-quality fish, and great sport. Standard patterns of fly will do fine.

LOCH AN ACHAIDH MHOIR 10/620424
LOCH BAD NA GALLAIG 10/630428

Permission: Paul Panchaud, The Altnaharra Hotel, Altnaharra.
Tel: Altnaharra (054981) 222

A series of five interlinked lochs which drain northwards into Loch Loyal. Bank fishing, for trout which average 8oz and fight furiously. Stream fishing also, in the linking burns, and on hot, midge-free days, swimming, too.

LOCH DIONACH-CARAIDH 10/559402

Permission: Paul Panchaud, The Altnaharra Hotel, Altnaharra.
Tel: Altnaharra (054981) 222

Park just before the forestry plantation to the west of the A836, near to Loch Staink (above). Dionach-Caraidh is approximately 1 mile west from the road. Bank fishing only, for small fish averaging 6–8oz.

LOCH COULSIDE 10/583437

Permission: Paul Panchaud, The Altnaharra Hotel, Altnaharra.
Tel: Altnaharra (054981) 222

An easily accessible loch, the headwaters of the Borgie River, amply supplied with small, wild brown trout and the occasional salmon. Park at Inchinloch at the south end of Loch Loyal and follow the outlet burn west, fishing as you go. This stream also holds some nice trout.

LOCH EILEANACH 10/593405

Permission: Paul Panchaud, The Altnaharra Hotel, Altnaharra.
Tel: Altnaharra (054981) 222

A lovely loch, to the north of the A836 and approached by walking round Staink and then east across the moor. The loch is divided into two sections by a narrow channel, with the northern part containing five small islands. A good fishing area. A boat is available, but bank fishing can be just as productive. Expect 8–10-oz trout which rise well to all the standard patterns of fly.

LOCH TARBHAIDH 16/637360

Permission: Paul Panchaud, The Altnaharra Hotel, Altnaharra.
Tel: Altnaharra (054981) 222

To the south of Loch Naver. The quick way is by boat across the loch to 628372, and then straight up the hill. Otherwise, the 'scenic' route is from the east end of Loch Naver, past the old churchyard at Achness. Also known as Tarvie, this is a 'designer' Scottish hill loch: clear, peat-stained water, happily rising trout of 8–10oz, sentinel rowan, sandy shores and birdsong all day long. Even better, some really super, much larger trout – when you are not looking.

LOCH NAVER 16/610360

Permission: Paul Panchaud, The Altnaharra Hotel, Altnaharra.
Tel: Altnaharra (054981) 222

Loch Naver is 6 miles long by about ½ mile wide and is principally renowned as a salmon and sea-trout fishery. But there are good brown trout as well and fish of over 6lb have been caught, although the average weight is about 8oz. The Altnaharra Hotel has a boat available at the north-east end of the loch, which is the best area for brown trout fishing.

LOCH LOYAL 10/620480

Permission: Paul Panchaud, The Altnaharra Hotel, Altnaharra.
Tel: Altnaharra (054981) 222
The Ben Loyal Hotel, Tongue.
Tel: Tongue (084755) 216

One of the most lovely lochs in the north, sadly much abused owing to its proximity to the Altnaharra–Tongue road. Wonderful fishing, nevertheless, particularly down the east shore, which is difficult to reach except by boat. The large, island-guarded bay, is an excellent fishing area, as is the south end, where a principal feeder stream enters, and the extreme south end, by the small island. Good trout lie here, and the occasional salmon. Loyal can be very windy so an outboard motor is really essential. Bank fishing is not very productive.

LOCH CRAGGIE 10/615515

Permission: Paul Panchaud, The Altnaharra Hotel, Altnaharra.
Tel: Altnaharra (054981) 222
The Ben Loyal Hotel, Tongue.
Tel: Tongue (084755) 216

6 Altnaharra Hotel gillies in the nineteenth century

To the north of Loyal, separated from it by a narrow causeway. An improving salmon fishery, Craggie can also offer excellent brown trout fishing for well-marked fish which average 8oz. The Tongue and District Angling Club has two super new boats on Craggie.

LOCH HOPE 10/460540

Permission: South End: Paul Panchaud, The Altnaharra Hotel, Altnaharra.
Tel: Altnaharra (054981) 222
North End: The Loch Keeper, Hope Estate, Keepers Cottage, Loch Hope.
Tel: Talmine (084756) 272

One of Scotland's most beautiful and outstanding sea-trout fisheries, which, against the current odds, still produces excellent sport from June to September. Book well in advance. Fly fishing and dapping only. Bank fishing is not allowed.

LOCH A'MHUILINN 10/568609

Permission: The Tongue and District Angling Club. Permits from: The Ben Loyal Hotel, Tongue.
Tel: (084755) 216
Permits also from Tongue Post Office and Royal Bank of Scotland in Tongue.

Cross the Kyle of Tongue and turn north, towards Talmine. Park at 580607 and follow a good track out to the loch. The west and north shore are the most productive areas, particularly where the feeder stream enters. Fish lie very close in, feeding in the flow from the stream. Trout average 11oz and a reasonable day should send you home with at least a couple of brace. Greenwell's Glory works well.

LOCH BHUALAIDH 10/537563
LOCH FHIONNAICH 10/555565

Permission: The Tongue and District Angling Club. Permits from: The Ben Loyal Hotel, Tongue.
Tel: (084755) 216
Permits also from Tongue Post Office and Royal Bank of Scotland in Tongue.

Turn south after crossing the Kyle and follow the minor road for about 1½ miles. Park where the road almost touches the Kyle and you will see a track on your right. The walk out takes about 30 minutes, passing Fhionnaich. Stop for a few casts, for Fhionnaich contains trout which average 8oz and they are great fun to catch. Bhualaidh has better fish and they fight hard. Take along standard pattern loch flies.

LOCH NA H-AIRIGH BIGE 10/550550

Permission: The Tongue and District Angling Club. Permits from: The Ben Loyal Hotel, Tongue.
Tel: (084755) 216
Permits also from Tongue Post Office and Royal Bank of Scotland in Tongue.

Continue south down the minor road round the Kyle, and park at 554544. A quick scramble up the course of the Garbh-allt burn brings you to this delightful little loch, with wonderful views south to Ben Hope and across the Kyle to Ben Loyal. Wonderful trout, too.

LOCH HAKEL 10/570530

Permission: The Tongue and District Angling Club. Permits from: The Ben Loyal Hotel, Tongue.
Tel: (084755) 216
Permits also from Tongue Post Office and Royal Bank of Scotland in Tongue.

Hakel lies south of the village of Tongue. Because of its proximity to the road, it suffers from illegal fishing but still manages to sustain a good population of trout of 8–12oz which are very pretty and fight well. Boat and bank fishing. In June 1991, a sea trout of 3lb 4oz was taken, which must have run the stream during the heavy rains in April and May. Gold coins were chucked into the loch in 1746 by supporters of Bonnie Prince Charlie who were ambushed there.

LOCHAN NA CULICE 10/585535

Permission: The Tongue and District Angling Club. Permits from: The Ben Loyal Hotel, Tongue.
Tel: (084755) 216
Permits also from Tongue Post Office and Royal Bank of Scotland in Tongue.

Known locally as Lily Loch, this water is 4 miles south from the village of Tongue, on the right of the road, close to Loch Hakel. It is difficult to fish, particularly as the season advances, but the Club has a boat, which helps greatly.

LOCH MODSARIE 10/649616

Permission: The Tongue and District Angling Club. Permits from: The Ben Loyal Hotel, Tongue.
Tel: (084755) 216
Permits also from Tongue Post Office and Royal Bank of Scotland in Tongue.

Modsarie, 700 yards long by 150 yards wide, lies to the east of the ring road out to Skerray from the A836. This is a very lovely loch, containing fine trout which average 12oz. They are not easy to catch, but well worth the effort. Offer them standard pattern loch flies. A good boat is available.

LOCH A'CHAORUINN 10/667600
LOCH SKERRAY 10/663600

Permission: The Tongue and District Angling Club. Permits from: The Ben Loyal Hotel, Tongue.
Tel: (084755) 216
Permits also from Tongue Post Office and Royal Bank of Scotland in Tongue.

Approach from the other end of the Skerray ring road, from Borgie Bridge. Skerray holds the best fish, and trout of up to 2lb 8oz are occasionally caught. Concentrate your efforts round the islands and use standard pattern loch flies.

LOCH AN TIGH-CHOIMHID 10/663608

Permission: The Tongue and District Angling Club. Permits from: The Ben Loyal Hotel, Tongue.
Tel: (084755) 216
Permits also from Tongue Post Office and Royal Bank of Scotland in Tongue.

Close to the Skerray ring road, and best approached from Modsarie. Walk out past Loch Modsarie and Loch Burag and you will find Tigh-Choimhid to the south-east. It holds modest fish that rise well to the usual flies.

LOCH DUBH BEUL NA FAIRE 10/648593

Permission: The Tongue and District Angling Club. Permits from: The Ben Loyal Hotel, Tongue.
Tel: (084755) 216
Permits also from Tongue Post Office and Royal Bank of Scotland in Tongue.

This small loch lies close to the A836 on the hill between Borgie and Tongue. It holds brown trout averaging 8–10oz and is a pleasant spot for a few evening casts. Standard pattern loch flies work well.

LOCH NAM BREAC BUIDGE 10/650567

Permission: The Tongue and District Angling Club. Permits from: The Ben Loyal Hotel, Tongue.
Tel: (084755) 216

Permits also from Tongue Post Office and Royal Bank of Scotland in Tongue. Approach from A836 by the Borgie Forest. There is a track leading southwards and the walk takes about 30 minutes. This is the best of the Tongue and District Angling Club waters and contains trout which average 12oz. It can be dour, but is a super place to fish and most outings should produce at least a brace. Use standard pattern loch flies bring them up.

THE CAPE WRATH FISHINGS

LOCH CROISPOL 9/390680

Permission: Cape Wrath Hotel, Keodale, by Lairg.
Tel: Durness (097181) 274

Croispol lies to the west of Balnakeil Craft Village and contains perfectly proportioned, beautifully marked trout. A boat is available and bank fishing is restricted to the west shore. The average weight is 1lb and all trout under 12oz must be returned. Trout of up to 4lb 8oz have been taken and all the standard pattern loch flies produce results. Dry fly and nymphs also work well. There is a deep of 40 feet towards the south-east corner of the loch, but otherwise fish rise and are caught all over.

LOCH CALADAIL 9/397667

Permission: Cape Wrath Hotel, Keodale, by Lairg.
Tel: Durness (097181) 274

This is without doubt one of the finest trout lochs in Europe, containing fish of outstanding quality. All fish under 1lb must be returned and baskets of trout in the order of four fish weighing 12lb are not uncommon. Avoid the deep water at the north end, but apart from that, trout are taken all over the loch where there are good weed beds, even in the middle. The best drift, in my opinion, is from the mooring bay, down towards the small island, about 60 yards out from the west shore. Try Ke-He, Woodcock & Hare-lug and Silver Butcher.

LOCH LANLISH 9/385684

Permission: Cape Wrath Hotel, Keodale, by Lairg.
Tel: Durness (097181) 274

A tiny loch with a huge reputation, where all fish under 2lb should be returned. In times past Lanlish regularly produced trout of over 12lb and in recent years trout of over 8lb have been caught. Bank fishing only and hard, hard work. But if you are a 'glass-case man', this little loch is the place to go to try and fill it.

LOCH BORRALIE 9/384670

Permission: Cape Wrath Hotel, Keodale, by Lairg.
Tel: Durness (097181) 274

The largest of the Durness limestone lochs and my personal favourite. The water is clear as crystal and the fish some of the hardest-fighting trout I have ever encountered. All fish under 1lb must be returned and Arctic char of over 2lb may also be caught. Borralie is over 100 feet deep and the best fishing area is from the island, down the east shoreline.

7 Five trout weighing 31lb from the finest trout loch in Europe, Loch Caladail, Durness

Another good drift is through the narrows, into the north bay, and up the east shore. Bank fishing can be very good, particularly in the evenings from the west shore, when large trout cruise into the shallows to feed. Offer them standard pattern loch flies, as well as Olives, Stone Flies, Sedges and Nymphs.

LOCH INSHORE 9/330696
LOCH NAM BREAC BUIDHE 9/337689

Permission: Cape Wrath Hotel, Keodale, by Lairg.
Tel: Durness (097181) 274

Two small lochs on the Parph Peninsula, close to the road out to the lighthouse. Approach from Keodale by ferry across the Kyle and then bus. Use standard patterns of fly, and expect large baskets of traditional highland trout averaging 6–8oz.

LOCH BAD AN FHEUR-LOCH 9/338672
LOCH AIRIGH NA BEINNE 9/325663

Permission: Cape Wrath Hotel, Keodale, by Lairg.
Tel: Durness (097181) 274

Cross the Kyle and walk up the Daill River. Bad an Fheur is first and contains trout which average three to the pound. Airigh na Beinne is a 30-minute walk further on. In the autumn it is always possible to encounter salmon, so be prepared. Otherwise, expect large baskets of small trout – in perfect surroundings.

LOCH NA GAINMHICH 9/306658
LOCH NA GLAIC TARSUINN 9/298662
LOCH NA GLAMHAICHD 9/290668

Permission: Cape Wrath Hotel, Keodale, by Lairg.
Tel: Durness (097181) 274

Three lochs to the south of the Cape Wrath road, involving a walk of about 3 miles. Wonderful scenery, provided that the weather is kind, and bank fishing for dozens of super little trout. Use standard pattern loch flies.

LOCH KEISGAIG 9/267680
LOCH GHEODHA RUAIDH 9/247675
LOCH NA CREIGE RIABHAICH 9/288633
LOCH A'PHUILL BHUIDHE 9/268631

Permission: Cape Wrath Hotel, Keodale, by Lairg.
Tel: Durness (097181) 274

The remotest waters on the Parph, a long walk out into the wilderness, but worth every step of the way. Observe the hill-walker's and climber's code by saying when you are going and when you expect to return. All these lochs have good stocks of traditional brown trout, but Keisgaig can produce fish of over 2lb. Standard pattern loch flies may tempt them.

THE RHICONICH FISHINGS

LOCH A'GARBH-BHAID BEAG 9/266505
LOCH A'GARBH-BHAID MOR 9/275480

Permission: Ray Graham, The Rhiconich Hotel, Rhiconich, by Lairg.
Tel: Kinlochbervie (097182) 224

Follow up the Rhiconich River from the hotel. Boat and bank fishing for salmon, sea trout and brown trout. Boat fishing is best. Wading is uncomfortable and, in many places, downright dangerous. A long walk, but glorious scenery and the chance of great sport. Use standard pattern loch flies for small, traditional, wild brown trout.

MATHAIR GHARBH UILT 9/279505

Permission: Ray Graham, The Rhiconich Hotel, Rhiconich, by Lairg.
Tel: Kinlochbervie (097182) 224

A series of small lochs south from Cnoc Laith and feeding into Loch a'Garbh-bhaid Beag via the Garbh-allt burn. Wonderful hill-walking country with bank fishing for traditional wild brown trout which rise readily to standard pattern loch flies.

LOCH NA THULL 9/253500
LOCH NA CAILLICH 9/250510

Permission: Ray Graham, The Rhiconich Hotel, Rhiconich, by Lairg.
Tel: Kinlochbervie (097182) 224

Easily accessible, scattered waters, with good bank fishing for 8–10-oz trout. Although they are close to the road, once over the hill and fishing you are completely alone and unlikely to be disturbed by anything other than the sound of rising trout. Na Caillich is a small extension of the main loch, at the west end.

LOCH NA CUL NA CARNAICH 9/280525
LOCH AN EAS GHAIRBH 9/268524
LOCHAN CUL NA CREIGE 9/280535

Permission: Ray Graham, The Rhiconich Hotel, Rhiconich, by Lairg.
Tel: Kinlochbervie (097182) 224

Na Carnaich is the largest water, linked to the others by small streams. Park at 266530 and a short walk over the hill, following the stream, brings you to Eas Ghairbh. There is a boat to help you explore this delightful loch, and trout average 8oz, but there are a few very much larger fish in the smaller lochs nearby. Use standard pattern loch flies.

LOCH TARBHAIDH 9/295555
LOCHAIN DUBHA 9/297554

Permission: Ray Graham, The Rhiconich Hotel, Rhiconich, by Lairg.
Tel: Kinlochbervie (097182) 224

Tarbhaidh is close to the A838, south from Gualin House, and easily accessible. Boat and bank fishing for trout which average 8oz. The Dubha lochs lie just to the east of Tarbhaidh, and consists of a series of interesting small lochans, well worth a cast or two. Use standard pattern loch flies.

LOCH CROACH 9/224527
LOCH NA DUIBHE 9/233523
LOCH CHAORUINN 9/240530
LOCH MOR CEANN NA SAITE 9/220545
LOCH A'PHREASAN CHAILLTEAN 9/213535
LOCH EILEANACH 9/209535

Permission: Ray Graham, The Rhiconich Hotel, Rhiconich, by Lairg.
Tel: Kinlochbervie (097182) 224

A superb series of lochs and lochans lying to the west of Rhiconich and north from Ardmore Point, of which Croach, on which there is a good boat, is the most productive. All the lochs are full of bright little fish which average 8oz and the odd larger fish to keep you alert and anxious. Magnificent scenery and peace, perfect peace.

LOCH SGEIR A'CHADHA 9/233510

Permission: Ray Graham, The Rhiconich Hotel, Rhiconich, by Lairg.
Tel: Kinlochbervie (097182) 224

Lies to the south of the track out to John Ridgeway's Adventure Centre at Ardmore. Three small lochs, all giving sport with trout which average 8–10oz. Standard pattern loch flies will work well.

LOCH AISIR MOR 9/226590

Permission: Ray Graham, The Rhiconich Hotel, Rhiconich, by Lairg.
Tel: Kinlochbervie (097182) 224

A good trout loch, near to Oldshoremore Lodge and the village of Oldshoremore. There is a boat on the loch and trout average 10oz. Ideal for the family, if they do not fish, because some of Scotland's finest beaches are close by.

THE SCOURIE FISHINGS

At the time of writing, most of the Scourie waters are the subject of an application for a Protection Order, under the terms of the Freshwater Fisheries (Scotland) Act 1976. This will provide for greater access and greater protection for the trout lochs in the area. The Reay Forest Estate and other riparian owners are to be congratulated for taking steps to preserve the outstanding quality of trout fishing in this area.

PARSONS LOCH 9/187422

Permission: Ian Hay, The Scourie Hotel, Scourie, by Lairg.
Tel: Scourie (0971) 2396

East from Lower Badcall, by Cnoc Thormaid. Bank fishing for trout which average 8oz but also the occasional fish of 2lb or more. Use Black Pennell, Grouse & Claret, and Invicta.

LOCH EILEAN NA CRAOIBHE MOIRE 9/209435

Permission: Ian Hay, The Scourie Hotel, Scourie, by Lairg.
Tel: Scourie (0971) 2396

Hutchinson's Loch, as it is known locally, lies to the east of Scourie, between Gorm Chnoc and Creag a'chlar Locha. The trout here fight hard and wading is not necessary since the bank shelves quickly and fish come into the shallows to feed. In the immediate vicinity there are a further 16 lochs, all containing traditional wild brown trout – and a few monsters of over 5lb.

LOCH NAN UIDH 9/195415

Permission: Ian Hay, The Scourie Hotel, Scourie, by Lairg.
Tel: Scourie (0971) 2396

A long straggle of interlinked lochs lying to the east of the A984, a few miles south from Scourie. Apart from 2 miles of main loch, there are several smaller lochs, all of which have fine trout. There is a good boat available on the main loch and the best fishing area is in the vicinity of the mooring bay.

GORM LOCH 9/217445
LOCH A'MHUIRT 9/203447
LOCH NA MHATHA 9/195440
LOCHAIN DOIMHAIN

Permission: Ian Hay, The Scourie Hotel, Scourie, by Lairg.
Tel: Scourie (0971) 2396

Apart from the waters noted above, there are dozens of other, smaller lochs, not named on the Ordnance Survey map. Local names for some of these little lochs are: Aeroplane, Boot, Pound and Otter, and they all hold good trout, some of which weigh up to 6lb. Park at 183450. Follow the gully up onto the moor and head south-west. Loch a'Mhuirt – The Murder Loch – is on your left and contains large numbers of small trout. Gorm Loch is divided into two sections with a boat moored at 211444. Finding the channel through into the north section is not as easy as it might look from the map – and finding the way back out is even more demanding. Take care. Great sport on the main lochs and even better in the surrounding, smaller lochs and lochans.

LOCHAIN NA CREIGE GILE 9/274454
CAOL LOCH A'MHIND 9/265455

Permission: Ian Hay, The Scourie Hotel, Scourie, by Lairg.
Tel: Scourie (0971) 2396

Another series of more than a dozen excellent little lochs. Start from the track at Stack Lodge and turn west up the outlet stream at 279444. Bank fishing only and trout average 8oz. There are also larger fish, so explore all the lochs, very carefully indeed.

LOCH AN TIGH SHELG 9/297486
LOCH NA TUADH 9/310473
LOCH AN EASAIN UAINE 9/325463
LOCH CUL UIDH AN TUIM 9/290494
LOCH NA STIOMA GILE 9/303492

Permission: Ian Hay, The Scourie Hotel, Scourie, by Lairg.
Tel: Scourie (0971) 2396

My favourite Scourie lochs, all reached after a not inconsiderable walk from Stack Lodge. An Easain Uaine – The Loch of the Green Waterfall – is furthest, Stioma Gile, the highest. All offer superb sport with trout from 6oz to 2lb and more. However, just being there is as important as fishing, and no words of mine could ever properly describe such a magnificent, wild landscape.

LOCH CROCACH 15/197395

Permission: Ian Hay, The Scourie Hotel, Scourie, by Lairg.
Tel: Scourie (0971) 2396

Drive south from Scourie towards Kylesku and park on the old road near 184384. Crocach is a short, stiff walk up the hill to the north. Take a compass and map as it is easy to get lost. There is a good boat and this lovely loch is capable of producing trout of up to 4lb. Best fishing areas are in the vicinity of the islands and standard pattern loch flies do the trick – or should. If the main loch proves dour, have a cast in the smaller, surrounding waters. You might get a pleasant surprise.

DUARTMORE 15/205370

Permission: Ian Hay, The Scourie Hotel, Scourie, by Lairg.
Tel: Scourie (0971) 2396

Greatly 'improved' recently, largely because of food escaping from the fish farm. Easily accessible, with trout averaging 12oz. A good boat is available and Duartmore offers respite from Scourie hill-walking, if required.

LOCH NA CLAISE FEARNA 9/200467
LOCH AN T-SEANA PHUILL 9/210458

Permission: Ian Hay, The Scourie Hotel, Scourie, by Lairg.
Tel: Scourie (0971) 2396

Claise Fearna is an ideal beginner's loch, close to the road, where dozens of small trout may be caught easily. There is a boat, and bank fishing also produces similar results. South from Claise Fearna lie two hill lochs, known locally at Mrs Little's Lochs, where there are larger trout of up to 2lb and more.

LOCH STACK 9/300425
LOCH MORE 15/330372

Permission: Ian Hay, The Scourie Hotel, Scourie, by Lairg.
Tel: Scourie (0971) 2396
The Reay Forest Estate, Estate Office, Achfary, by Lairg.
Tel: Lochmore (097184) 221

These lochs are most famous for salmon and sea trout, although they also contain some really excellent brown trout. Boat fishing only. Gillies are not available and outboard motors are not allowed. Be prepared for some hard oar work – or take along a strong young friend.

LOCH EILEANACH 9/244426
LOCH NA SEILGE 9/255435

Permission: Ian Hay, The Scourie Hotel, Scourie, by Lairg.
Tel: Scourie (0971) 2396
The Reay Forest Estate, Estate Office, Achfary, by Lairg.
Tel: Lochmore (097184) 221

Park at the bothy on the A838 at 265438, just before Loch Stack. Find the stalker's track, south up Ben Stack, and follow it up the hill. Na Seilge is to your right, at the foot of the hill, and contains huge numbers of small fish. It is a long hike down and up again for breakfast. March on, and after 45 minutes you will see Eileanach, sparkling silver, to your right, at the bottom of the hill. Trout of 2–3lb are taken regularly from this super loch and don't ignore the smaller loch to your left, on the way down the hill – it also contains good trout. Standard pattern loch flies produce results.

8 Loch Stack from Ben Stack

9 Ann Sandison on Loch Tighan Sheilg looking towards Foinaven

LOCH DRUIM NA COILLE 9/189492
LOCH NAM BRAC 9/180480
LOCH GOBHLOCH 9/174491
LOCH LAICHEARD 9/180460
LOCHAIN BEALACH AN EILEIN 9/158462
LOCHAN AN FHEIDH 9/200479
LOCH A'PHREASAIN CHALLTUINNE 9/187467

Permission: Mr A. Thompson, The Scourie Angling Association, 2 Handa Terrace, Scourie, by Lairg.
Tel: Scourie (0971) 2420

These are the principal waters of the local angling club, lying to the north of Scourie, and they offer visitors excellent, easily accessible sport. Loch nam Brac is the most scenic and the most productive, being scattered with little islands, bays and promontories where, even in very windy conditions, shelter may be found. A convenient road circles the area, from Claisfearn on the A894, leading round the peninsula, past Tarbet (the starting-point for visits to Handa Island Nature Reserve) and back via Fangmore.

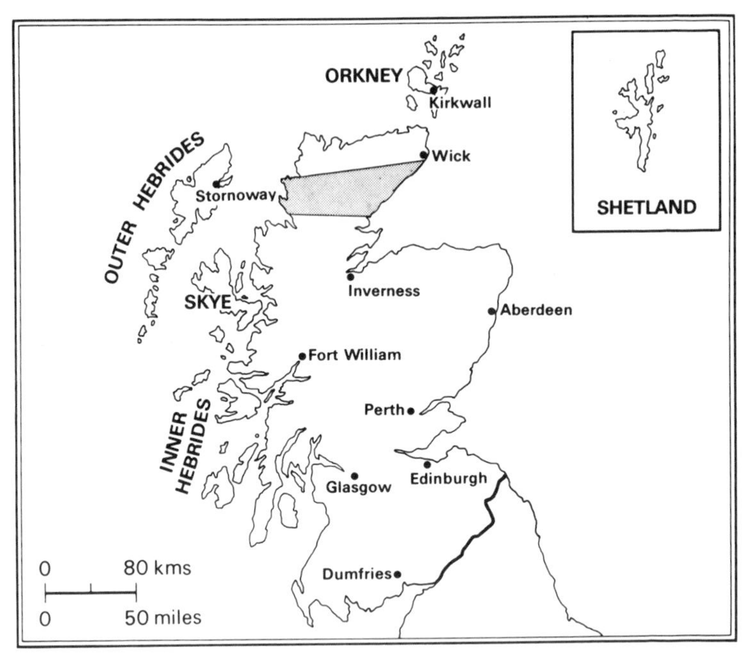

7 Sutherland

3 Sutherland

Many of the lochs described in this section contain *ferox* trout, which can grow to enormous size – Fionn, Assynt, Shin, Merkland, Cam, Veyatie. Catching them requires 'trolling', although from time to time some are taken on the fly when they come to the shallows to feed on small trout. All the lochs offer visiting anglers great sport with traditional highland wild brown trout amidst absolutely glorious scenery, and many have good numbers of fish of 2–3lb.

When boat fishing, always make sure that your craft is sound and that the outboard motor is in good order. Wear a life-jacket, and tie in the oars and outboard. Never, never stand up to fish. These lochs can be astonishingly wild and windy and you should never take chances, under any circumstances. Since the last edition of this book, boats have ceased to be available to members of the public through the Assynt Angling Club. However, bank fishing, more often than not, will produce just as good results. Assynt, Inchnadamph and the Elphin area are stunningly beautiful, with plenty for non-fishing members to do and see: bird-watching, limestone caves, rare Alpine plants, prehistoric monuments, castles, fine hill-walking and climbing. Tom Strang, at Birchbank, Elphin, a noted Scottish mountaineer, author and angler, is always ready to help visitors, and I highly recommend his lodge and adventure centre at Knockan where nothing is ever too much trouble.

ASSYNT ANGLING CLUB WATERS

LOCH CUL FRAIOCH 15/025330

Permission: Tourist Information Office, Lochinver.
Tel: Lochinver (05714) 330

Near the cliffs on the Point of Stoer, 'the loch behind the heath', Cul Fraioch is about 1 mile long by 700 yards wide. The loch, which is managed by the Assynt Angling Club, has a reputation for being dour, but it contains good stocks of trout which average 8oz. Use standard pattern loch flies.

LOCHAN SGEIREACH 15/040290

Permission: Tourist Information Office, Lochinver.
Tel: Lochinver (05714) 330

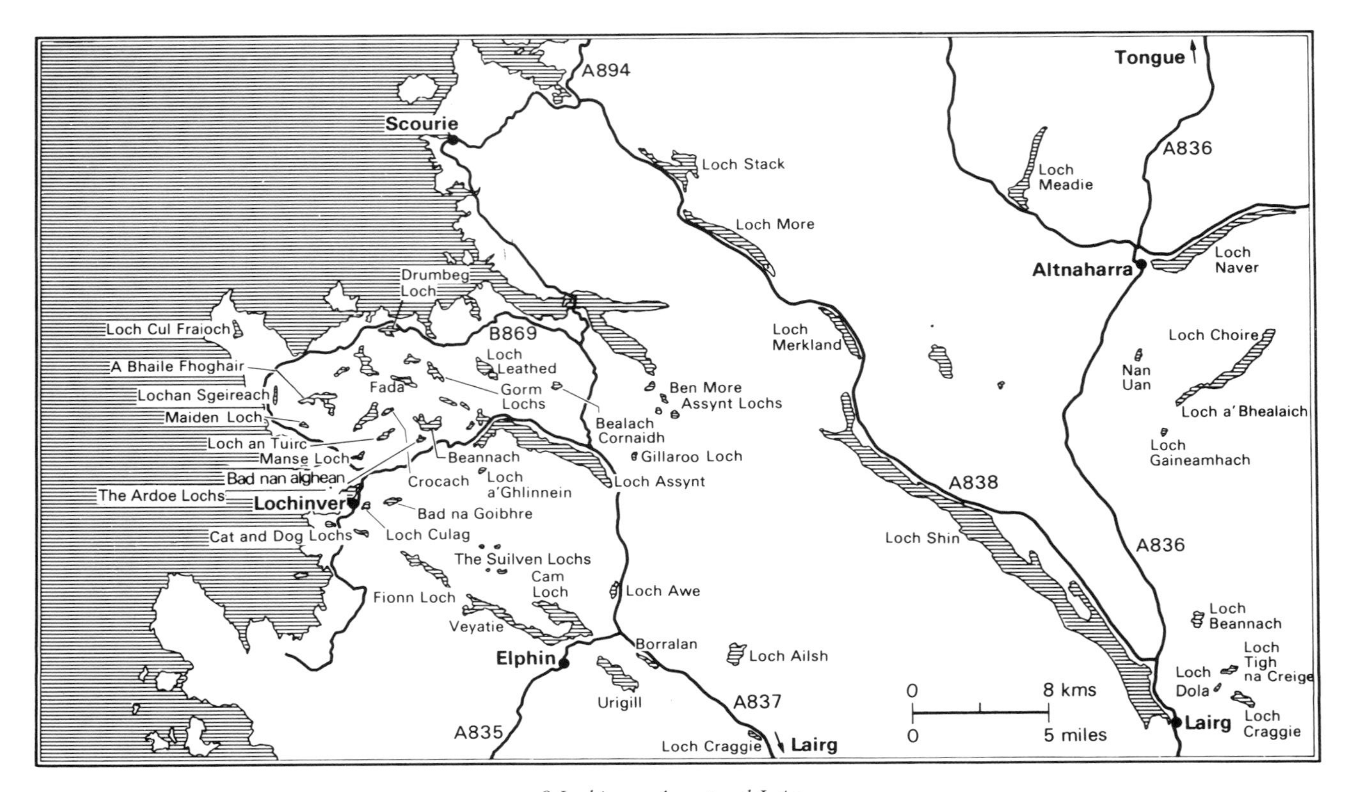

8 *Lochinver, Assynt and Lairg*

Sgeireach lies to the north of the village of Store, adjacent to the B869. It is easily accessible and about 350 yards long by 100 yards wide. Wading requires care but good baskets of 8-oz trout are frequently taken and the loch's roadside position makes it a favourite with visitors.

LOCH POLL DROIGHINN 15/053288
LOCH LEATHED A'BHAILE FHOGHAIR 15/055280
LOCH LEATHAD NAN AIGHEAN 15/058274

Permission: Tourist Information Office, Lochinver.
Tel: Lochinver (05714) 330

These are Assynt Angling Club waters, east of the B869, near to Clachtoll, and easily accessible. The average weight of trout is around 8oz. A'Bhaile Foghair, also known as Lexy's Loch, has larger fish, and trout of up to 4lb have been taken in the past. Use standard pattern loch flies.

THE MAIDEN LOCH 15/050268
LOCH NA H-AIRIGH BIGE 15/053269

Permission: Tourist Information Office, Lochinver.
Tel: Lochinver (05714) 330

Adjacent to the B869 near Clachtoll, the Maiden Loch is one of a series of small, trout-filled lochs which extend from the Bay of Stoer to Drumbeg. The average weight of fish is around 8oz. Maiden is joined by a short stream to Loch na h-Airigh Bige, with its attractive little island, which is also worth fishing.

LOCH CULAG 15/098217

Permission: Inver Lodge Hotel, Lochinver, by Lairg.
Tel: Lochinver (05714) 496

The loch lies to the south of Lochinver and holds salmon, sea trout and brown trout. Inver Lodge guests have priority. It is a shallow loch with an average depth of only 3½ feet and fishes best in a strong wind. Boat fishing only. (The boat is locked to the Hydro Board pole.) Brown trout are small and the loch is of more interest to salmon anglers.

LOCH DRUIM SUARDALAIN 15/115218
LOCH NA H-AIRIGH FRAOICH 15/133213
LOCH NA ALLTAIN DUIBH 15/146206

Permission: Inver Lodge Hotel, Lochinver, by Lairg.
Tel: Lochinver (05714) 496

Reserved for the use of Inver Lodge guests, these lochs are part of the Culag system, linked by the Abhainn Bad na h-Achlaise burn.

THE MANSE LOCH 15/092248

Permission: The Tourist Information Office, Lochinver, by Lairg.
Tel: Lochinver (05714) 330

A small loch to the north of Lochinver, part of the Loch Roe system, managed by the angling club and stocked during the recent past with sea-trout fry. Fishes best during August for brown trout which average 8oz, with the odd fish of over 1lb.

LOCH BAD NA GOIBHRE 15/107227

Permission: Inver Lodge Hotel, Lochinver, by Lairg.
Tel: Lochinver (05714) 496

A small, shallow loch to the east of Lochinver which holds very good trout indeed. Bank fishing only for pink-fleshed, fighting-fit trout. Easily accessible, and hotel guests have priority. Use standard pattern loch flies.

LOCH CROCACH 15/105275

Permission: Inver Lodge Hotel, Lochinver, by Lairg.
Tel: Lochinver (05714) 496

A very lovely loch, reached by a good track which leads out from the B869 north of Lochinver at Rhicarn. Crocach is shallow, with an average depth of 15 feet, and is 1½ miles long by ½ mile wide at its widest. Boat and bank fishing among a multitude of small islands and bays which make for interesting and exciting sport. The average weight of trout is 10–12oz and large baskets are frequently taken. Use standard pattern loch flies.

LOCH AN TURIC 15/115260

Permission: Tourist Information Office, Lochinver, by Lairg.
Tel: Lochinver (05714) 330

The loch is at the head of the Loch Roe system and joined to the Manse Loch by the Allt Loch an Turic burn. There is no bank fishing on this scattered water of narrow bays and sheltered corners. A delightful setting, where trout average 8oz and large baskets may be taken on standard pattern loch flies.

LOCH BAD NAN ALGHEAN — 15/133256

Permission: Tourist Information Office, Lochinver, by Lairg.
Tel: Lochinver (05714) 330

A small, triangular-shaped loch, lying to the north of the A837 near Little Assynt. Bank fishing only for 8-oz trout. It is easily accessible, and baskets of 8–12 fish are common, taken on standard pattern loch flies.

LOCH BEANNACH — 15/140265

Permission: Inver Lodge Hotel, Lochinver, by Lairg.
Tel: Lochinver (05714) 496

A shallow, island-dotted loch to the north of the A873 at Little Assynt, 1¾ miles long by some 600 yards wide, and with a maximum depth of 40ft. The average weight of trout is 8–12oz and baskets of 10–20 fish are often caught. This is a rocky loch, so take care. Fish rise and are caught everywhere, and because Beannach is easily accessible it is the perfect place for a family picnic.

LOCH A'GHLINNEIN — 15/170234

Permission: Inver Lodge Hotel, Lochinver, by Lairg.
Tel: Lochinver (05714) 496

The loch lies to the south of the A837, and is approached from Little Assynt, over the bridge across the River Inver. Follow the track to the right for a few hundred yards, then turn left up the Allt an Tiaghaich burn to the loch. A'Ghlinnein is a circular loch, with bank fishing only, and the best fishing area is in the north-east corner, depending upon wind direction. Trout are of good quality and average 12oz. Standard pattern loch flies will do.

LOCH FEITH AN LEOTHAID — 15/185224
LOCH NA BEINNE REIDHE — 15/213216
LOCH NAM MEALLAN-LIATHA — 15/222200
LOCH COIRE NA CREIGE — 15/170215
LOCH AN LEOTHAID — 15/143226
LOCH CROM — 15/145219
LOCH BAD AN T-SLUIC — 15/153218

Permission: Inver Lodge Hotel, Lochinver, by Lairg.
Tel: Lochinver (05714) 496

All these lochs lie to the south of Loch Assynt and may be approached from Little Assynt, at the west end of the loch, or from the track that leads out from Lochinver, past Glencanisp Lodge. They all contain good stocks of wild brown trout which average 8oz, but there are larger fish to be taken, and one of the joys of walking and fishing in this glorious area is finding out where the large fish lie. Offer them Ke-He, Black Pennell and Silver Butcher.

THE ARDOE LOCHS

LOCH INEIG 15/080243
LOCHAN AN TAIRBH 15/085240
LOCH DUBH 15/074240
LOCH NA GAINEAMHAICH 15/076233
LOCH CAMUS NA FRAITHEARACHD 15/069233
LOCH BRAIGH A'BHAILE 15/066237
LOCH THORMAID 15/066235

Permission: Tourist Information Office, Lochinver, by Lairg.
Tel: Lochinver (05714) 330

These are Assynt Angling Club waters, but readily available to visitors. They lie to the north-west of Lochinver and are approached either from the B869 or along the track that wends out over the moor from Baddidarach on the north shore of Loch Inver. Trout average 8oz and standard pattern loch flies produce results.

LOCH ASSYNT 15/200250

Permission: Inchnadamph Hotel, Assynt, Lochinver, by Lairg.
Tel: Assynt (05712) 202
Inver Lodge Hotel, Lochinver, by Lairg.
Tel: Lochinver (05714) 496

The loch is adjacent to the A837 Lochinver–Ledmore Junction road. It is 6 miles long and up to 1 mile wide, dropping to a depth of nearly 300 feet and covering an area of some 2000 acres. Best results come from boat fishing and while bank fishing is allowed it can be very dangerous because of the depth of the water close to the shore. This is a wild, windy loch where anglers must take the greatest care. Storms can appear suddenly and you should never take chances. If in doubt, don't set out. Loch Assynt has salmon, sea trout and brown trout. About 50 salmon are taken each season, as well as large *ferox* trout which can weigh over 10lb. There are also good numbers of 3–4-lb trout but the average weight is more like 8oz. The best fishing areas are in the shallow water, close to the shore. All the standard patterns of flies will produce good results.

LOCH AWE 15/245154

Permission: Inchnadamph Hotel, Assynt, Lochinver, by Lairg.
Tel: Assynt (05712) 202
Inver Lodge Hotel, Lochinver, by Lairg.
Tel: Lochinver (05714) 496

Loch Awe lies close to the A837 Inchnadamph–Ledmore Junction road and is ¾ mile long by up to 500 yards wide. The occasional salmon makes its way up to the loch via the River Loanan, depending upon water levels, but Loch Awe is best renowned for its sporting, wild brown trout. The average depth is only 5 feet, so the loch tends to weed up as the season advances. However, this weed provides good cover and the best place to fish is near the weed patches, and around the little islands. The burns that run into Loch Awe also hold good trout – and they make a perfect fishing and picnic location if things prove difficult on the loch.

LOCH NA GRUAGAICH 15/242159
LOCH NA SAIGHE DUIBHE 15/233159
LOCH DUBH MEALLAN MHURCHAIDH 15/213195
LOCH NA FAOILEIGE 15/213191

Permission: Inchnadamph Hotel, Assynt, Lochinver, by Lairg.
Tel: Assynt (05712) 202
Inver Lodge Hotel, Lochinver, by Lairg.
Tel: Lochinver (05714) 496

Na Gruagaich and na Saighe Duibhe lie just to the west of Loch Awe, on the route up Canisp (846m). Meallan Mhurchaidh and na Faoileige can be visited on the way down. This makes for a wonderful day out, fishing and walking, with spectacular views from the summit of Canisp, which is an easy walk, and great sport with traditional wild brown trout.

LOCH BEALACH CORNAIDH 15/209282

Permission: The Inchnadamph Hotel, Assynt, Lochinver, by Lairg.
Tel: Assynt (05712) 202

Chose a good day, as far as possible, for the walk out to this delightful little loch. Bealach Cornaidh lies on the upper slopes of the east face of Quinag (808m) and although the trout are not very large, averaging three to the pound, the setting is majestic. Approach from the A894 Skiag Bridge–Unapool road. Two miles north from Skiag you will see a track on your left. Follow this for 1¼ miles and from where it ends march straight on up the Allt na Bradhan burn to the loch.

LOCH A'CHOIRE DHUIBH 15/252281
LOCH A'CHOIRE DHERIG 15/252272
LOCHAN A'CHOIRE GHUIRM 15/261268
LOCH BEALACH A'BHUIRICH 15/261280
LOCH BEALACH NA H-UIDHE 15/264256
LOCH NAN CUARAN 15/291239
LOCH FLEODACH COIRE 15/273248
LOCH NAN CAORACH 15/290234
LOCH MEALL NAN CAORACH 15/290230

Permission: The Inchnadamph Hotel, Assynt, Lochinver, by Lairg.
Tel: Assynt (05712) 202

These are the high lochs of Ben More Assynt, approached from either Loch na Gainmich on the Skiag Bridge–Unapool road, or from the Inchnadamph track. Be prepared for some tough walking, be properly dressed and take a compass and map. There are excellent trout waiting to be caught, some of which reach more than 3lb. This is hill loch fishing at its finest. Use Black Pennell, Black Zulu, Ke-He and Silver Butcher.

LOCH MAOL A'CHOIRE 15/276194

Permission: The Inchnadamph Hotel, Assynt, Lochinver, by Lairg.
Tel: Assynt (05712) 202

Better known as the 'Gillaroo Loch', because of the similarity of the trout it used to contain to their more famous Irish cousins. It is a long time since any were caught but this fine loch now has good brown trout which average 12oz. The southern end, where the feeder burn enters, is perhaps the best fishing area, although fish rise and are caught all over this beautiful loch. Use standard pattern loch flies.

LOCH BORRALAN 15/260110

Permission: The Alt Bar, Altnacealagach, Elphin, by Lairg.
Tel: Strathkanaird (085486) 220

A delightful roadside loch, with both boat and bank fishing. Recently four rods recorded 31 trout weighing 21lb, including a fish of 2lb 4oz. Borralan also holds Arctic char which average 8oz. If and when the going gets tough, retire to the Alt Bar, 20 yards from the lochside.

LOCH URIGILL 15/240100

Permission: Tom Strang, Birchbank Activity Lodge, Knockan, Elphin, by Lairg.

10 Cul Mor from Loch Borralan

Tel: Strathkanaird (085486) 215 or 203
Facilities for Disabled Anglers: As above. A boat seat can be fitted and other facilities are available by prior arrangement.

Approach via a forestry track, 1 mile east from the Ledmore Junction on the A837. Remember to take the key for the locked gate. Park on Cnoc Bad na h-Achlaise (207m), and a five-minute walk brings you to the loch; and to an ideal picnic location – the large, sandy bay on the north shore. The most productive fishing areas are in the vicinity of the lovely little islands in the south-west corner, where trout of 1–2lb may be encountered. The average weight is more modest, 8oz, but in 1987 a superb trout of 8lb 4oz was landed. Use standard pattern loch flies, but there is a mayfly hatch in late June, when Greenwell's Glory produces results.

CAM LOCH 15/210140

Permission: Inver Lodge Hotel, Lochinver, by Lairg.
Tel: Lochinver (05714) 496

'The Crooked Loch' is a large, beautiful loch, adjacent to the A835 road at Elphin. Boats are moored at the east end, directly below the little cemetery. Cam can be wild and windy, when it is advisable to remain in the first bay and concentrate your efforts round the island, which is also a good place for lunch. Keep close to the shore when fishing Cam, because it shelves very quickly and a short distance out puts you over water which can be as much as 30 feet deep. Cam holds large *ferox* and good stocks of 8-oz trout. Expect great sport, large baskets and a few big fish. Standard pattern loch flies all work well.

LOCH VEYATIE 15/190130
LOCH A'MHADAIL 15/154144

Permission: Inver Lodge Hotel, Lochinver, by Lairg.
Tel: Lochinver (05714) 496

Loch Veyatie has a more sombre feel about it than its neighbour, Cam Loch (above). Cul Mor (849m) towers over the south shore and Suilven (731m) dominates the northern skyline. Veyatie is a long, narrow, deep loch dropping to 126 feet at the north end, and, as with Cam, you should take great care when boat fishing. The east end offers the best sport but there are dozens of small bays and corners where good fish may be caught.

Loch a'Mhadail lies at right angles to Veyatie, at the west end, separated from Veyatie by a narrow rock bar. During times of high water, a'Mhaidail becomes joined to Veyatie and this is a good place to fish. A trout of 9lb was taken here recently. An outboard motor is really essential when fishing Veyatie. The average weight of trout is 8oz, but there are good numbers of larger fish. There is a mayfly hatch in late June; otherwise, use standard patterns.

FIONN LOCH 15/130176

Permission: Inver Lodge Hotel, Lochinver, by Lairg.
Tel: Lochinver (05714) 496

Regarded by many as the best loch in the area, Fionn Loch lies in a valley formed by Cul Mor to the south and Suilven to the north. It is best approached from Inverkirkaig, south from Lochinver, up the track that follows the Kirkaig River, past Achin's Bookshop, the remotest bookshop on mainland Britain. Fionn is 2½ miles long by about 500 yards wide and holds good stocks of trout which average 8oz, and good numbers of larger fish of 3–4lb, as well as *ferox*. The western end is perhaps the most productive, but it is hard to resist the temptation to explore the remote eastern bays and corners. Flies to use include Blue Zulu, Invicta and Silver Butcher. If trout are dour, park at 133172 and climb Suilven by Belach Mor. Savage entertainment.

THE NORTH SUILVEN LOCHS

LOCH NA BARRACK 15/157188
LOCH A'CHOIRE DHUIBH 15/160188

Permission: Inver Lodge Hotel, Lochinver, by Lairg.
Tel: Lochinver (05714) 496

A series of some 15 little lochs and lochans which lie below Caisteal Liath, the highest point on Suilven, the 'Pillar Mountain' of the Vikings. Utterly wonderful. Approach from Lochinver and Glencanisp Lodge.

THE SOUTH SUILVEN LOCHS

LOCH GLEANNAN A'MHADAIDH 15/160161
LOCH NAN RAC 15/170159
LOCHAN NIGHEAD 15/182147

Permission: Inver Lodge Hotel, Lochinver, by Lairg.
Tel: Lochinver (05714) 496

These superb hill lochs all lie between Suilven and Veyatie and are most easily approached by taking a boat up Veyatie and walking north into the hills with compass and map. They are very special, with fierce-fighting, bright little trout which average 8oz and rise well to all the standard patterns of flies. Hard walking.

THE SOUTH CANISP LOCHS

LOCH A'CHROISG 15/220155
LOCHAN FADA 15/206167
LOCH MEALL A'MHUTLAICH 15/190167
LOCH NA GAINIMH 15/175185

Permission: Inver Lodge Hotel, Lochinver, by Lairg.
Tel: Lochinver (05714) 496

Spend a whole day fishing these super lochs. Set out from the east end of Cam Loch, near Elphin, at 229121 and follow the stalkers' path along the north shore of Cam. These lochs are the ideal place to introduce beginners to both fly fishing and to hill-walking. All the lochs have large stocks of traditional wild brown trout and large baskets are the rule rather than the exception.

DRUMBEG LOCHS

LOCH DRUMBEG 15/117326

Permission: Inquiries to Alasdair Hay, The Keeper, North Lochinver Estate, Torbeck, Lochinver, by Lairg.
Tel: Lochinver (05714) 220

An easily accessible, scattered loch, full of bays, promontories and small, tree-covered islands. It contains brown trout which average 8–10oz but fish of up to 2lb are sometimes taken. Best results come from boat fishing. The loch is naturally divided into two sections by a channel known as 'The Narrows' and the eastern shore of the west bay is the most productive area; on the main loch, round the islands is the place to concentrate. Use Grouse & Claret, Greenwell's Glory, Black Pennell, Blae & Black and Silver Butcher.

LOCH POLL 15/100303

Permission: Inquiries to Alasdair Hay, The Keeper, North Lochinver Estate, Torbeck, Lochinver, by Lairg.
Tel: Lochinver (05714) 220

The largest of the Drumbeg waters, a short walk over the moor, south from the B869 at 095317. Poll fishes best in a good south-west wind and the south-west bay is the most productive area, eastwards, along to the principal inlet burn. Use standard pattern loch flies.

LOCH SKERRACH 15/119308
LOCH BAD AN OG 15/116314
LOCH NAM BREAC 15/106317

Permission: Inquiries to Alasdair Hay, The Keeper, North Lochinver Estate, Torbeck, Lochinver, by Lairg.
Tel: Lochinver (05714) 220

A number of small lochs adjacent to the peat track that leads southwards from Drumbeg. Bank fishing only for trout averaging 8–10oz. Use nymphs, Blae & Black, Invicta and Ke-He.

LOCH FADA 15/113304
LOCH AN TOLLA BHAID 15/117295
LOCH NA LOINNE 15/126293

Permission: Inquiries to Alasdair Hay, The Keeper, North Lochinver Estate, Torbeck, Lochinver, by Lairg.
Tel: Lochinver (05714) 220

These lochs lie to the south of Drumbeg and are easily reached by following a good peat track which starts at the west end of Loch Drumbeg. Bank fishing only, but great sport with trout averaging three to the pound.

LOCH A'BHRAIGHE 15/131308
GORM LOCH MOR 15/142298
GORM LOCH BEAG 15/143288
LOCH ODHAR 15/152296

Permission: Inquiries to Alasdair Hay, The Keeper, North Lochinver Estate, Torbeck, Lochinver, by Lairg.
Tel: Lochinver (05714) 220

The lochs are approached from the village of Nedd on the A869. Follow the surfaced track south for ½ mile to the crofts. A grass track leads south. A'Bhraighe is the first loch, and contains traditional, small highland wild brown trout; Mor and Beag also have fish which average 8oz, but there are a few larger trout as well. Loch Odhar might surprise you. Flies to use include Invicta, Greenwell's Glory, Mallard & Claret and Black Pennell.

SOUTH AND EAST SUTHERLAND LOCHS

LOCH A'MHEALLAIN 15/289108

Permission: The Oykle Bridge Hotel, Rosehall, by Lairg.
Tel: Rosehall (054984) 218

A classic hill loch, 1 mile north from the A837 Oykle Bridge–Ledmore Junction road. A stiff climb, but wonderful sport with 8-oz wild brown trout and a few larger fish. Bank fishing, using the standard fly patterns.

LOCH CRAGGIE 15/325055
LOCH EILEAG 15/309063

Permission: The Oykle Bridge Hotel, Rosehall, by Lairg.
Tel: Rosehall (054984) 218

Two easily accessible roadside lochs to the south of the A837, now surrounded by commercial forestry plantations. Rainbow trout have been stocked in Craggie in the past, and from time to time sea trout are taken. Brown trout average 8oz. Bank fishing, using the standard fly patterns.

LOCH AILSH 15/315110

Permission: The Oykle Bridge Hotel, Rosehall, by Lairg.
Tel: Rosehall (054984) 218

The loch is north from the A837, and approached from the estate road which leads out to Benmore Lodge. It was notable in days past as a sea-trout fishery, and is still capable of producing good sport. Brown trout average 12oz and fish of over 2lb are sometimes taken. The best areas are the north and south ends, where the infant River Oykle enters and leaves, and where the odd salmon is also taken. Best flies include Black Pennell, Soldier Palmer, Black Zulu and various Butchers. Superbly scenic and a perfect place to spend a day, fishless or otherwise.

LOCH SHIN 16/500160

Permission: Don Keniston, The Lairg Angling Club, Main Street, Lairg.
Facilities for Disabled Anglers: As above.
Tel: Lairg (0549) 2239
Sutherland Arms Hotel, Lairg.
Tel: Lairg (0549) 2291
The Overscaig Hotel, by Lairg.
Tel: Merkland (054983) 203

One of the largest lochs in Scotland, and one of the most productive, Loch Shin is full of 8-oz traditional, wild brown trout and a good number of much larger fish weighing 2lb and more. *Ferox* are regularly taken and during 1991 the Inverness branch of the Royal British Legion took trout weighing 7lb 2oz, 5lb 10oz and 4lb 8oz. One double-figure trout was lost at the net, being too big to land. However, an average basket is more likely to be about 20 fish totalling 12lb. Favourite fishing areas are around Gull Island and the mouth of the Fiag River. Flies to use include Black Pennell, Black Zulu, Invicta and Loch Ordie. A boat is essential, as is great care when afloat, for Shin can be a windy, dangerous water.

LOCH CRAGGIE 16/625075

Permission: The Sutherland Arms Hotel, Lairg.
Tel: Lairg (0549) 2291

This is the best loch in the area, with easy access via a new forestry road to the west end, where boats are moored. Bank fishing is not allowed. Trout average 12oz and fight hard, with fish of 3–4lb taken regularly. Good fishing areas are in Boathouse Bay and along the south shore. The east end of the loch is also excellent, particularly by the little island and opposite the wood at the south-east end. Take care here, because there are large boulders just below the surface. An outstanding, not-to-be-missed fishery.

LOCH DOLA 16/607080
LOCH TIGH NA CREIGE 16/615093

Permission: The Sutherland Arms Hotel, Lairg.
Tel: Lairg (0549) 2291

Two lochs to the west and north of Craggie, approached by the same forestry road. Dola is full of super fish which average 8–10oz and may be taken anywhere on the loch. Tigh na Creige has smaller fish, but there is a good chance of trout of over 2lb. The north shoreline is the best fishing area on Creige, particularly where the feeder burn enters the loch.

LOCH BEANNACH 16/599125

Permission: Don Keniston, Lairg Angling Club, Main Street, Lairg.
Tel: Lairg (0549) 2239

The loch lies to the east of the A836 Lairg–Altnaharra road, sheltered by Dalchork Forest, and is ¾ mile long by about 700 yards wide. Boat fishing only. Recent catches (1991) show 5 fish of 7lb 8oz, 10 fish of 9lb and 6 fish of 8lb 3oz. Flies to use are Loch Ordie (essential), Kate Maclaren, Grouse & Claret, Soldier Palmer and Peter Ross.

LOCH MERKLAND 16/393310

Permission: Overscaig Hotel, by Lairg.
Tel: Merkland (054983) 203

Adjacent to the A838 Lairg–Scourie road, the loch is 3 miles long and up to ¼ mile wide. It holds good stocks of 8-oz trout and some huge *ferox*. This is a deep loch, so keep close to the shore when fishing and use standard pattern loch flies.

LOCH A'GHRIAMA 16/390260

Permission: Overscaig Hotel, by Lairg.
Tel: Merkland (054983) 203

An extension of Loch Shin and joined to Loch Merkland by the Merkland River. It offers good sport with traditional trout averaging 8oz, and, particularly in the autumn, the chance of much larger specimens. Do not ignore the Merkland River; on windy days when it is not possible to launch a boat on either Shin or Merkland, the river can be great fun.

LOCH NAM BREAC BEAGA 16/651188

Permission: Sutherland Estates, Estate Office, Golspie.
Tel: Golspie (04083) 268

A small loch in the Ben Armine Forest, lying on a ridge on the slopes of Meallan Liath Mor (461m). Fishing is from the bank only and the loch has a plentiful supply of good 8-oz trout. There are a few larger

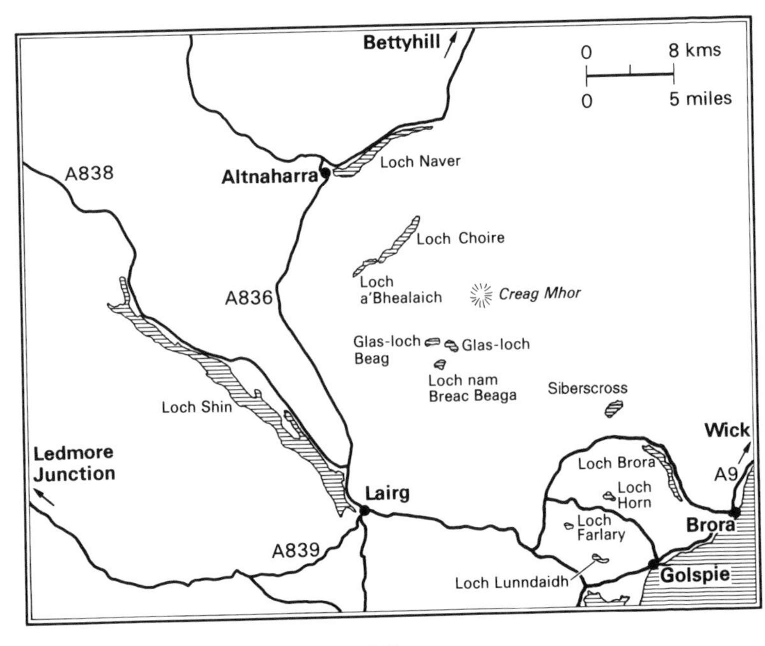

9 Brora

fish and from time to time trout of up to 2lb are taken. The loch is also known as the Dhli Loch and an average basket should account for 10–15 fish. Approach from Brora and use Soldier Palmer, Zulus, Loch Ordie and Gold Butcher.

GLAS-LOCH BEAG

16/660202

Permission: Sutherland Estates, Estate Office, Golspie.
Tel: Golspie (04083) 268

A small, triangular loch to the west of Glas Loch, shallow and full of small trout. Getting up to the loch may make you catch your breath a bit, but once there the scenery is spectacular and baskets of 30–40 fish common. Approach as for Breac Beaga (above) and use the same patterns of flies.

THE GLAS LOCH

16/670195

Permission: Sutherland Estates, Estate Office, Golspie.
Tel: Golspie (04083) 268

The Glas Loch lies on a ridge to the west of Creag Dubh Dail nan Gillean and reaching it involves a long, stiff climb. It is worth the effort, because the trout average 12oz and fight furiously – and fish of up to 3lb are also taken. It holds Arctic char as well. Use standard pattern loch flies. Approach from Brora.

LOCH FARLARY 17/772050

Permission: Sutherland Estates, Estate Office, Golspie.
Tel: Golspie (04083) 268

An easily accessible roadside loch, 5 miles up Dunrobin Glen. It is shallow, and both boat and bank fishing are available. Trout average 8–10oz and rise well to the standard patterns of fly. Ideal for beginners.

LOCH LUNNDAIDH 17/785006

Permission: Lindsay & Co, Main Street, Golspie.
Tel: Golspie (04083) 212

A pleasant loch, involving an enjoyable walk of about 40 minutes along a good track. Loch Lunndaidh lies between Lunndaidh (446m) and Aberscross Hill (257m) and trout average 12oz, with the occasional fish of up to 2lb. The far end, where the loch narrows, is the best fishing area and always have a Peter Ross as the tail fly on your cast.

LOCH HORN 17/796060

Permission: Lindsay & Co, Main Street, Golspie.
Tel: Golspie (04083) 212

A beautiful loch, lying 1000 feet up on the southern slopes of Ben Horn (521m). The walk out takes about 30 minutes from Bridge of Horn at 800048. The Golspie Angling Club stocks this excellent loch and a boat is available. Trout average 12oz and fight hard. There are larger fish in Loch Horn but they tend to stay there, being very hard to catch. Concentrate round the margins using standard pattern loch flies.

LOCH BAD NA H-EARBA 17/765138
LOCH NA GLAIC 17/760131
LOCHAN CUL NA H-AMAITE 16/759142

Permission: Siberscross Lodge, Strath Brora, Rogart.
Tel: Rogart (04084) 246

Go north from the lodge, up a good track, to these easily accessible lochs. There is marvellous sport with bright, small trout in all three and a few much larger fish as well. Ideal lochs for beginners of any age, and an ideal place for a day out in the hills.

LOCH BRORA 17/850080

Permission: Rob Wilson (Rods & Guns), Rosslyn Street, Brora.
Tel: Brora (04082) 21373

The principal attractions here are sea trout and salmon, although Loch Brora also holds good stocks of brown trout, including fish of up to 5lb. The best trout fishing area is at the south end of the loch and all the standard patterns of fly produce results. Boat fishing only.

11 Far from the madding crowd

LOCH BUIDHE 21/660984
LOCH LARO 21/605995
LOCH AN LAGAIN 21/660955
LOCH LAOIGH 21/730958
LOCH LANNSAIDH 21/737945
LOCH A'GHOBHAIR 21/659936

Permission: W. A. Macdonald, Ironmonger, Castle Street, Dornoch.
Tel: Dornoch (0862) 810301
The Trentham Hotel, The Poles, Dornoch.
Tel: Dornoch (0862) 810391 or 810551

These are the Dornoch Angling Club waters and all are readily available to visiting anglers. Reaching Loch Laro requires a four-wheel drive vehicle, but the others are easily accessible. Anglers will find sport with good-quality brown trout averaging 8–10oz and a few much larger fish, in glorious surroundings.

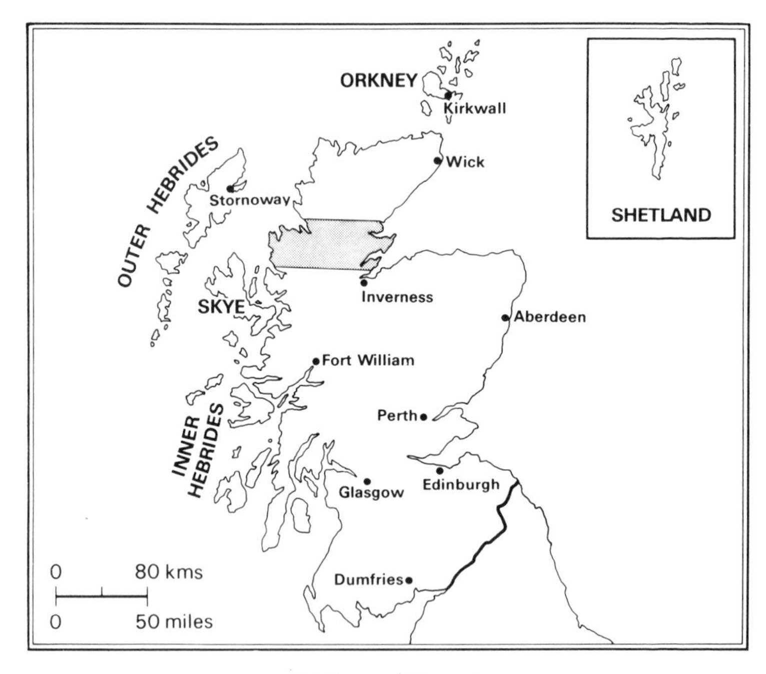

10 Ross and Cromarty

4 Ross and Cromarty

Of all the lochs in Scotland, I think that Sionascaig, near Ullapool, is one of the finest. It is remote, beautiful and lovely, and surrounded by some of the finest scenery in the world. It also contains excellent trout, and nearby are many other lochs and lochans all of which offer great sport. This area is Scotland and the Highlands at their finest and no words of mine could ever do justice to its majestic grandeur. In spite of many efforts, I have yet to take a photograph which really captures the true magnificence of the region and so I suppose all I can advise you to do is to go and see for yourself. You will not be disappointed, either with the scenery or the trout fishing. From Ullapool to Shieldaig and Golspie to Strathpeffer, there are trout lochs to suit all tastes and all degrees of physical fitness. You may chose a roadside reservoir or walk miles into the hills and there is now a small commercial rainbow fishery as well. Ross and Cromarty is well worth a visit and an excellent centre for a fishing holiday.

THE DAM LOCHS

LOCH BEINN DEIRG 15/15500020/153000
LOCH NA MAOILE 15/16000020/157998
LOCH BAD NA H-ACHLAISE 20/158995
LOCH DUBH 20/150985

Permission: Ullasports, West Argyle Street, Ullapool.
Tel: Ullapool (0854) 612621

These lochs cover an area of nearly 1 square mile and lie to the north of Ullapool. There is good access to them via a Hydro Board road which branches off the A835 1 mile south of Strathkanaird. The water levels of the lochs fluctuate, but this does not seem to affect the fishing adversely. Boats are available and good catches are taken from the bank, particularly from the south-eastern shore of Loch Dubh where several feeder burns enter the loch. The Dam Lochs are stocked from time to time and hold brown and rainbow trout. Loch Beinn Deirg holds the largest fish and the average weight is around 1lb 8oz. It is a dour loch though and you should not expect the fish to come leaping into the boat with their hands up. Loch Dubh trout average 1lb and na Maoile and na h-Achlaise average 8–12oz. An average basket should

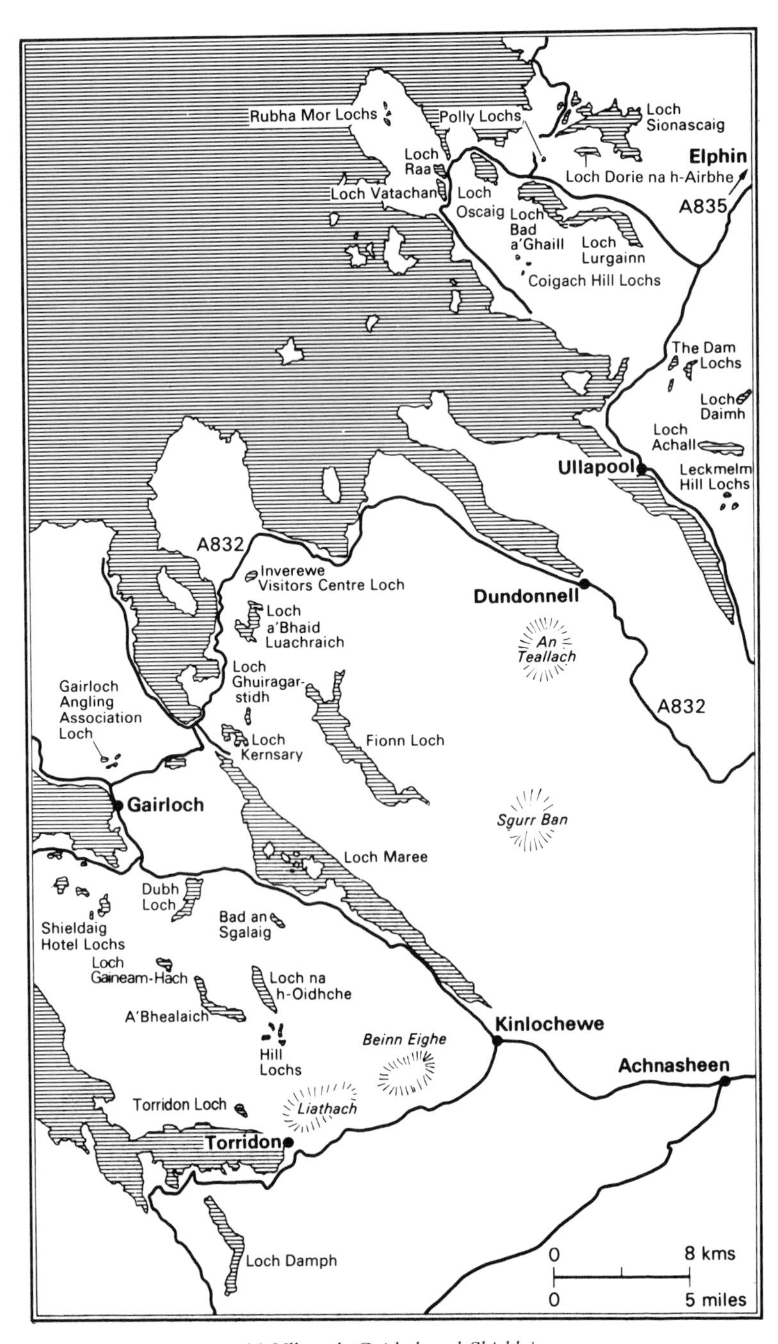

11 Ullapool, Gairloch and Shieldaig

bring you six fish weighing 4–6lb – on a good day, but trout of over 3lb are also caught. Best flies to use are Black Pennell, Grenwell's Glory, Grouse & Claret and Butchers.

LOCH ACHALL 20/175950

Permission: Lochbroom Hardware, Quay Street, Ullapool.
Tel: Ullapool (0854) 612356

Loch Achall is to the east of Ullapool on the Rhidorroch Estate and there is a good road out to the loch. Boat and bank fishing are available. Some sea trout and a good run of salmon move into the loch from June onwards. Brown trout are small, averaging 8oz but large baskets are taken and 20–30 fish would not be an exceptional catch. The best fishing areas are in the bays close to the shore and a good drift is along the south shore where several feeder burns enter the loch from Deinn Eildeach. Teal & Green, Invicta, Black Pennell and Butchers produce the best results. A very pleasant loch for a day out in the hills.

LECKMELM ESTATE HILL LOCHS

LOCH COIRE NA BA BUIDHE 20/200981
LOCHANAN FIODHA 20/192295
LOCHANAN A'MHUILINN 20/195918
LOCH AN ACHA 20/198915
LOCH SARRAIDH MHOIR 20/181924
LOCH THORMAID 20/211927
LOCH NA BEINNE BRICE 20/219928

Permission: Leckmelm Estate Holiday Enterprises, Leckmelm, Ullapool.
Tel: Ullapool (0854) 612471

These hill lochs are to the east of Leckmelm on the A835 Ullapool–Loch Broom road. They are stocked from time to time and all contain brown trout with an average weight of 12oz. The odd larger fish is sometimes taken and trout of 2lb–2lb 8oz are not infrequent, while the largest trout taken weighed 4lb. Access is via an estate road, on foot only, involving a walk of up to 2½ miles. It is bank fishing only, with good baskets of well-shaped, excellent trout. Lovely surroundings and a great place to fish.

LOCH DAIMH 20/275944

Permission: Highland Coastal Estates, Argyle Street, Ullapool.
Tel: Ullapool (0854) 612548

Loch Daimh is a remote, delightful loch to the east of Ullapool on the Rhidorroch Estate. It lies in a steep-sided valley with Cnoc Camh (591m) to the north and Mullach a'Chadha Bhuidhe (442m) to the south. The fishing is let with Rhidorroch Lodge (boat included) and is reserved for lodge guests. Trout average 12oz and excellent baskets of up to 20 fish are taken frequently on Soldier Palmer, Grouse & Claret and Butchers. Good fishing in superb scenery.

12 Loch Lurgainn from Stac Pollaidh, looking south-east

LOCH LURGAINN 15/110090

Permission: Inverpolly Estates, Estate Office, Inverpolly, Ullapool.
Tel: Achiltibuie (085482) 452

Loch Lurgainn lies adjacent to the minor road out to the Summer Isles and is 4 miles long by ½ mile wide. Ragged hills rise from the shoreline with the Coigach Mountains dominating the southern horizon and Cul Beag and Stack Polly northwards. Lurgainn contains trout which average 8oz but each season usually produces a few much larger fish, including *ferox*. The largest trout in recent years weighed 5lb 12oz. The western section of the loch, with its sheltered bays and islands, is the best fishing area where all the standard pattern loch flies will produce results.

LOCH BAD NA H-ACHLAISE 15/083090

Permission: Inverpolly Estates, Estate Office, Inverpolly, Ullapool.
Tel: Achiltibuie (085482) 452

This small loch, known locally as the Green Loch, lies between Loch Lurgainn and Loch Bad a'Ghaill. In high water levels it is sometimes possible to haul a boat over to it. Bad na h-Achlaise offers great sport with brown trout, as well as occasional sea trout and salmon.

LOCH BAD A'GHAILL 15/080100

Permission: Inverpolly Estates, Estate Office, Inverpolly, Ullapool.
Tel: Achiltibuie (085482) 452

Loch Bad a'Ghaill is 2 miles long by ½ mile wide, and lies adjacent to the Summer Isles road out from the A835 at Drumrunnie. In recent years this loch has lost its reputation for being dour, and during 1990 a magnificent trout of 5lb was taken; also salmon and sea trout of up to 4lb 12oz. Daily permits are available for both boat and bank fishing, and Bad a'Ghaill is also let with a well-furnished self-catering cottage, including fishing on the River Garvie and Loch Oscaig. Outboard motors may be hired from the estate office. Use standard pattern loch flies.

LOCH OSCAIG 15/042123

Permission: Inverpolly Estates, Estate Office, Inverpolly, Ullapool.
Tel: Achiltibuie (085482) 452
The Summer Isles Hotel, Achiltibuie, Ullapool.
Tel: Achiltibuie (085482) 282

Oscaig is the last in the chain of lochs that lie between Inverpolly and Coigach. From Oscaig, the system drains through the rocky little River

Garvie to the sea in Garvie Bay. Loch Oscaig is best known as a sea-trout fishery although some good brown trout are taken as well, particularly along the wooded south-west shore. The average weight of brown trout is about 1lb; of sea trout, up to 3lb 8oz; of salmon, up to 11lb.

LOCH GARVIE 15/039138

Permission: Inverpolly Estates, Estate Office, Inverpolly, Ullapool.
Tel: Achiltibuie (085482) 452
The Summer Isles Hotel, Achiltibuie, Ullapool.
Tel: Achiltibuie (085482) 282
Mrs T. G. Longstaff, Badentarbat Lodge, Achiltibuie, Ullapool.
Tel: Achiltibuie (085482) 225

Loch Garvie is an extension of the River Garvie, just before it enters the sea. As the season advances, the loch tends to become weedy, but it can produce outstanding sport with sea trout, and the occasional salmon. Bank fishing only, and the west shore is best. Sea trout may also be caught from the beach where the river flows out into the bay.

LOCH RAA 15/017120
LOCH VATACHAN 15/017110

Permission: The Summer Isles Hotel, Achiltibuie, Ullapool.
Tel: Achiltibuie (085482) 282
Mrs T. G. Longstaff, Badentarbat Lodge, Achiltibuie, Ullapool.
Tel: Achiltibuie (085482) 225

Delightfully situated, close to the road out to the Summer Isles. Splendid brown trout averaging 8oz with the occasional larger fish, especially in May and June. Bank fishing only, using standard pattern loch flies.

COIGACH HILL LOCHS

LOCHAN SGEIREACH 15/048097
LOCHAN LEACACH 15/055095
LOCHAN FADA 15/055093
LOCHAN EALLACH 15/063094

Permission: The Summer Isles Hotel, Achiltibuie, Ullapool.
Tel: Achiltibuie (058482) 282

The Coigach Hill Lochs are all about an hour's walk from the Summer Isles Hotel. You will not catch any record-breaking fish but you will have great sport with typical highland wild brown trout – and there are few more dramatic places to catch them.

RUBHA MOR LOCHS

LOCH A'MHEALLAIN	15/992110
LOCH CAMAS AN FHEIDH	15/994118
LOCH NA CREIGE DUIBHE	15/006117
LOCH NA BEISTE	15/005125
LOCHAN DEARG	15/999129
LOCH TOTAIG	15/980160
LOCH AIRIGH BLAIR	15/986170
LOCH NA PLOYTACH	15/983177
LOCH AIRIGH CHALUIM	15/991159
CLAR LOCH BEAG	15/991155
CLAR LOCH MOR	15/994150

Permission: Mrs T. G. Longstaff, Badentarbat Lodge, Achiltibuie, Ullapool.
Tel: Achiltibuie (085482) 225

This remote corner of Ross-shire offers all that is best for a complete family holiday: excellent game fishing, superb hill walks and climbs, marvellous empty, shining white sands and glorious bird and plant life. The lochs detailed above will all provide good sport with 6–8-oz trout, but there are a few very large trout lurking in some of the lochs, so be prepared. My own favourites are the remote waters, not because they are any better, but because they are yours for the day to share only with curlew and lark – not another human for miles.

POLLY LOCHS

LOCH CALL AN UIDHEAN	15/092146
LOCH BUINE MOIRE	15/097155
LOCH UIDH TARRAIGEAN	15/095139
LOCH NA DAIL	15/084136

Permission: Inverpolly Estate, Estate Office, Inverpolly, Ullapool.
Tel: Achiltibuie (085482) 452

These lochs lie to the north of Polly Farm and fishing is mostly from the bank, although there is now a boat on Loch na Dail, which is also known as Lower Polly. The average weight of brown trout in Tarraigean and Dail is about 12oz and a good day should produce four to six fish. Trout of up to 5lb have been caught and most years produce a few 3-lb fish. Salmon and sea trout are regularly caught in the lochs from July onwards. Call an Uidhean and Buine have small, 6–8-oz trout.

LOCH SIONASCAIG 15/120140
LOCHAN GAINMHEICH 15/140114
LOCHAN DOIRE DHUIBH 15/137106
LOCH LON NA H-UAMHA 15/128110

Permission: Inverpolly Estate, Estate Office, Inverpolly, Ullapool.
Tel: Achiltibuie (085482) 452

Sionascaig lies at the heart of the Inverpolly National Nature Reserve to the north-east of Ullapool and must be one of the most dramatically beautiful lochs in all of Scotland. It is a large scatter of shimmering water, studded with little islands and a shoreline that meanders in and out over 16 miles of bays and headlands in a vista of mountain, moorland and water. There are three adjacent lochs, joined to Sionascaig, and these, too, offer excellent sport, as does the principal feeder burn that enters Doire Dhuibh from the Drumrunie Forest. Boats are moored in Boat Bay at 098152, a short walk from the road.

Fish amidst the beauty of Stack Polly, Cul Beag, Cul Mor and Suilven, and if you are discovering this area for the first time you will be overwhelmed by the sheer size of the landscape. Sionascaig is a deep loch and near the largest island, Eilean Mor, the water drops to nearly 200 feet. Fishing is best, therefore, round the margins and in the shallow water. The annual catch is around 700 fish from three boats and bank fishing, with trout averaging 8–12oz. A number of 5–7-lb fish are also taken, as are *ferox,* which can weigh up to 17lb. The 1989 season produced one *ferox* which weighed 16lb 12oz. Yes, you will have blank days as well, but this is a loch that you must fish. You will not be disappointed.

LOCH DOIRE NA H-AIRBHE 15/105127

Permission: Inverpolly Estate, Estate Office, Inverpolly, Ullapool.
Tel: Achiltibuie (085482) 452

There is no easy way in. Getting to Doire na h-Airbhe involves a stiff walk, from all directions. Park at 082136 and head east towards Stack Polly. An alternative approach is by boat, via Sionascaig; come ashore at 102131 and walk up the hill, south-west. Whichever way you choose, once there this fine loch will more than repay your efforts. The most productive area is the south-east shoreline, particularly along the wooded east end. Trout average 12oz and this is my favourite Inverpolly loch.

THE SHIELDAIG LOCHS

THE FAIRY LOCH 19/810712

Permission: Shieldaig Lodge Hotel, Badachro, Gairloch.
Tel: Badachro (044583) 250

13 Ann Sandison, above Loch Doire na h-Airbhe looking towards Cul Mor

The Fairy Loch is a 1-mile walk from the hotel and guests have priority. There is one boat available and bank fishing is also allowed. This loch holds excellent trout and fish of up to 3lb 8oz are caught. Best flies to use are Soldier Palmer and Grouse & Green. This is a small loch dotted with islands and fishing is best round them. Bank fishing is good from the points and headlands, but you will count your fish on the fingers of one hand rather than on both. Excellent trout, though, if you do tempt them to rise.

SPECTACLES 19/817705

Permission: Shieldaig Lodge Hotel, Badachro, Gairloch.
Tel: Badachro (044583) 250

This is the highest of the Shieldaig Lochs and fish average 12oz. Bank fishing only and an average basket will account for up to 10 fish. Standard loch fly patterns produce results and the loch is an easy walk from the hotel. Guests have priority.

THE AEROPLANE LOCH 19/808711

Permission: Shieldaig Lodge Hotel, Badachro, Gairloch.
Tel: Badachro (044583) 250

If the midges are not too bad this is an ideal spot for some after-dinner casting and good baskets are taken. Trout average 8oz and 15–20 fish are frequently caught. Best flies include Kingfisher Butcher, Red Tag, Peter Ross and Wickham's Fancy. A good loch to restore one's confidence if things get a bit hard on Fairy Loch.

THE DIAMOND LOCH 19/810702

Permission: Shieldaig Lodge Hotel, Badachro, Gairloch.
Tel: Badachro (044583) 250

This is a small loch about 500 yards by 200 yards and the average weight of trout is 12oz. It is a short walk from the hotel and fishing is from the bank only. Catches in double figures are not uncommon and trout rise to all the standard patterns of loch flies. The south-east bank, in the vicinity of the small island, is a favourite spot, although fish are caught from all round the shore.

LOCH BAD NA H-ACHLAISE 19/770737

Permission: Shieldaig Lodge Hotel, Badachro, Gairloch.
Tel: Badachro (044583) 250

Bad na h-Achlaise is a beautiful roadside loch to the west of the hotel along the B8056 road to Redpoint. It fishes best early in the season and both boat and bank fishing are possible. There are two boats available. The loch is in two sections and the best area is in the western section on the northern bay, towards Port Henderson. Two feeder burns enter the southern section of the loch from Meall Bad a'Chrotha and this also is a good area to try. Flies to use include Silver Butcher, Blue Charm, Peter Ross and Dunkeld. Bad na h-Achlaise is sometimes very calm, and this is when dry-fly fishing can bring good results. Excellent trout averaging 12oz, and a delightful loch to fish.

LOCH SGEIREACH 19/810708

Permission: Shieldaig Lodge Hotel, Badachro, Gairloch.
Tel: Badachro (044583) 250

This is a small loch in the group known as the Fairy Lochs and is a short walk from the hotel. Trout average 12oz and rise well to all the standard pattern loch flies. Fishing is from the bank only and good baskets are taken regularly.

LOCH BAD A'CHROTHA 19/786728

Permission: Shieldaig Lodge Hotel, Badachro, Gairloch.
Tel: Badachro (044583) 250

This is an extension of the River Badachro and the loch is also known locally as Badachro Loch. The main interest here is salmon and sea trout and there are two boats available. The brown trout average only three to the pound. Easy fishing and ideal for a day off from the hill lochs.

LOCH BRAIGH HORRISDALE 19/797705

Permission: Shieldaig Lodge Hotel, Badachro, Gairloch.
Tel: Badachro (044583) 250

This loch is on the same track as the route out to the Fairy Lochs, to the south of the hotel. It lies adjacent to the track and is full of bright little fish with suicidal tendencies. This is the ideal loch for newcomers to fly fishing and perfect for a picnic with the family. There is a boat on the loch and wading is safe all round, although it is 50 feet deep in the middle. Baskets of 20 fish are often taken and 50 fish would not really raise any eyebrows in the hotel. Best flies are Peter Ross, Blue Zulu, Silver Butcher and Invicta. Sandy beaches, peace and quiet, free-rising trout and a pleasant day out.

LOCH CLAIR 19/773718
LOCH NAM BREAC ODHAR 19/768720
LOCH AIRIGH UILLEIM 19/755719
LOCH DOIRE NAN EALA 19/779713
LOCHAN NA GLAIC GILLE 19/765709

Permission: Shieldaig Lodge Hotel, Badachro, Gairloch.
Tel: Badachro (044583) 250

These lochs all lie to the west and south of the hotel, between Shieldaig and South Erradale. They are easily accessible via a good track which leaves the B8056 at 783732, by Badachro Farm. Trout average about 8oz, but there are a few much larger fish, particularly in nam Breac Odhar and Airigh and an Uilleim. Getting them out is the only problem. Use standard pattern loch flies and crossed fingers.

LOCH A'BHEALAICH 19/870640

Permission: Shieldaig Lodge Hotel, Badachro, Gairloch.
Tel: Badachro (044583) 250

This is the largest loch in the Shieldaig Forest and it lies to the west of

Baosbheinn (875m) 'The Wizard's Mountain', 8 miles south from the hotel. The loch is 1¾ miles long by ½ mile wide and both boat and bank fishing are available. Although over 100 feet deep in places, the loch shallows to a mere 2–3 feet and the shallows are the best fishing areas. Pay particular attention to where the many feeder burns enter the loch and also try the depths for *ferox*. Trout of up to 3lb have been caught and standard patterns do the trick – or should. In spite of the considerable walk involved, this is a very attractive loch to fish – the surroundings could not be grander.

LOCH GAINEAMHACH 19/834670

Permission: Shieldaig Lodge Hotel, Badachro, Gairloch.
Tel: Badachro (044583) 250

Loch Gaineamhach is a 6-mile walk south from the hotel and lies to the left of the track up the Abhainn Braigh Burn. This is a shallow loch over ½ mile long by ¼ mile wide and fishing is from the bank only. Wading is easy and the best fishing areas are along the west bank and the north shore. Large baskets of small trout are caught here and the average weight is 8oz. Great sport, and the flies to attract them with are Invicta, Woodcock & Hare-lug and Greenwell's Glory. A very pleasant loch to fish, amidst lovely surroundings.

LOCHAN FADA 19/922627
LOCH A'CHAORAINN 19/929621
LOCHAN CARN NA FEOLA 19/920619
LOCH NAN CABAR 19/926605
LOCH COIRE MHIC FHEARCHAIR 19/942608

Permission: Shieldaig Lodge Hotel, Badachro, Gairloch.
Tel: Badachro (044583) 250
Harry Davis, Creag Beag, Charleston, Gairloch.
Tel: Gairloch (0455) 2322

These lochs lie at the head of Strath Lungard at the end of a 9- or 10-mile walk south from the A832. Follow the line of the Allt Strath Lungard burn to reach them and expect to catch lots of small, brightly marked, traditional highland wild brown trout. You are surrounded here by some of the most dramatic scenery in the north, with Beinn an Eoin (855m), Liathach (1054m) and Beinn Eighe (972m) towering over the lochs. Hard walking, but utterly wonderful. Coire Mhic Fhearchair is the most difficult to reach. My favourite is Loch nan Cabar.

LOCH NA H-OIDHCHE 19/890650

Permission: Harry Davis, Creag Beag, Charleston, Gairloch.
Tel: Gairloch (0445) 2322

A long, exciting walk out into the wilderness, starting from 856721 on the A832 Gairloch–Loch Maree road. A good track runs south along the line of the Abhainn a'Gharbh Choire burn and within a couple of hours brings you to the north end of the loch. There is a boat house here, with a good boat and outboard motor. Sail down the loch to Poca Buidhe, a well-furnished and well-equipped bothy, at the south end, and spend a few days amidst some of the most wonderful scenery in Scotland. Trout average 12oz and are remarkable in that they are all perfectly matched in both size and weight. The loch fishes best early in the morning and during the evening. Use Black Pennell, Black Zulu, Greenwell's Glory and Grouse & Claret.

GORM-LOCH FADA 19/899639
GORM-LOCH NA BEINNE 19/903636

Permission: Harry Davis, Creag Beag, Charleston, Gairloch.
Tel: Gairloch (0445) 2322

Outstanding lochs in an outstanding setting, where excellent trout of up to 3lb may be caught. Stay at Poca Buidhe and fish the Gorm lochs during the day, launching your attack on na h-Oidhche as night falls. I defy anyone not to be impressed and deeply moved by the magnificence of the surrounding scenery – regardless of rising trout.

14 Ann Sandison at the Loch of the Night

LOCH A'BHAID-LUACHRAICH 19/890860

Permission: Inverewe Visitors Centre, Poolewe.
Tel: Poolewe (044586) 229

This loch lies to the south of the A832 near Drumchork and is 1½ miles long by 1 mile wide. Spurs from Carn Bad na h-Achlaise and Maol na Bruaich almost divide the loch into two and the approach is from Drumchork via a good track. Only bank fishing is available. There are good bays and points all round the loch and the southern, shallower bay is the best fishing area. Trout average 8–12oz and rise well to the standard patterns of loch flies.

LOCH GHUIRAGARSTIDH 19/890810

Permission: Inverewe Visitors Centre, Poolewe.
Tel: Poolewe (044586) 229

This loch drains out of Loch Kernsary and is approached from Poolewe via Kernsary by a rough track and an hour's walk. It is a small, shallow loch about ¾ mile long by 350 yards wide. The loch contains brown trout and the most productive area is in the vicinity of the small islands. Standard loch fly patterns work well.

LOCH KERNSARY 19/880804

Permission: Inverewe Visitors Centre, Poolewe.
Tel: Poolewe (044586) 229

Fishing on Kernsary is managed by the National Trust for Scotland and the loch is a ragged, beautiful water nearly 1½ miles in length by ½ mile wide. This is a deep loch, nearly 100 feet deep towards the eastern end, and it contains good brown trout, stocked by the National Trust. Sea trout sometimes wander up from Loch Maree and there are dozens of good fishing points all round the shore. A lovely loch and well worth a visit.

FIONN LOCH 19/950785
LOCHAN BEANNACH BEAG 19/947773
LOCHAN BEANNACH MOR 19/940765

Permission: Harry Davis, Creag Beag, Charleston, Gairloch.
Tel: Gairloch (0445) 2322
K. Gunn, Strath, Gairloch.
Tel: Gairloch (0445)2400

Fionn lies to the north of Loch Maree and is one of the most lovely lochs in the north. It is immortalized for anglers in a passage from

Osgood Mackenzie's book, *A Hundred Years in the Highlands*. It relates the story of a basket of 12 trout taken from the loch by trolling which weighed 87lb 12oz. Difficult to match today, but nevertheless big trout are still caught. Fionn is 5 miles long by 1½ miles wide and is an endless delight of small bays and fishy points. Along the south shore a short stream leads into Lochan Beannach Beag and Lochan Beannach Mor, which are also worth a cast or three. This is magnificent country and the loch is surrounded by superb peaks: Slioch (980m), Meall Mheinnidh (720m) and Beinn Airigh Charr (791m) dominate the horizon. Well worth fishing and highly recommended. Standard pattern loch flies do fine.

LOCH NAN CLACH DUBHA 19/929780
LOCH NA MOINE 19/924775
LOCH AN GAINEAMH 19/920795

Permission: Harry Davis, Creag Beag, Charleston, Gairloch.
Tel: Gairloch (0445) 2322
K. Gunn, Strath, Gairloch.
Tel: Gairloch (0445)2400

Walk out from Kernsary Farm and follow the line of the Allt Creige burn, with the crags of Spidean nan Clach (703m) towering to your

15 Ready for action on Scotland's most famous trout water, the Fionn Loch

right. All these lochs offer good sport with 8-oz trout which rise readily to standard pattern loch flies.

LOCH MAREE 19/920730

Permission: Lochmaree Hotel, by Achnasheen.
Tel: Lochmaree (044589) 200
Shieldaig Lodge Hotel, Badachro, Gairloch.
Tel: Badachro (044583)250

The most famous of all Scottish sea-trout lochs, sadly fallen on hard times because of the absence of fish. In times past, a day's catch would be more than a year's catch now, and great efforts are being made to discover why numbers of fish have declined so drastically. It is not all bad news, however, and the new owners tell me that during the 1990 season more than 300 sea trout were taken – and salmon of up to 20lb.

LOCH BAD AN SGALAIG 19/850710
LOCH DUBH 19/845700

Permission: The Wildcat Stores, Gairloch.
Tel: Gairloch (0445) 2242

These two lochs lie to the south of the A832 Gairloch–Kinlochewe road and have been joined together by the construction of a dam. They cover an area of 2 miles by 1/2 mile and are easily accessible from the road. The fishing is managed by the Gairloch Angling Club and both boat and bank fishing is available. Trout average 8–12oz but in 1991 a fish of 2lb 8oz was taken. Bad an Sgalaig also contains some very large pike.

LOCH TOLLAIDH 19/840785
LOCH FEUR 19/809781
LOCHAN NAM BREAC 19/815783
LOCH NAM BUAINICHEN 19/855735
LOCH DOIRE NA H-AIRIGHE 19/875740
LOCH NA FEITHE MUGAIG 19/860745
LOCH AIRIGH A'PHUILL 19/840755
LOCH AIRIGH MHIC CRIADH 19/830765

Permission: The Wildcat Stores, Gairloch.
Tel: Gairloch (0445) 2242

These are all Gairloch Angling Club waters which lie between Loch Gairloch and Loch Maree. While the club makes its fishing readily available to visiting anglers, bookings are not taken more than four days before fishing. Both boat and bank fishing are available and the trout range from hard-fighting little 8-oz fish up to trout of 4lb and more. The best way of exploring these waters is to contact Derek Roxborough, a local gillie and casting instructor who knows the area better than most and offers guided hill-loch fishing tours. Write to Derek at: The Old Police Station, Gairloch, Ross-shire IV21 2BP, tel: Gairloch (0445) 2057.

LOCH NA BA CAOILE 19/872827

Permission: Inverewe Visitors' Centre, Poolewe.
Tel: Poolewe (044586) 229

This is a little loch by the A832 Poolewe–Drumchork road and it is 350 yards long by 50 yards wide. The name means 'the loch of the lean cow' and fishing is from the bank only. The loch is stocked and trout average 12oz. Easily accessible and ideal for a couple of hours' fishing.

LOCH NA DAILTHEAN 19/877830

Permission: Inverewe Visitors' Centre, Poolewe.
Tel: Poolewe (044586) 229

The National Trust manage this pleasant roadside loch. It is shallow, averaging only 10 feet deep, and drains out to the sea at Loch Thurnaig, so in spate conditions there is the chance of salmon and sea trout. A boat is available and brown trout average 12oz. This loch is stocked and good baskets are often taken on standard loch fly patterns.

LOCH DAMPH 24/862510

Permission: Loch Torridon Hotel, Torridon, by Achnasheen.
Tel: Torridon (044587) 242

The principal Torridon Hotel water, this long, narrow loch is most famous as a salmon and sea-trout fishery with fish entering the system via the River Balgy. Sadly, as is the case with most of our west coast fisheries, salmon and sea trout have been most notable by their absence in recent years, but some excellent brown trout of up to 11lb have been taken by trolling. The average weight of trout in this lovely loch is 1lb.

LOCH AN UILLT-BHEITHE 25/920524
LOCHAN DOMHAIN 25/919519
LOCH AN EION 25/923510

Permission: Loch Torridon Hotel, Torridon, by Achnasheen.
Tel: Torridon (044587) 242

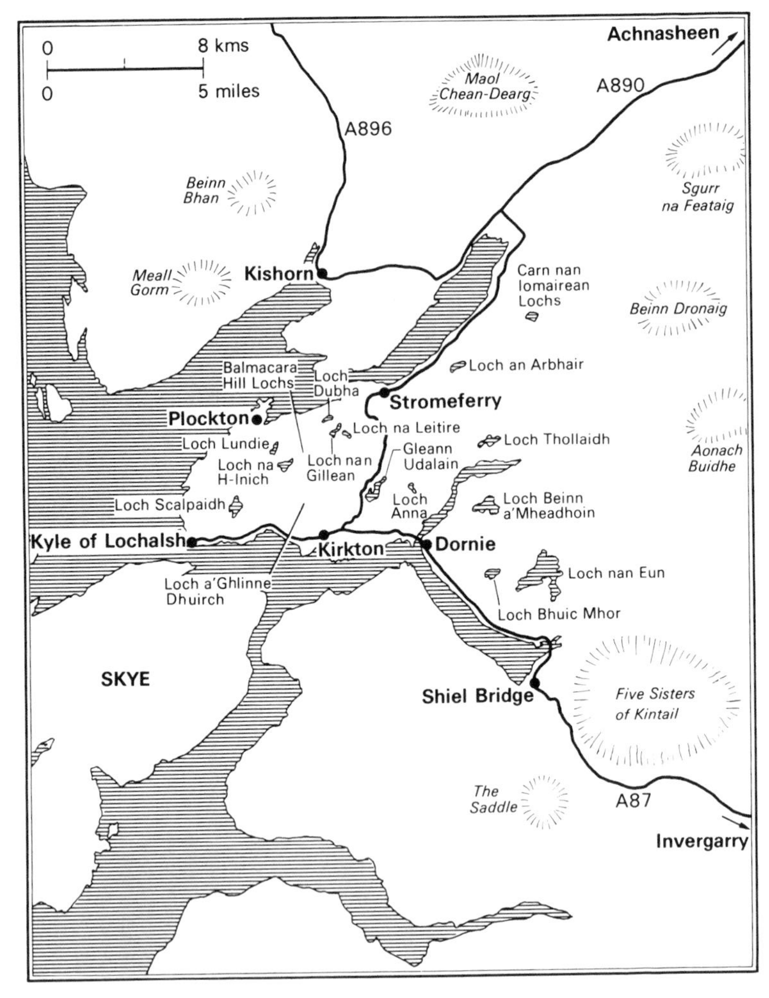

12 Ross-shire

Three excellent trout lochs in superb surroundings, at the end of a two-hour walk from the A896, south-east from the hotel. A stalkers' track winds round the lower slopes of Beinn na h-Eaglaise (737m), skirting the east shore of Loch an Eion, which is furthest out into the hills. Eion has two tiny islands and the best fishing area is in the vicinity of these islands and in the south-west corner where a small feeder burn tumbles in from Loch na Craoibhe-caorainn. Fish average 12oz.

LOCH NAN EUN 33/952266
LOCH BHUIC MHOR 33/923260
LOCH BEINN A'MHEADHOIN 33/923286

Permission: The Factor, Inverinate Estate, Dornie, by Kyle, Ross-shire.
Mrs E. Huggett, Bundalloch, Dornie, by Kyle, Ross-shire.

These small lochs lie in the hills to the north of the A87 Shiel Bridge–Kyle of Lochalsh road, and involve a good walk to reach them. The trout are small but great fighters and good baskets will be taken using standard loch fly patterns. The greatest attraction is the marvellous scenery. The hills and mountains on the Inverinate Forest dominate the horizon and the Five Sisters of Kintail line the southern sky. This is a truly magnificent place to fish. Get permission, fasten your boots and have a memorable day out.

LOCH SCALPAIDH 33/780288
LOCH LUNDIE 24/807317
LOCH NA H-INICH 24/812308

Permission: Not required

These lochs are to the north of Kyle of Lochalsh and easily accessible. Trout on Scalpaidh average three to the pound and good baskets are taken on most of the standard loch fly patterns. Loch Lundie was stocked some years ago with rainbow and brook trout but both Lundie and na h-Inich have a reputation for being dour. There are good trout in na h-Inich, as well as pike, and fish of 2½–3½lb are sometimes caught.

LOCH NAN GILLEAN 24/840325
LOCH NA LEITIRE 24/844322
LOCH DUBHA 24/832328

Permission: Not required

This group of small lochs, known locally as the Craggs, lies to the south-east of Plocton and may be approached via a good track which leaves the minor ring road round Loch Lundie. The first part of the walk is fairly steep but the effort involved is well worth while since the scenery is grand and the trout fishing excellent. Loch Dubha holds the largest fish and trout of up to 5lb have been taken. Baskets of four to five fish are usual, with trout averaging 8–12oz. Best fly on Loch Dubha is the Kingfisher Butcher. Otherwise, standard pattern loch flies will all produce good results.

BALMACARA HILL LOCHS

LOCH NAM BREAC MORA 24/838308
LOCH NA DOIRE MOIRE 24/827304
LOCH NA SMEORAICH 24/844304
LOCH A'GHLINNE DHUIRCH 33/837299

Permission: Not required

You will puff and pant a bit getting there, but these are excellent little trout lochs and should be visited. Fishing is all from the bank and trout average 12oz, with fish of 2lb and more not infrequently taken. Flies to use are Butchers, Greenwell's Glory, Blue Zulu and Peter Ross.

GLEANN UDALAIN 33/853290

Permission: Not required

This is a small reservoir to the east of the A890 Stromeferry–Kyle road. It suffers from great fluctuations in water level and the trout average three to the pound. However, it is easily accessible and when water conditions are right fish of up to 1lb are sometimes caught.

LOCH ANNA 33/879292

Permission: Not required

This is a hill loch on the north side of Ardelve on the A87. It is a fair walk out to Loch Anna and the water has a reputation for being dour; nevertheless, it can produce excellent results and trout of up to 2lb are caught. Fishing from the bank and standard pattern loch flies will do.

LOCH THOLLAIDH 24/896306

Permission: Not required

This is a tiny hill loch to the north of Conchra and trout average 8oz. The fish are very pretty, being bright and golden. Flies to use should match the trout's colour and patterns such as Kingfisher Butcher, Dunkeld and Silver Invicta work well. Only the left-hand bank is worth fishing.

LOCH AN ARBHAIR 24/883342

Permission: Not required

An easily accessible loch to the east of Stromeferry, Loch Arbhair has a reputation for holding very large trout indeed. It is getting them out that causes all the trouble and you will have a lot of blank days trying. But trout of up to 10lb are caught here, which may have something to do

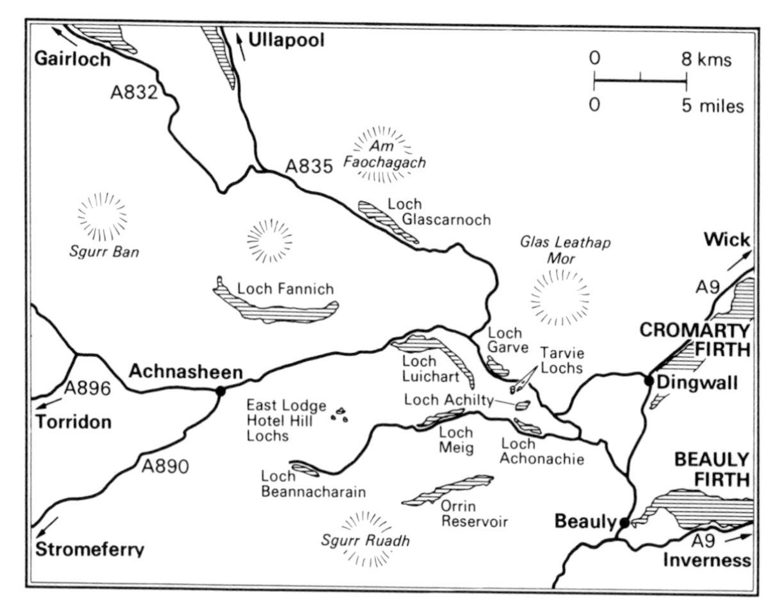

13 Strathpeffer

with why folks keep trying. Just what flies to use to tempt them I do not know, but persevere.

CARN NAN IOMAIREAN LOCHS 25/915357

Permission: Not required

These lochs all lie to the south of Attadale on Loch Carron and are hill lochs containing trout which average three to the pound. Really good baskets are taken and fish rise readily to the standard pattern loch flies. Lovely countryside and a great place for a day out in the hills.

LOCH FANNICH 20/210650

Permission: Conon Bridge Post Office, Conon Bridge.
Tel: Dingwall (0349) 61201

Fannich is a hydro-electric loch 7 miles long by ¾ mile wide. It is approached from the A832 Dingwall–Gairloch road, just before the power station at the River Grudie. Loch Fannich is a wild, desolate place but a track runs the length of the north shore, giving good access for bank fishing and this is productive at the head of the loch where the main feeder burn enters. This is also the shallowest part of the loch and fishes best from the boat. Another good boat drift is eastwards from the forestry plantation, among the bays and inlets below Torran Ruadh. Trout average 8–10oz, with good baskets being taken using Black Pennell, Grouse & Claret and Butchers.

LOCH GLASCARNOCH 20/300735

Permission: Aultguish Inn, Aultguish, by Garve.
Tel: Aultguish (0995) 514254

Loch Glascarnoch is a recently formed loch, part of the Conon Valley Hydro-Electric Scheme. The loch is 4½ miles long by 1 mile wide. Bank fishing only and take great care on the edges. Frequent water-level changes make the margins very soft in places. This is a dour loch, wild and windy, and trout are difficult to catch. The average weight is 8oz but fish of up to 4lb have been caught. The A835 Garve–Ullapool road follows the south shore, so Glascarnoch is easily accessible, if somewhat public.

LOCH BEANNACHARAIN (Loch Scardroy) 25/230515

Permission: The East Lodge Hotel, Strathconon.
Tel: Strathconon (09977) 222
J. H. MacMillan, The Square, Strathpeffer.
Tel: Strathpeffer (0997) 421346
Mr Burr, The Tackle Shop, Cromartie Buildings, Strathpeffer.
Tel: Strathpeffer (0997) 421561

This loch is known locally as Loch Scardroy and it lies to the south of Achnasheen. Approach from Inver on the A890, or from Marybank on the A832, up the River Meig. Beannacharain is 1¾ miles long by 400 yards wide and both boat and bank fishing is available. The loch is over 150 feet deep in the middle and the best fishing is to be found in the shallow water round the margins, especially at the western end. The loch has been stocked in the past with Loch Leven trout and fish average 8oz. Trout of up to 4lb are sometimes taken and eight fish would be a good basket.

LOCH BHAD GHAINEANHAICH 26/325590
LOCH AN ALLTAIN BHEITHE 26/319595
LOCH AN EILEIN 26/305584
LOCH CUL 26/305586

Permission: East Lodge Hotel, Strathconon.
Tel: Strathconon (09977) 222

A series of hill lochs west of the small town of Milltown, which the River Meig runs through. Getting to them involves a vigorous walk. Trout average 8oz, with the occasional larger fish, and they rise well to standard patterns of loch flies. Expect baskets of four to six fish.

ORRIN RESERVOIR 26/376496

Permission: The Fairburn Estate Office, Muir of Ord.
Tel: Urray (09973) 273

Orrin Reservoir is 5 miles long by ½ mile wide and fishing on it is strictly controlled by the estate. Access is via an estate road only. The occasional day may be made available to visitors and anglers should contact the estate office for details. Orrin is a remote and beautiful water containing good trout and baskets of six to eight fish may be expected. Standard pattern loch flies work well. There is no fishing after 31 August.

LOCH LUICHART 20/340620-26/380593

Permission: The Sports & Model Shop, Tulloch Street, Dingwall.
Tel: Dingwall (0349) 62346

Loch Luichart is a hydro-electric loch and fishing is managed by the Dingwall & District Angling Club. It is approached directly off the A832 at Lochluichart Station and is a long, dour loch of 5½ miles by 1 mile wide. The average weight of trout is 8oz but it is reputed to hold much larger fish as well. There are miles of interesting shoreline to explore and all the standard loch fly patterns work well.

LOCH MEIG 26/367557

Permission: East Lodge Hotel, Strathconon.
Tel: Strathconon (09977) 222
Mr Burr, The Tackle Shop, Cromartie Buildings, Strathpeffer.
Tel: Strathpeffer (0997) 421561
J. H. MacMillan, The Square, Strathpeffer.
Tel: Strathpeffer (0997) 421346

Loch Meig lies to the east of Strathpeffer and is a long, narrow water 2 miles long by 400 yards wide. It is a very lovely loch and can offer good sport, particularly early in the season. There are three boats, but outboard motors are not allowed. Bank fishing is available and can be good. The most productive areas are in the north-west corner, where several feeder burns enter the loch, and in the bay on the south shore, at the widest part of the loch. If the water level is high, Loch Meig does not fish well, but in normal conditions expect trout averaging about 1lb. Trout of up to 3lb are also taken, usually towards the end of the season. Meig is stocked, and evening fishing is generally best. Use Black Pennell, Peter Ross, Coachman, Kingfisher Butcher, Black Zulu and Greenwell's Glory. Well worth a visit.

LOCH GARVE 20/405600-26/410595

Permission: Conon Bridge Post Office, Conon Bridge.
Tel: Dingwall (0349) 61201

Loch Garve lies adjacent to the A832 and is 1½ miles long by ½ mile wide. Good brown trout are caught, of up to 4lb, but this is a dour loch and it also contains very large pike of up to 19lb. Boat fishing is best, in the shallow waters at the north end, and standard pattern loch flies should produce results.

LOCH AN EICH BHAIN 26/423580

Permission: Murray Douglas, Inchdrean, Tarvie.
Tel: Tarvie 250

These lochs, also known as the Tarvie Lochs, lie to the north of Conon on the A832 road from Muir of Ord and are easily accessible. Both boat and bank fishing are available. Fishing is for natural brown trout and stocked rainbow trout which rise well to all the usual patterns of fly.

LOCH ACHONACHIE 26/433550

Permission: Mr Burr, The Tackle Shop, Cromartie Buildings, Strathpeffer.
Tel: Strathpeffer (0997) 421561
J. H. MacMillan, The Square, Strathpeffer.
Tel: Strathpeffer (0997) 421346

Loch Achonachie lies adjacent to the minor road from Marybank on the A832 and contains brown trout, perch, pike and the occasional salmon. Bank fishing is allowed, but fishing from the boat brings the best results. Trout of up to 4lb are sometimes caught, but the loch has the reputation for being dour. Try standard pattern loch flies and fish the east end of the loch, below Torrachilty Wood, and in the bay in the south-east corner where the feeder burn enters by the roadside. An outboard motor is useful.

LOCH ACHILTY 26/435566

Permission: Achilty Hotel, Contin.
Tel: Strathpeffer (0997) 421355

Loch Achilty is a sheltered loch, ¾ mile long by 700 yards wide. It is easily accessible from the A832 and is surrounded by trees. The loch contains brown trout and has been stocked in the past. Trout average 8–10oz, with the odd fish of up to 4lb, but the loch has a dour reputation. However, on its day, sport can be fast and furious – it is just being there on that day that is the difficult bit. Use standard loch fly patterns and fish the shallows.

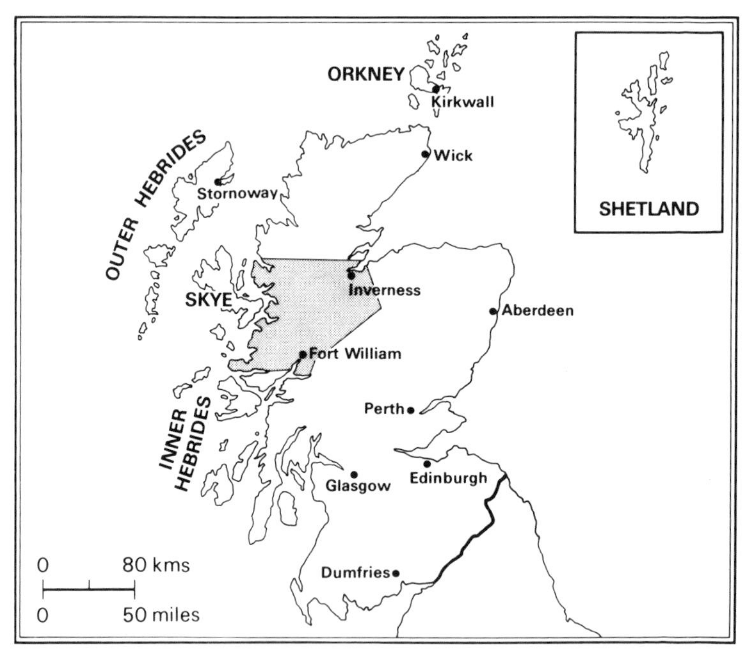

14 Inverness-shire

5 Inverness-shire

Inverness-shire covers a vast area and contains hundreds of trout lochs. There are a number of hydro-electric waters, desolate, windy and dour, but holding really monster trout of up to 20lb; and dozens of hill lochs, such as the Invermoriston waters and the remote lochs of the far west. You can't travel far in this area without coming across evidence of the 1745 rebellion, and I have often mused upon what Scotland might have been like today if Prince Charles Edward Stewart had travelled round with a trout rod, rather than a ragged army of highlanders. Certainly a lot of heads would have remained a lot more firmly attached to a lot of shoulders and the Highlands would have been spared the ungentle administrations of Butcher Cumberland after the Battle of Culloden. The route followed by Bonnie Prince Charlie after the battle takes you past some of the best trout waters in the area, from Ruthven, up Glen Garry and over to Loch Quoich. In fact, it would make an excellent path to follow for a present-day fishing holiday, and give an added sense of excitement to the occasion. My own favourite lochs are the Invermoriston and Tomich hill lochs and Ruthven and A'Choire, to the south-west of Inverness; and, of course, distant, vast Loch Morar – and never enough time to fish and explore them all. I hope that the waters I have described will help you start your journey and see the first trout safely into the net.

GLENMORISTON LODGE ESTATE LOCHS

DUNDREGGAN LOCH 34/355157

Permission: Glenmoriston Lodge Estate, Invermoriston, Inverness.
Tel: Glenmoriston (032051) 300

Dundreggan Loch lies on the upper River Moriston and is ½ mile long by some 200 yards wide. It is easily accessible from the A887, which runs along the north shore. This is an excellent loch, pleasant with wooded banks and containing first-class fish. The estate stocks Dundreggan regularly and the average weight of trout is 1lb. Best results come from boat fishing and there are two boats available for visitors. The most favoured fishing area is in the shallower water at the western end of the loch. Another good drift is down the north-west shore. Evening fishing during July and August frequently produces

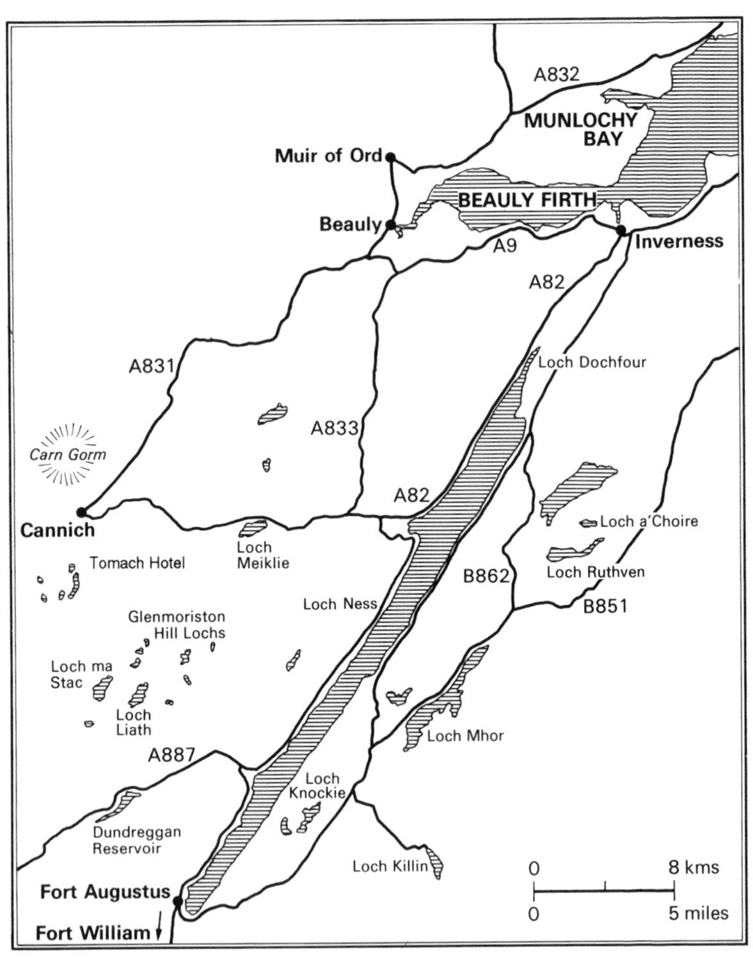

15 Loch Ness

baskets of 15–20 fish and the best trout taken recently was a fish weighing 7lb 2oz. Flies to use include Black Pennell, Silver Butcher, Black Zulu, Blue Zulu and Grouse & Claret. A lovely loch and well worth a visit.

LOCH LIATH 34/335197

Permission: Glenmoriston Lodge Estate, Invermoriston, Inverness.
Tel: Glenmoriston (032051) 300

This loch lies to the north of Invermoriston and is 4 miles from Bhlaraidh on the A887. Access is by an estate road and a high-wheelbased vehicle is recommended – or stout walking boots. Liath contains excellent trout and fishing is from the bank only. The loch is well managed and regularly stocked by the estate and the trout average 12oz. Baskets of up to 20 fish are not uncommon and Liath also holds good Arctic char. This is a classic hill loch, some 1500 feet above sea level, and the surrounding countryside and views are magnificent.

LOCH MA STAC 26/340215

Permission: Glenmoriston Lodge Estate, Invermoriston, Inverness.
Tel: Glenmoriston (032051) 300

Loch ma Stac is the best trout loch in the area and lies to the north of Invermoriston and the A887. Approach via the estate road from Bhlaraidh. Loch ma Stac is at an altitude of 1600 feet and is 1 mile long by 1/3 mile wide. There is a boat, but bank fishing can produce just as good results. The trout average 1lb, but each year much larger fish are taken and trout of up to 6lb have been caught on this fine loch. Loch ma Stac is over 40 feet deep by the east shore and the best fishing area is down the western bank, which is fringed with inviting bays and headlands. The area round the island should also be 'worked over' most carefully. The estate restocked the loch in 1985 and it continues to fish very well indeed. A perfect loch with fine views all round and the Five Sisters of Kintail lining the western horizon. Highly recommended.

LOCH AN DUBHAIR 26/390202
LOCH NA FEANNAIG 26/397202
LOCHAN AN RUIGHE DHUIBH 26/380207
LOCH A'CHRATHAICH 26/364210
LOCH A'MHUILINN 26/363230
LOCH NA LEIRISDEIN 26/370230
LOCHLOCH NA RUIGHE DUIBHE 26/381236
LOCH NAM MEUR 26/390230
LOCH NAM BRATHAIN 26/392219
LOCHCOIRE NA RAINICH 26/398218

Permission: Glenmoriston Lodge Estate, Invermoriston, Inverness.
Tel: Glenmoriston (032051) 300

There are more than 20 hill lochs on the estate and all are readily available to members of the public through the estate office. All these lochs contain excellent trout of from 8oz up to real monsters of 6lb. Most of the lochs involve a fair walk but the angler will be assured of peace and quiet in superb surroundings – and a good basket of fish at the end of the day. The lochs are well managed and regularly stocked and the estate can also arrange good accommodation in well-situated chalets. There are not many better places for a few days' fishing, and these lochs are highly recommended. There is good salmon fishing also on the River Moriston and in Loch Ness.

LOCH NESS

Sheets 24-26

Permission: Glenmoriston Lodge Estate, Invermoriston, Inverness.
Tel: Glenmoriston (032051) 300
Foyers Hotel, Foyers, Inverness-shire.
Tel: Gorthleck (04563) 216
Inchnacardoch Lodge Hotel, Fort Augustus.
Tel: Fort Augustus (0320) 6258

Because of its Monster, Loch Ness has become one of the best known lochs in the world, and there is, I am sure, something there. Just what flies to use to tempt it, what breaking strain of nylon or length of rod would be best, I don't care to say. Suffice to advise you when fishing on Loch Ness, keep a sharp look out – you never can tell! Loch Ness is a most beautiful loch and displays throughout its length every aspect of game fishing. It is easily accessible and often very busy, both along the shore and on the water, but there is always some secret, quiet corner to be found and the angler on Loch Ness can be as secluded and remote as he wishes. It is not too great a generalization to say that brown trout can be caught over most of the loch. Very large fish are sometimes caught off Glenmoriston and there is good bank fishing along the south shore from Dores, before the loch opens out. There are miles of unfrequented bays and corners near Foyers. Trout average 8–10oz, and are well shaped and in some areas almost golden. Standard pattern loch flies work fine and Loch Ness is well worth a visit. You may not catch a glimpse of the Monster, but you will most certainly catch a few trout.

LOCH DOCHFOUR

26/605385

Permission: The Shop, Dochgarroch Locks, Inverness.
Tel: Inverness (046386) 333

Loch Dochfour extends from the outflow of Loch Ness to where the weir divides the flow into the canal and the River Ness. The loch contains brown trout and pike and the average size of trout is 1lb. Fishing is from the bank only and the loch is easily accessible from the A82, which runs along the north shore. It is a rather public place to fish, but a very lovely setting. The fish tend to be dour, but large trout are caught and standard loch fly patterns should be used.

LOCH RUTHVEN 26/620275

Permission: A. Humphrey, Loch Ruthven, Flichity, Inverness.
Tel: Farr (08083) 283
John Graham & Co, 71 Castle Street, Inverness.
Tel: Inverness (0463) 33178

Loch Ruthven is an excellent loch providing first-class sport in beautiful surroundings. It is 2¼ miles long by ½ mile wide with an average depth of 10 feet. This is a well-managed water and it is regularly stocked. The average weight of fish is 1lb and trout of 4–5lb are often caught. An average basket should produce six to eight fish and the best flies to use are Grouse & Claret, Black Pennell, Yellow Invicta and Greenwell's Glory. Bank fishing is not allowed. Boats are moored at the north end of the loch where there are good car parking facilities. Highly recommended as a lovely loch to visit and fish. Mr Humphrey has a number of well-furnished, comfortable, self-catering cottages, ideally situated for a perfect Highland holiday.

LOCH A'CHOIRE 26/630293

Permission: A. Humphrey, Loch Ruthven, Flichity, Inverness.
Tel: Farr (08083) 283
John Graham & Co, 71 Castle Street, Inverness.
Tel: Inverness (0463) 33178

This is a lovely hill loch to the north of Loch Ruthven (above), north

16 Loch Ruthven, no outboard engines allowed, pack a strong, young friend

from Mr Humphrey's cottage. The loch contains brown trout averaging 12oz and Arctic char. The best fishing areas are in the north-west bay, and at the western end of the loch. Both boat and bank fishing are allowed and the flies that do most damage are Grouse & Claret, Black Pennell and Invicta. The loch is an easy after-dinner walk from the self-catering cottages and is highly recommended.

LOCH ASHIE 26/615350
LOCH DUNTELCHAIG 26/620310
LOCHAN EION RUADHA 26/610320
LOCHAN NA CURRA 26/605323
LOCH CEOTHLAIS 26/585287

Permission: John Graham & Co, 71 Castle Street, Inverness.
Tel: Inverness (0463) 331178

These lochs lie to the north of Ruthven (above) and all contain good stocks of brown trout averaging 8–10oz. Duntelchaig is the largest, with crystal-clear water, and it also contains much larger fish. Getting them out will test both your skill and temper – but they are well worth catching. Smaller flies (size 14–16) seem to work best, including Black Pennell, Woodcock & Hare-lug and Kingfisher Butcher.

LOCH KNOCKIE 34/455135

Permission: Knockie Lodge Hotel, Whitebridge, Stratherrick, Inverness-shire.
Tel: Gorthleck (04563) 276
The Whitebridge Hotel, Stratherrick, Inverness-shire.
Tel: Gorthleck (04563) 226

This loch lies to the west of the B862 between Whitebridge and Fort Augustus. It is very pleasantly situated and is over 1¼ miles long by 600 yards wide. The most favoured drifts are near to the islands in the north bay and the loch contains brown trout as well as Arctic char. Trout average 12oz and in 1991 a fish of 2lb was caught. Black Pennell, Black Zulu and Blue Zulu do well. Boat fishing only and a perfect setting, with outstanding bird life.

LOCH NAN LANN 34/443130
LOCHAN MAM-CHUIL 34/436112
LOCH NA SGORTHAICH 34/448148

LOCHAN NAN NIGHEAN 34/455150

Permission: Knockie Lodge Hotel, Whitebridge, Stratherrick, Inverness-shire.
Tel: Gorthleck (04563) 276

These lochs are managed by Knockie Lodge Hotel and nan Lann is an easy after-dinner stroll from the hotel. It contains a few large fish, and good stocks of 8-oz trout. Reaching the others, particularly mam-Chuil, requires a little effort, but this will be well rewarded by the quality of sport. Knockie Lodge is superbly comfortable, offering the highest possible standard of food and accommodation.

LOCH KILLIN 35/529105

Permission: The Head Keeper, Garrogie Estate, Gorthleck, Inverness-shire.
Tel: Gorthleck (04563) 284

Loch Killin is to the south-west of Whitebridge and is a dramatic loch lying in a narrow valley with Carn Dubh (726m) to the west and Carn a'Choire Ghlaise (778m) to the east. Easily accessible, with fishing from the bank only. The east bank produces the best results and although trout only average 8oz the occasional monster is taken. Use standard pattern loch flies to tempt them.

17 Loch Killin, Stratherrick

LOCH MHOR 35/540197
LOCH BRAN 35/507193

Permission: The Whitebridge Hotel, Stratherrick, Inverness-shire.
Tel: Gorthleck (04563) 272
Foyers Hotel, Foyers, Inverness-shire.
Tel: Gorthleck (04563) 216

Both these lochs lie adjacent to the B862 Inverness–Fort Augustus road in Strath Errick and are easily accessible. Loch Mhor used to be two lochs, Loch Farraline and Loch Garth, and these were joined to form the present hydro-electric loch. A gravity-feed system is used to run turbines at Foyers and this nightly operation does not help the fishing. It effects Loch Farraline least, where the average weight of trout is about 12oz. Fish of up to 4lb have been taken and 1991 produced a trout of 2lb 8oz. Concentrate your efforts round the bays at Aberchalder and Migovie, using standard pattern loch flies.

Loch Bran is a small forest loch to the north of Loch Mhor with a main section and two small adjoining bays. The water is peaty and fish average 12oz, but large fish are often taken and trout of up to 3lb have been caught.

LOCH MULLARDOCH 25/190305

Permission: Glen Affric Hotel, Cannich, Inverness-shire.
Tel: Cannich (04565) 214
John Graham & Co, 71 Castle Street, Inverness.
Tel: Inverness (0436) 33178

Loch Mullardoch is a remote, beautiful loch 8 miles long by ½ mile wide. It is surrounded by magnificent mountains and is in one of the least populated areas of Scotland. Westwards is roadless to the Atlantic and this is a truly majestic loch to fish. Approach from Cannich village via the A831 from Lovat Bridge on the A9. Trout average 12oz and a day's fishing should bring you six to eight fish. There is a track for much of the north shore, giving access to many good bays and points where fish lie. Boats are also available. Best flies include Black Pennell, Greenwell's Glory, Butchers and Alexandra. There are much larger fish in the loch, so be prepared for that big one all the time. A superb loch in matchless scenery.

LOCH BEINN A'MHEADHOIN 25/240250

Permission: Glen Affric Hotel, Cannich, Inverness-shire.
Tel: Cannich (04565) 214
John Graham & Co, 71 Castle Street, Inverness.
Tel: Inverness (0436) 33178

This loch is 5 miles long by 700 yards wide and lies at the head of lovely Glen Affric. Mountains rise from the tree-lined shore of the loch and the trout are good fighters averaging 8–10oz. A reasonable basket would be eight fish and trout rise well to all the usual patterns of fly.

TOMACH HOTEL LOCHS

LOCH NA BEINNE MOIRE 26/325264
LOCH NA GREIDIL 26/319260
LOCH NAN LUCH 26/329257
LOCH NA BEINNE BIGE 26/328252
LOCH NAM FIODHAG 26/319236
LOCH NAM FREUMH 26/328269
LOCH GAOIREACH 26/325272

Permission: The Tomach Hotel, Tomach, Inverness-shire.
Tel: Cannich (04565) 399

A series of well-managed hill lochs which offer something for everyone, beginner and expert alike. Na Beinne Moire is the largest water, containing trout which average 12oz and some fish of up to 4lb. Close by is na Greidil, an absolute gem of a loch, where trout of over 7lb have been caught. Dour nam Fiodhag will drive you mad, hunting for very large fish, while the others all have good stocks of 8–10-oz trout – and nan Luch has been stocked with rainbow trout, ideal for beginners. The hotel arranges transport out to the lochs, organized by

18 Loch na Greidil, where trout of over 7lb have been caught

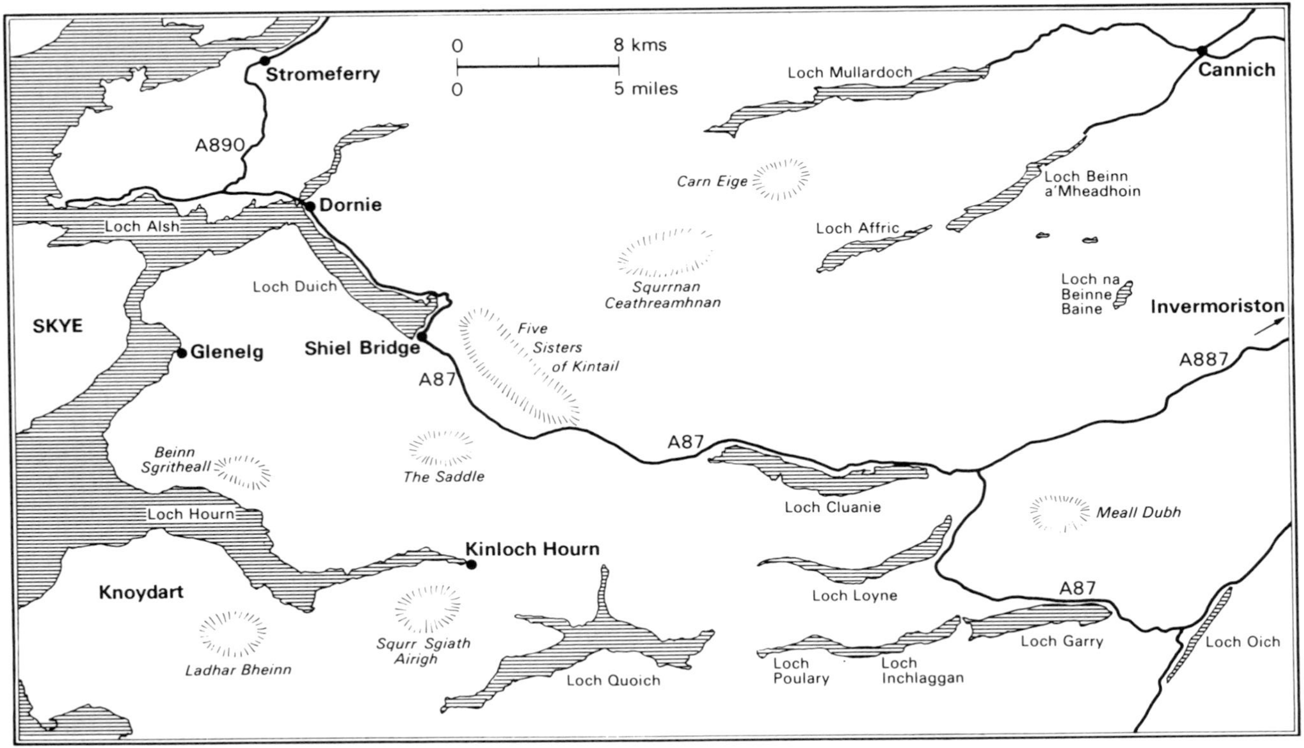

16 Glen Garry

the Fishery Manager, Kyle Laidlay, who also offers fly-casting lessons, and nothing is ever too much trouble for the staff. This is one of the most comfortable and welcoming hotels in Scotland. There are also, first-class, self-catering cottages – complete with heated indoor swimming pool and games room. Outstanding accommodation in a delightful conservation village and highly recommended.

LOCH OICH 34/320010

Permission: Miss J. Ellice, Tigh An Lianach, Aberchalder Estate, Invergarry.
Tel: Invergarry (08093) 287

The Caledonian Canal runs through Loch Oich and the loch is 4 miles long by 900 yards wide. The loch contains salmon and brown trout but the trout are dour and hard to catch. However, they have a good average weight of over 1lb and fish of up to 3lb 8oz are often taken. Bank fishing only and the best places to fish are in the bays on the north shore. Particularly good is the bay to the west of where the River Garry enters the loch. The best time to fish Loch Oich is during June, July and August, either in the early morning or at dusk. Flies to use are Peter Ross, Alexandra, Black Sedge and Wickham's Fancy. On its day, one of the best lochs in Scotland.

LOCH GARRY 34/230020
INCHLAGGAN 34/180017
LOCH POULARY 34/125014

Permission: Tomdoun Hotel, Invergarry, Inverness-shire.
Tel: Tomdoun (08092) 218
Garry Gualach Adventure Centre, Invergarry, Inverness-shire.
Tel: Tomdoun (08092) 230

Loch Garry and the surrounding lochs are some of the most beautiful in Scotland and cover a vast area of over 8 miles by 1 mile. There are very large fish in these lochs and trout of up to 18lb 2oz have been caught. That fish was landed in 1956 and at the time was a record for Britain. More recently, in 1985, a trout of 16lb was caught and each season double-figure fish are taken from these waters. The level of the lochs was considerably raised when they became part of the hydro-electric scheme and one of the best places to fish on Inchlaggan is on the line of the old River Garry. Both boat and bank fishing are available and the lochs are easily accessible. Fishing on Poulary is best from the boat since the margins are very shallow and weedy.

Glen Garry has a lot to offer the angler and is a pleasant place to spend some time. The Tomdoun Hotel offers all the comforts of a good fishing hotel whereas Garry Gualach on the other side is a holiday activity centre where the accommodation is more simple. Whichever you choose, or indeed if you are passing through, this area will captivate you with its marvellous scenery. All the standard pattern loch flies work well in this 'one for the glass case' country.

LOCH QUOICH 33/020020

Permission: Tomdoun Hotel, Invergarry, Inverness-shire.
Tel: Tomdoun (08092) 218

Loch Quoich, at the head of Glen Garry, is one of the remotest lochs in the north and is a wild, windy, lonely place. It was amidst these ragged wastelands the Prince Charles Edward Stewart hid from encircling searchers, and it was through these inhospitable hills that he finally escaped to the west. Quoich offers good sport, although it can be very dour at times. The loch is easily accessible via the road from Invergarry to the high dam at the eastern end. The average weight of trout is about 12oz but Quoich holds the British record with a fish of just over 19lb 9oz. Each year produces double-figure fish, caught by trolling, and good numbers of 5–10-lb trout are also taken regularly. An outboard motor is essential on this vast, often dangerous water and Quoich offers an endless delight of bays and headlands to explore. Use standard pattern loch flies.

LOCH CLUANIE 33/090115-34/140095

Permission: Duncan Stoddart, Stalkers Cottage, Cluanie Lodge, Invergarry, Inverness-shire.
Tel: Dalchreichart (0320) 40208
Cluanie Hotel, Glenmoriston, Inverness-shire.
Tel: Dalchreichart (0320) 40238

Loch Cluanie is to the south of the A87 Invermoriston–Kyle of Lochalsh road and is 7½ miles long by ¾ mile wide. The loch has a depth of over 200 feet and around it tower Sgurr na Conbhairean (1109m) and Beinn Loinne (789m). This is majestic countryside, wild and lovely. Trout in Cluanie average 1lb, with much larger fish frequently taken. Both boat and bank fishing are available. Fishing from the boat is most productive and outboard motors may be hired. All the standard patterns of loch flies will catch fish and an average day might bring you five trout. Fish the shallows where the many feeder burns enter the loch. The vicinity of the islands can also be very good, as can Lundie Bay. Outstanding scenery will make up for perhaps hard fishing, but there is always the chance of a 7-lb trout 'bumping' into your flies, so watch out for it.

LOCH LOYNE

34/160050

Permission: Tomdoun Hotel, Invergarry, Inverness-shire.
Tel: Tomdoun (08092) 218
Cluaine Hotel, Glenmoriston, Inverness-shire.
Tel: Dalchreichart (0320) 40238

Loch Loyne is 7 miles long by ½ mile wide and is a hydro-electric loch, the level having been raised to join two waters to make one. Mountains tower all round this distant water and it is approached from the A87 Invergarry–Kyle of Lochalsh road from the south, or via the A887 Inverness road from the east. This is a very deep loch and fishing is from the bank only, so do be careful. There are good bays to fish along the north shore, and the west end of the loch, from Glenloyne to the inlet burn, is also a good place to try. Loyne holds trout which average 8–10oz – and some much larger fish, including pike of up to 30lb. Indeed, I have heard reports of pike of over 40lb being encountered in Loyne.

LOCH LOCHY

34/190860-280950

Permission: None required

Loch Lochy is 10 miles long by ¾ mile wide and is part of the Caledonian Canal system. This is a beautiful loch with wooded shores and the bulk of Ben Nevis dominating the southern view. Loch Lochy holds some very good trout indeed but they are shy and very hard to catch. Persevere, since there are fish of up to 7lb. The east shore is very public, being close to the A82 Fort William–Inverness road, but the west shore, approached from Laggan Locks, is peaceful and remote. Use standard pattern loch flies.

LOCH ARKAIG

33/990915-34/160890

Permission: Rod & Gun Shop, 18 High Street, Fort William.
Tel: Fort William (0397) 2656

This romantic loch with its association with Bonnie Prince Charlie, sunken treasure and the Commandos of the last war, lies 15 miles north of Fort William at the end of the Great Glen. Leave the A82 at Spean Bridge and follow the B8004. This narrow, twisting road passes up the Mile Dorcha (The Dark Mile) and eventually ends at Muiraggan. Arkaig is surrounded by mountains and is nearly 12 miles long by up to ¾ mile wide. The deepest part is near Eilean a'Ghiubhaid, where it drops to 350 feet. On both shores dozens of small feeder burns cascade down the hills into the loch and these are the most productive areas to fish. Loch Arkaig holds brown trout, *ferox*, salmon, sea trout, Arctic char and pike. Very large trout of over 15lb are taken by trolling, but the average weight is about 8–10oz. Arkaig can be dour and frustrating but on a warm June evening – trout or no – there are few more delightful places to fish.

LOCH SHIEL

40/680680-905807

Permission: Loch Shiel Hotel, Acharacle, Inverness-shire.
Tel: Salen (096785) 224
The Stage House Inn, Glenfinnan, Inverness-shire.
Tel: Kinlocheil (039783) 246
Rod & Gun Shop, 18 High Street, Fort William, Inverness-shire.
Tel: Fort William (0397) 2656
Morar Hotel, Morar, by Mallaig, Inverness-shire.
Tel: Mallaig (0687) 2346

Loch Shiel lies to the west of Fort William and is one of the longest lochs in Scotland, being 17 miles long by ½ mile wide. The loch is deepest by Meall na Creag Leac (755m) where it drops to over 400 feet deep, although, towards the southern end, in the middle, there are areas where the depth is barely 6 feet. Shiel is a wild, beautiful place to fish, with a seemingly unending range of mountains crowding both shores. The loch is best known as a sea-trout fishery, with the occasional salmon, although in recent years these beasts have been few and far between. Brown trout average 10oz with the odd fish of 2–3lb. The best place to fish is at the south end amidst the bays and corners, particularly along the north shore. Use standard pattern loch flies and, if possible, employ the services of a gillie, for there is a lot of water to cover.

LOCH DOILET

40/810677

Permission: Ben View Hotel, Strontian, Sunart, Inverness-shire.
Tel: Strontian (0967) 2333
Forestry Commission District Office, Strontian, Acharacle, Inverness-shire.
Tel: Strontian (0967) 2165
Facilities for disabled anglers: As above

Loch Doilet is joined to Loch Shiel (above) by the River Pollach and contains sea trout and some salmon. It is surrounded by forestry plantations and the hills and mountains of Sunart and Moidart. Fishing is from the boat only and the eastern bay is the most productive area. Sea trout, when they are there, run to 4lb, salmon to 8lb. Brown trout are more modest – 6–8oz.

LOCH EILT
40/815825

Permission: Lochailort Inn, Lochailort, Inverness-shire.
Tel: Lochailort (06877) 208
Rod & Gun Shop, 18 High Street, Fort William.
Tel: Fort William (0397) 2656
Morar Hotel, Morar, by Mallaig, Inverness-shire.
Tel: Mallaig (0687) 2346

Loch Eilt is adjacent to the A830 Fort William–Mallaig road and is 3¼ miles long by some 400 yards wide. The loch contains mainly salmon and sea trout, or should: the numbers caught in recent years could be counted on the fingers of one hand. Brown trout average 10–12oz, with the odd heavier fish taken from time to time, but it was sea trout for which this lovely loch was most famous.

LOCH MORAR
40/690920-865905

Permission: Morar Hotel, by Mallaig, Inverness-shire.
Tel: Mallaig (0687) 2346
The Superintendent, Alt an Loin, Morar, by Mallaig, Inverness-shire.

Morar is the deepest freshwater loch in Europe and plunges to a depth of over 1000 feet between South Tarbet Bay and Camas Luinge Bay, where the River Meoble enters. Loch Morar lies at the end of 'The Road to the Isles' and this desolate, magnificent water is 12 miles long by up to 1½ miles wide. The best way to explore Morar is by boat, the

19 Loch Morar – and the islands

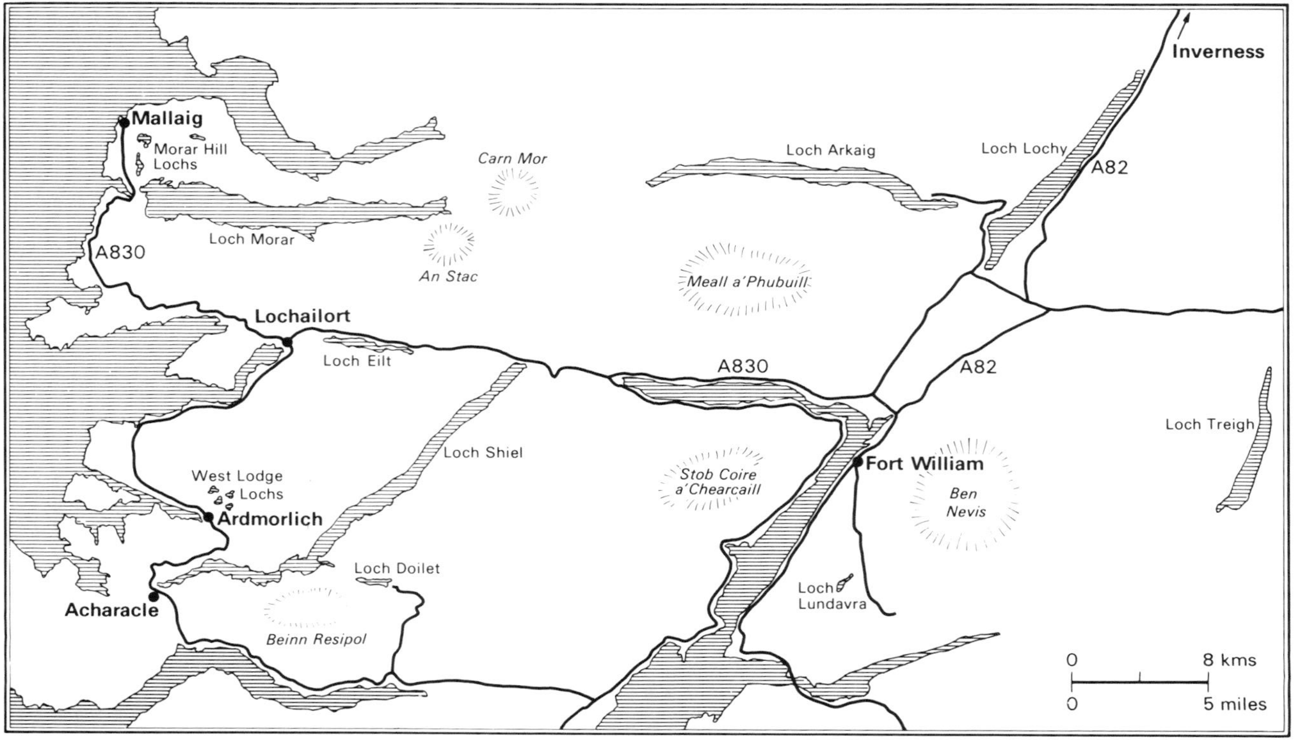

17 Fort William

south shore being almost trackless and the public road on the north shore ending after 5 miles at Bracorina. The loch has excellent brown trout and the odd salmon and sea trout. Members of the Morar Angling club, fishing for salmon on 12 July 1991, took 14 salmon weighing 87lb. Donny MacLellan and John MacVarrish had four fish, the heaviest of which weighed 15lb. The best trout fishing is to be found at the west end of the loch, around the islands (where Lord Lovat was captured in 1746 after the Jacobite Rebellion). The Morar Hotel has three boats available and bank fishing is also allowed; but because the water shelves so rapidly, take great care if wading – it is a long way down. Trout average 12oz and fight well and a decent day should bring you four to six good fish. Trout of over 11lb have been caught and each season produces fish of 5–8lb. Best flies to use include Butchers, March Brown, Black Pennell, Greenwell's Glory and Grouse & Claret. Keep a weather eye open for 'Morag' as you do – Loch Ness has a rival here – and you never can tell what you might hook in the depths.

NORTH MORAR HILL LOCHS

LOCH A'GHILIE GHOBAICH 40/687940
LOCH A'BHADA DHARAICH 40/696946
LOCHAN A'MHEADHOIN 40/695945
LOCH AN NOSTARIE 40/690955
LOCH NA BA GLAISE 40/715940
LOCH MHIC LEANNAIN 40/713949
LOCH EIREAGORAIDH 40/720956
Permission: Not required

These delightful hill lochs lie to the north of Loch Morar (above) and may be approached either from a good track that leads east from Glasnacardoch, 1 mile south from Mallaig, or from a similar track heading north from Loch Morar at 698932, where the Allt an Loin burn enters the loch at Bun an Loin Bay. Bank fishing only for good baskets of wild trout which average around 8–10oz, with the odd larger fish to catch you unawares. Wonderful walking country for a splendid day out in the hills.

LOCHAN INNIS EANRUIG 40/738930
LOCHAN ROPACH 40/743927
LOCHAN STOLE 40/746935
LOCHAN NAN UAN 40/753934
GASKINE LOCH 40/761919

LOCHAN NAN RI-CHRIOCHAN 40/769924
LOCH A'BHRGNAID 40/772920

Permission: Not required

These lochs and lochans are even nicer than those described above – but they are also much harder to reach. They all lie to the east of Bracorina and although there is a track along the north shore of Loch Morar, to help you on your way, sooner or later you have to strike north into the wilderness. The going is tough, compass and map country, but if you enjoy exciting hill-loch fishing amid some of the most wonderful scenery in Scotland, then this is the place to go. Take along standard pattern loch flies.

LOCH NAM PAITEAN 40/725740

Permission: Mrs N. D. Stewart, Kinlochmoidart House, Kinlochmoidart, Lochailort, Salen, Inverness-shire.
Tel: Salen (096785) 609

This is a hill loch to the north of Ardmolich on the A861 from Acharacle to Lochailort. A track leads off the minor road to the east of Ardmolich at Brunery and wends up Coire Mor and Leached Fheadacach. It is a stiff climb but worth the effort. The average weight of trout is 1lb and a reasonable day should produce four to six fish. The loch was stocked many years ago and the native population has thrived and is of really first-class quality. The best time to fish Paitean is May and June, when good baskets are taken. The loch has a multitude of bays and points with a scattering of small islands. Trout of up to 2–3lb are sometimes caught and this excellent loch is well worth visiting. Boat and bank fishing, using standard pattern loch flies.

LOCHAN MEALL A'MHADAIDH 40/717750

Permission: Mrs N. D. Stewart, Kinlochmoidart House, Kinlochmoidart, Lochailort, Salen, Inverness-shire.
Tel: Salen (096785) 609

This lovely loch lies at an altitude of 2000 feet in a setting of supreme beauty. The walk up to it takes about an hour and half and fishing is from the bank only. Meall a'Mhadaidh is a classic hill loch with scattered islands, and trout are caught from all round the shores. The fish are a good average weight, 1lb 8oz, but they are also hard to catch. Larger trout are taken most years and this fine loch has produced fish of up to 6lb. You may puff and huff a bit on the way up to Meall a'Mhadaidh – but it is well worth the effort.

LOCH A'MHUILLINN 40/700742
LOCH NA CAILLICH 40/705747
LOCH DEARG 40/737742
LOCHAN NA CRAOIBHE 40/727751
LOCHAN NA CAILLICH 40/705747
UPPER LOCHAN SLIGEANACH 40/715744

Permission: Mrs N. D. Stewart, Kinlochmoidart House, Kinlochmoidart, Lochailort, Salen, Inverness-shire.
Tel: Salen (096785) 609

Fishing any of these hill lochs involves a good walk, but they are delightfully remote and surrounded by some of the most dramatic scenery in Scotland. You will need to be prepared – full-service hiking gear and compass and map – but you will have an unforgettable day out. Trout are not particularly large, averaging around 8–10oz, but some of the lochs do have big fish. Finding them is one of the great joys of fishing in Moidart. Detailed directions will be given on booking and fishing is from the bank only. Take standard pattern loch flies – and you will need strong legs and lungs.

ARDNAMURCHAN ESTATE LOCHS

LOCH MUDLE 47/544660
LOCHAN A'MHADAIDH RIABHAICH 47/557656

Permission: Mike MacGregor, Glenmore Cottage, Glenborrodale, Salen, Inverness-shire.
Tel: Glenborrodale (09724) 263

Fishing on these lochs is managed by the Ardnamurchan Estate and they are situated between Kilchoan and Glenborrodale on the B8007. The lochs contain brown trout which average 8–12oz, with some larger fish of up to 1lb 8oz being caught occasionally. Salmon are sometimes taken on Loch Mudle and permits are issued on the understanding that anglers make proper returns of catches. Both boat and bank fishing are available and baskets of 10–12 trout are often taken. A'Mhadaidh Riabhaich is best for trout but both lochs are pleasant to fish, and in lovely surroundings. Use standard loch fly patterns.

ARDTORNISH ESTATE LOCHS

LOCH ARIENAS 49/685510
LOCH DOIRE NAM MART 49/660525
LOCH TEARNAIT 49/750470
CROSBEN BLACK LOCHS 49/703530

EIGNIGG BLACK LOCHS 49/780454
LOCH NAN CLACH 49/785465
LOCHAN AN FHAING 49/767487
LOCHAN NAN CRAOBH 49/773485
LOCH NA SULA MOIRE 49/777464
LOCHAN BEINN LAOAIN 49/699533
LOCH AN UISG ADMAIR 49/725485

Permission: Ardtornish Estate, Estate Office, Morvern, by Oban, Argyll.
Tel: Morvern (096784) 288

Ardtornish is high on my list of outstanding fishing locations, not only because of the quality of the surrounding landscape and of the sport, but also because of the whole experience: good salmon and sea-trout fishing, superb hill loch fishing for wild brown trout, comfortable, well-furnished, self-catering cottages, and excellent facilities for non-fishing members of your party.

The 1990 season produced 61 salmon, 257 sea trout and 638 brown trout. The brown trout are from 8–10oz up to 2lb 8oz, with the best fish recorded weighing 6lb 8oz; sea trout of up to 9lb have been taken and the heaviest salmon was a fish of 26lb. My favourite trout loch is Tearnait, which involves a delightful walk of about 3 miles. Arienas is best for sea trout although most salmon and sea trout are caught in the River Aline and White Glen. If you are looking for a place for an all-round family holiday, look no further: Ardtornish will satisfy all your requirements.

20 Bruce Sandison on Loch Tearnait

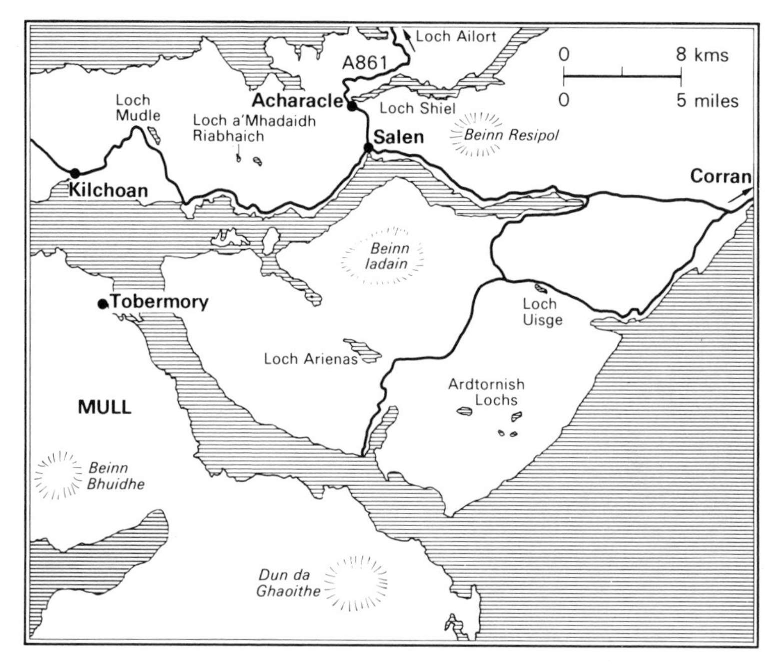

18 Ardtornish

LOCHAN LUNN DA BHRA (Loch Lundavra) 41/090660

Permission: Mrs MacCullum, Lundavra Farm, Fort William.
Tel: Fort William (0397) 702582

This is a beautiful loch to the south of Fort William, high up on the slopes of Ben Nevis. A narrow, single-track road leads up from the town and drivers should be very careful on the blind summits. The loch is about 1 mile long by 250 yards wide and both boat and bank fishing are available. Trout of 3–5lb are frequently taken; the heaviest fish caught on Lundavra was a trout of 8lb and the average weight is 12oz. Fish are caught all round the loch but the favoured areas are where the feeder burn enters at the west end of the loch and in the vicinity of the island. Book in advance and take along Peter Ross, Soldier Palmer and Black Pennell. A lovely loch, easily accessible and well worth a visit.

LOCH TREIGH 41/335720

Permission: British Alcan Highland Estates, Estate Office, 33 High Street, Fort William, Inverness-shire.
Tel: Fort William (0397) 702433

Loch Treigh is 6 miles long by 3/4 mile wide and contains brown trout and pike. It is a distant, remote and dramatic water, with Stob Coire Easain (1116m) to the west and Stob Coire Sgriodain (960m) to the east. Turn south from the A86 at Inverlair Falls on the River Spean. This is a deep loch, over 300 feet in parts, and great care should be taken when wading. The shallows are the most productive areas to fish, particularly at either end of the loch. There are very large trout in Treigh, some weighing well over 10lb, but an average day should produce a basket of three to four fish totalling 2–3lb. Standard pattern loch flies work well.

AVIEMORE LOCHS

AVIELOCHAN 36/907165

Permission: G. Mortimer, 61 High Street, Grantown-on-Spey, Morayshire.
Tel: Grantown-on-Spey (0479) 2684
Allen's, Deisher Road, Boat of Garten, Morayshire.
Tel: Boat of Garten (047983) 372
Mrs Macdonald, Loch Cottage, Avielochan, Aviemore.
Tel: Aviemore (0479) 810847

Avielochan lies adjacent to the A95, 2½ miles north of Aviemore. There are two sessions: 10.00am–6.00pm, and 6.00pm until dusk. The loch is stocked with both brown and rainbow trout. Brown trout average 1lb 1oz, rainbow trout, 15oz. The largest brown trout caught during 1991 weighed 3lb and the heaviest rainbow, 2lb 8oz. Rods are limited to 10 and so it always advisable to book in advance if you wish to fish this easily accessible, somewhat public little lochan.

LOCH VAA 36/913175

Permission: G. Mortimer, 61 High Street, Grantown-on-Spey, Morayshire.
Tel: Grantown-on-Spey (0479) 2684
Allen's, Deisher Road, Boat of Garten, Morayshire.
Tel: Boat of Garten (0479783) 372

Loch Vaa is in the middle of a fine old forest of pine trees, close to Aviemore, and covers an area of some 35 acres. Boat fishing only is allowed on this delightful, secluded loch which is regularly stocked with both brown and rainbow trout. The average weight of brown trout is 1lb 4oz, while rainbow trout average 1lb. During 1991 a brown trout of 4lb was landed and the heaviest rainbow weighed 3lb 8oz. There is a limit of 10 fish per boat per day and trout respond well to all the standard patterns of loch flies.

LOCH DALLAS 36/932160

Permission: G. Mortimer, 61 High Street, Grantown-on-Spey, Morayshire.
Tel: Grantown-on-Spey (0479) 2684
Allen's, Deisher Road, Boat of Garten, Morayshire.
Tel: Boat of Garten (0479783) 372

Loch Dallas lies south from Boat of Garten, close to the River Spey, and is best approached from Boat of Garten along Kinchurdy Road, past the 30mph sign until you come to where the road turns left under the Strathspey Railway Company line; then on until you see the loch on your right. The loch covers an area of 8 acres and is regularly stocked with both brown and rainbow trout. Brown trout average 1lb 1oz, rainbows, 15oz. The heaviest brown trout taken during 1991 weighed 3lb, and the heaviest rainbow, 2lb 8oz. Boat fishing only and there is a bag limit of 10 fish per boat per day. This is a most attractive loch, intimate and pleasant to fish, with magnificent views to the Cairngorms.

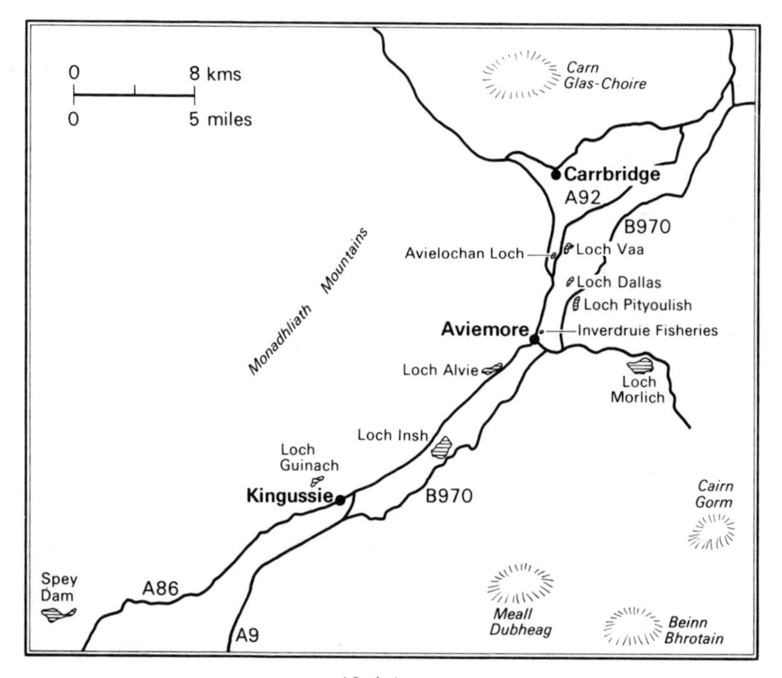

19 Aviemore

LOCH PITYOULISH 36/920135

Permission: Rothiemurchus Fishing Centre, Aviemore, Inverness-shire.
Tel: Aviemore (0479) 810703

Pityoulish is to the east of Aviemore and is approached from the B970 Coylumbridge–Nethybridge road. This is a deep loch over 1/2 mile long by 1/4 mile wide, surrounded by trees and nestling at the foot of Creag a'Ghreusaiche (435m). Fishing is from the boat only and the loch contains some very shy, very large brown trout – and some much less shy, voracious, large pike. Average weight of trout is about 12oz.

LOCH MORLICH 36/965095

Permission: Warden's Office, Glenmore Campsite, Glenmore, by Aviemore, Inverness-shire.
Tel: Cairngorm (047986) 271
Facilities for disabled anglers: As above

There are circumspect brown trout and pike in this very beautiful loch, which is popular and often very busy with water sports and other activities. Perhaps a good place to take the children for a picnic. A glorious setting.

LOCH ALVIE 36/865095

Permission: Alvie Estate, Estate Office, Kincraig, Kingussie, Inverness-shire.
Tel: Kincraig (0540) 651255 or 651249

21 Big trout country, Loch Pityoulish, Aviemore

Loch Alvie is now overlooked by the new A9 and is 1 mile long by 1/2 mile wide. The loch is between 33 and 66 feet deep and contains brown trout and pike. A pike of 15lb was caught in 1990, and returned to the water, which will help to keep the 8–12-oz brown trout alert and on their toes. Boat and bank fishing are available.

LOCH INSH 36/830045

Permission: Loch Insh Watersports & Skiing Centre, Insh Hall, Kincraig, Inverness-shire.
Tel: Kincraig (05404) 272

Loch Insh is easily accessible, lying 5 1/2 miles north-east of Kingussie at Kincraig. Insh is an expansion of the River Spey and contains brown trout, Arctic char, salmon, sea trout and pike. The best brown trout fishing area is at the southern end and round the island at the northern end. Loch Insh is shallow over most of its area although there are parts where it drops to more than 100 feet. Trout average 8–10oz, with the odd fish of up to 4lb, and standard pattern loch flies produce results. The loch is also a very popular water-sports centre.

ROTHIEMURCHUS FISH FARM 36/901112

Permission: Rothiemurchus Fish Farm, Inverdruie, by Aviemore, Inverness-shire.
Tel: Aviemore (0479) 810703

Rothiemurchus Fish Farm is the base for fishing Rothiemurchus Estate waters, including the River Spey for trout and two hill lochs with boats, as well as an 8-acre loch stocked with rainbow trout and a beginner's pond at the trout farm. Tackle and instruction are provided. Loch and river fishing from April until September, rainbow trout fishing all year round.

SPEY DAM 35/570935

Permission: The Paper Shop, Kingussie, Inverness-shire.
Tel: Kingussie (05402) 207
Facilities for disabled anglers: As above

Spey Dam, on the upper reaches of the River Spey, is 1 mile long by 1/2 mile wide. Approach via the minor road at Laggan Bridge. The loch is surrounded by magnificent hills and mountains and contains excellent brown trout. The local angling association stocks Spey Dam and both boat and bank fishing are available. Trout average 12oz, although there are also good numbers of larger fish. As always, the only problem is getting them out. Use standard pattern loch flies to try.

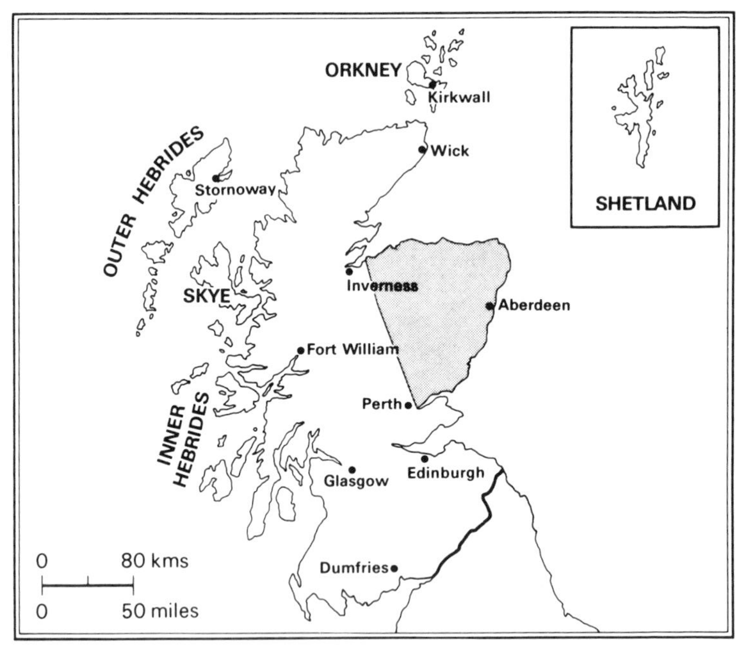

20 Angus and the North-East

6 Angus and the North-East

All too often the potential of the trout fishing in this area is underestimated. Most visiting anglers fish for increasingly rare salmon on the great rivers such as the Don, Dee and Findhorn and very few try the many lovely trout lochs. There are few waters in Scotland that can match the excellent returns produced by Rescobie Loch near Forfar and few lochs in more remote and magnificent settings than Lochs Brandy and Wharrl in Glen Clova. The Loch of Strathbeg is one of the least-known and most attractive lochs in Scotland, while Lochindorb Loch, with its dramatic ruined castle, is a perfect place to spend a day. I began fishing in this area in the early 1960s and it was in the forests of Glen Isla that my wife and I saw our first wildcat. We spent an unforgettable few days walking and fishing among some of the most lovely scenery in all of Scotland. The Forth and Tay road bridges have made the area more easily accessible and I highly recommend it to you.

LOCH OF LINTRATHEN 53/280550

Permission: J. Yule, Lintrathen Loch.
Tel: (05756) 327
Dr David Parratt, 91 Strathern Road, Broughty Ferry, Dundee.
Tel: Dundee (0382) 21164
Club membership available by post from: J. Bowman, 5F Brassie Court, Dundee.
Facilities for disabled anglers: At the loch

The Loch of Lintrathen lies to the north of Alyth and is 1½ miles long by ¾ mile wide. Fishing is from boats only and 11 are available for anglers. The season runs from April until September and the loch is stocked with brown trout. Outboard motors are not allowed and two boats are held daily until 5.00pm for the use of visiting anglers who are not members of the Lintrathen Angling Club. There is an excellent clubhouse at the loch and a water bailiff is on hand to advise on the best places to fish and which flies to use. Trout average 12oz but a number of fish of 2lb are taken each season. There is a limit of 18 fish per boat and individual catches of six to ten fish are common. The Lintrathen trout have a great reputation, fight hard and are of good

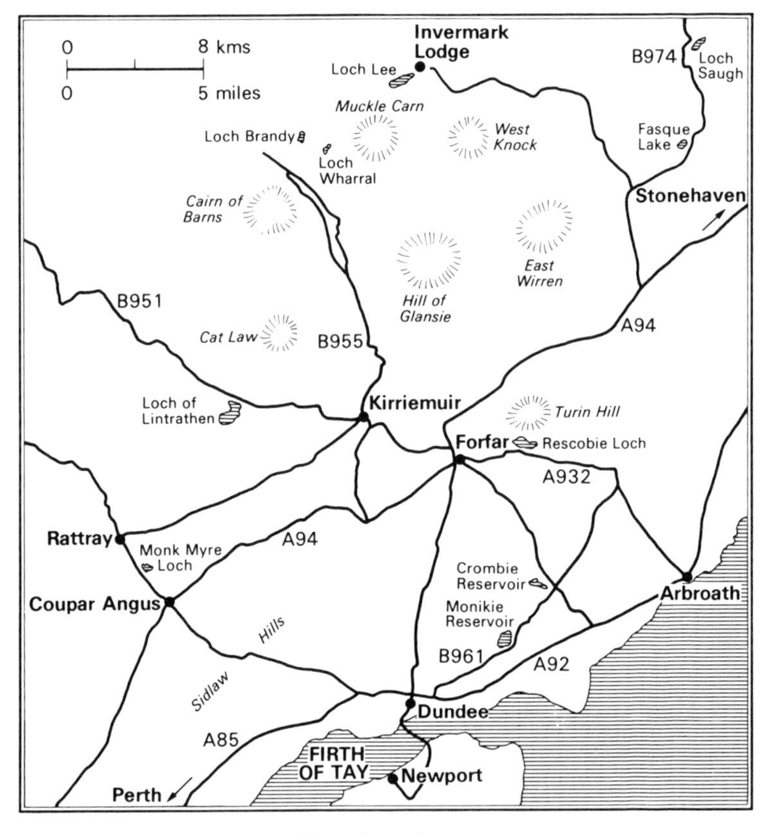

21 Dundee and Angus

quality. The most favoured fishing areas are around the island off the north-west shore, and along the south shore. Standard loch fly patterns do well and in calm conditions great sport can be had using dry fly. This is a lovely loch in very pleasant surroundings, easily accessible and well worth fishing. Bookings may be made up to seven days in advance.

MONK MYRE LOCH 53/210427

Permission: David Simpson, Post Office, Cupar, Angus.
Tel: Cupar (08282) 329

Monk Myre lies to the north of Cupar, east of the A923 Blairgowrie road and covers 14 acres. Bank fishing is not allowed but four boats are available for anglers. The loch is stocked with both brown and rainbow trout and the average weight is just over 1lb. There is a limit of eight fish per rod and the best flies to use are Greenwell's Glory, Invicta and Grouse & Claret, all in sizes 14–16. Trout of up to 3lb are taken each season and an average basket is three or four fish. Monk Myre fishes best during June and July and the most productive area is in the middle, and then closer to the margins as darkness falls. The season extends from May until the end of October and this is a very popular loch – so book early.

RESCOBIE LOCH 54/520515

Permission: The Rescobie Loch Development Association, Jack Yule, The Bailiff, South Lodge, Reswallie, by Forfar, Angus.
Tel: Letham (Angus) (030781) 384
Facilities for disabled anglers: Contact above

The objective of the Development Association is to provide good fishing at a reasonable price and these aims are being achieved very well indeed if results from Rescobie are anything to go by. Rescobie covers 190 acres and lies between Forfar and Friockheim on the A932. This is an easily accessible loch in attractive surroundings of good farming land and wooded slopes. Electric outboard motors are available for hire at the boat house and the loch is stocked each year. During

22 Everything right at Rescobie

1991 3000 brown trout were introduced, as well as 5500 rainbow trout of 8oz and 9000 rainbow trout of between 1 and 4lb. The average weight of brown trout caught during 1991 was 2lb 2oz and rainbow trout averaged 1lb 8oz. The largest brown trout landed weighed 7lb 2oz and was a record for the loch, while the largest rainbow weighed 5lb 11oz. The best basket from boat fishing was six fish totalling 14lb 9oz, while the best basket taken bank fishing was six fish totalling 13lb 12oz. Flies that do the damage on Rescobie include Dunkeld, Black Pennell, Alexandra, Wickham's Fancy, Cinnamon & Gold, and standard reservoir lures. Visitors will find the bailiff, Jack Yule, an experienced and helpful angler, always ready to offer advice and assistance, and the mainstay of the whole operation. Rescobie is highly recommended and is the best loch in the area. Book in advance.

MONIKIE RESERVOIR 54/505380

Permission: William H. Bell, Hon. Secretary, Monikie Angling Club, 12 Forfar Road, Dundee.
Tel: Dundee (0382) 459811
Facilities for disabled anglers: As above

There are two waters here, separated by a narrow peninsula, and they are within the confines of Monikie Country Park, to the north of Monifieth. Fishing is from boats only and two are held daily until 5.00pm for the use of visitors who are not club members. The lochs are stocked with brown trout and the average weight is 12oz. There is a bag limit – frequently achieved – of 12 fish per boat and trout of 2lb are taken, with fish of over 1lb being common. Best flies include Wickham's Fancy, Butchers, Black Pennell, Greenwell's Glory and Invicta. Two sessions operate: 8.00am–4.30pm and 5.00pm until dusk. Late-evening fishing brings best results. Man-made lochs, but nevertheless attractive, and first-class fishing.

CROMBIE RESERVOIR 54/525407

Permission: William H. Bell, Hon. Secretary, Monikie Angling Club, 12 Forfar Road, Dundee.
Tel: Dundee (0382) 459811
Facilities for disabled anglers: As above

Crombie is in a woodland setting to the north of Carnoustie. Approach from the B961 just past the junction with the A958 Forfar–Carnoustie road. The reservoir is in a country park and wildlife sanctuary and is a long, narrow water which wends its way through the trees for 1½ miles. It is stocked with brown trout and they average 8–12oz. The most productive area is round the large island at the western end of the reservoir and in the 'Cut', where the feeder burn enters. Boat fishing only and an average basket should produce six to eight trout. Fish of up to 1lb 8oz have been caught and the most favoured flies are Wickham's Fancy, Black Pennell, Greenwell's Glory, Invicta and Ke-He. Fishing is divided into two sessions, as at Monikie Reservoir, and there is a deposit required when you collect the key for the boat. The deposit is returned after fishing – provided the key is also. An easily accessible and very pleasant water to fish, well managed and worth a visit.

LOCH WHARRAL 44/358745

Permission: The Factor, Airlie Estate Office, Cortachy, Kirriemuir, Angus.
Tel: Cortachy (05754) 222

Loch Wharral is 700 yards long by 200 yards wide and lies at an altitude of 1800 feet. There is an invigorating 2-mile walk to get to Wharral and you should approach from the B966 at Wheen. The crags of Ben Tirran (896m) rise sharply from the margin of the loch. Although the trout are not very large they give a good account of themselves. Fishing is from the bank only and wading is reasonably comfortable, although carrying waders up the hill is not. Fish the north-east corner and the south shore using standard pattern loch flies. Loch Wharral is a very lovely loch, infrequently fished, and can give excellent sport. A trout of 1lb would be considered very large for this delightful water, but it is worth the effort required to get to it because of the dramatic setting. Peaceful and remote.

LOCH BRANDY 44/340765

Permission: The Factor, Airlie Estate Office, Cortachy, Kirriemuir, Angus.
Tel: Cortachy (05754) 222

Loch Brandy lies at the head of Glen Clova in a horseshoe basin formed by the slopes of Green Hill (870m). This is a remote and lovely little loch and may be approached via a good track which leaves the B955 just behind the Ogilvy Arms Hotel. Brandy contains a good stock of hard-fighting, 8-oz trout, but warm weather is required before they can be tempted to rise. When they do, baskets of up to 30 fish can be taken and there is the odd 1-lb trout from time to time – generally when you are looking somewhere else. The best area is below the crags on the north-west shore and size 14–16 flies should be used. Try

Butchers, Zulus and Black Pennell. A good walk up, but worth the effort. You will be rewarded with peace and quiet and surrounded by superb scenery.

LOCH LEE 44/420795

Permission: Fred Taylor, Invermark Estate Office, Glenesk, Angus.
Tel: Tarfside (03567) 208

Loch Lee is 1½ miles long by some 500 yards wide and lies in a hollow surrounded by Monawee (696m) to the north, Cairn Caidloch (674m) to the south and ragged Craig Maskeldie (687m) to the west. Loch Lee can be dangerously windy and at times fishing is cancelled because of high winds. Take along an outboard motor and a drogue. Bank fishing is not allowed but there are three boats available for anglers. Lee is a deep loch and the best fishing area is at the western end, where the water is shallow, and round the western margins. The loch contains brown trout which average 8–12oz, and some Arctic char. Fish of up to 4lb have been caught, and a char weighing 1lb 4oz. Catches vary considerably according to weather conditions but you should take home a basket of six to a dozen fish, and size 10–12 flies seem to do best. Use Blue Zulu, Black Zulu, Black Pennell, Grouse & Claret and Kingfisher Butcher. No Sunday fishing and the estate prefers to receive bookings by post giving at least two weeks' notice. This is a most attractive loch to fish, out in the wilds amidst splendid scenery.

LOCH SAUGH 46/676788

Permission: Drumtochty Arms Hotel, Auchenblae, Kincardineshire.
Tel: Auchenblae (05612) 210
Facilities for disabled anglers: As above

This is a long, narrow loch between Thorter Hill (416m) to the west and Strathfinella Hill (414m) to the east. Approach from the B966 from Auchenblae, or from the north via the B974, turning east at Clatterin Brig. The loch is managed by the Brechin Angling Association, who have stocked it with both brown and rainbow trout. Fishing is from the bank only and the trout average 12oz. Fish of over 2lb are taken occasionally and standard loch fly patterns will do.

FASQUE LAKE 45/645747

Permission: Peter Gladstone, Fasque, Fettercairn, Laurencekirk, Kincardineshire.
Tel: Fettercairn (05614) 201

Fasque Lake lies to the west of Laurencekirk and is approached via the B974 from Fettercairn. This is a man-made lake of about 20 acres in a beautiful setting within the Fasque Estate. The loch – sorry, lake – was built in 1840 and has excellent natural spawning grounds. It contains brown trout and rainbow trout which average 1lb, although fish of up to 5lb have been taken. There is a bag limit of three fish per rod per day but should a trout of more than 3lb 8oz be caught after this limit has been reached the angler is allowed to keep it. Boat fishing only and there are two available. The estate has first-class accommodation available and guests have priority for the fishing. If you wish for privacy, peace and quiet and excellent fishing in beautiful surroundings, this is for you.

LOCH VROTACHAN 43/123785

Permission: Martin Holroyd, The Ballater Angling Association, 59 Golf Road, Ballater, Aberdeenshire.
Tel: Ballater (03397) 55365
Countrywear, 15 & 35 High Street, Ballater, Aberdeenshire.
Tel: Ballater (03397) 55453

This loch lies above the ski slopes at Spittal of Glenshee. It may be reached in relative comfort by hitching a ride up on the chair-lift and then by striking out north-west for about 1 mile. Loch Vrotachan lies at an altitude of over 2000 feet amidst the wild corries and crags of the mountains of Mar. There is a good fishing hut with all facilities and a boat. Brown trout average 8oz but during 1991 one of 2lb 15oz was taken on a Black & Peacock Spider. The season has been extended to 5 October and this is a wonderful loch in lovely surroundings, well worth a visit.

LOCH NAN EUN 43/063780

Permission: Estate Office, Invercauld Estate, Braemar, by Ballater, Aberdeenshire.
Tel: Braemar (03397) 41224

Loch nan Eun lies at the head of Glen Taitneach, 6 miles north-west of the Spittal of Glenshee. Follow the track on the north side of the bridge at Spittal, where the A93 makes the sharp bend east. The loch lies at an altitude of 2000 feet and Beinn Lutharan Mor towers a further 1000 feet over the loch. Trout average 8oz with the odd larger fish. But visit Loch nan Eun as much for the beauty of the surroundings as for the fishing. The season closes on 11 August. Best flies are Butchers, Blue Zulu, Teal & Green, Black Pennell and Stoat's Tail.

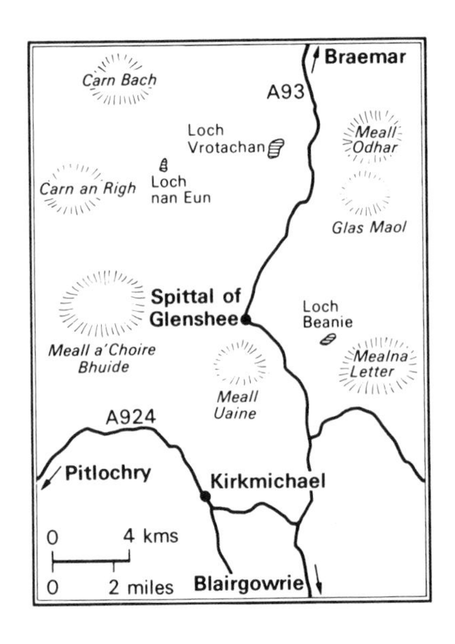

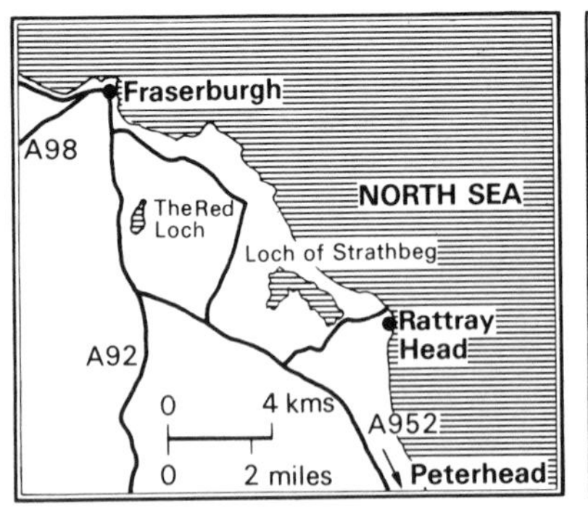

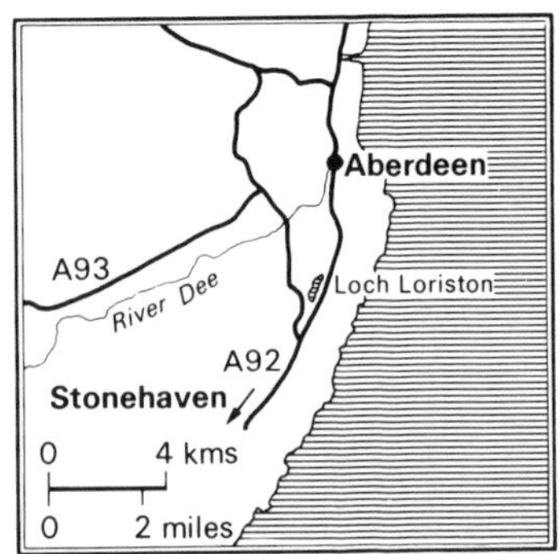

22 Aberdeen

LOCH BEANIE (Loch Shechernich) 43/160688

Permission: Estate Office, Invercauld Estate, Braemar, by Ballater, Aberdeenshire.
Tel: Braemar (03397) 41224
The keeper: R. Hepburn, Wester Binzian, Glenshee.
Tel: Glenshee (025085) 206
To reserve a boat, contact the keeper in Glenshee.

Loch Beanie is 700 yards long by about 250 yards wide. It nestles in a hollow below Meatna Letter (702m) to the south and Craigenloch Hill (738m) to the north. Beyond, peaks and summits march into the distance and this is a really wonderful setting. The loch contains brown trout averaging 8oz but fish of up to 2lb 4oz are sometimes taken. Boat and bank fishing are available and the season closes on 11 August. Approach Beanie from Runavey Farm (130690) or from Invereddrie Farm (137681) and expect a splendid walk of about 2 miles. Take along standard pattern loch flies.

LORISTON LOCH 38/940010

Permission: J. Somers & Sons, 40 Thistle Street, Aberdeen.
Tel: Aberdeen (0224) 50910

Loriston Loch lies 4 miles to the south of Aberdeen between the A92 and A956 roads. Fishing is from the bank only and the loch has been stocked with rainbow trout which average 12oz. Loriston is 700 yards long by 200 yards wide and can be a very windy loch. Wind direction dictates which shore to fish, but trout are taken all round the loch. An average basket should produce three or four fish and trout of up to 2lb 3oz have been caught. Evening fishing is best and Red Buzzers and orange-coloured flies, size 12–14, work well. An easily accessible loch with a bag limit of six trout per rod per day.

THE LOCH OF STRATHBEG 30/070590

Permission: All enquiries to the Royal Society for the Protection of Birds, 17 Regents Terrace, Edinburgh.

Disaster has struck at Strathbeg, with hardly any fish being seen, let alone being caught. Various theories are propounded, including the effect of upwards of 20,000 greylag geese roosting on the loch. Scientists are working on the problem, but it will be some years before Strathbeg recovers its stature as one of the finest trout lochs in Scotland – and one of my personal favourites.

LOCH OF THE BLAIRS 27–023555

Permission: Department of Recreation, Moray District Council, District Headquarters, Elgin, Morayshire.
Tel: Elgin (0343) 543451
Jim Mitchell, The Tackle Shop, 97B High Street, Forres, Morayshire.
Tel: Forres (0309) 72936
Facilities for disabled anglers: As above

This is an easily accessible loch lying 2½ miles south of Forres. It is stocked regularly with both brown and rainbow trout and three boats are available for anglers. Bank fishing is not allowed. The loch is delightfully situated, surrounded by trees and has two small islands. There is super bird life, squirrels and roe deer in the forest and the chance of an osprey, proving that the fish are still there. There is a limit of six trout per rod per day – the osprey ignores this – and fish average 12oz. Trout of up to 3lb are taken most seasons and an average basket should bring you four fish. Concentrate on the area round the island and the margins of the loch, although fish can be taken all over. Most anglers use standard pattern loch flies, but more and more are turning to reservoir lures and there is a restriction here on the size of lure permissible, with size 8 being the largest allowed. Two sessions: 8.00am–5.00pm and 5.00pm until dusk. A lovely loch and well worth a visit.

MILLBUIES LOCHS 28/242570

Permission: Department of Recreation, Moray District Council, District Headquarters, Elgin, Morayshire.
Tel: Elgin (0343) 543451
The Warden, Millbuies Lochs, Elgin, Morayshire.
Tel: Longmorn (034386) 234
Facilities for disabled anglers: As above

The Millbuies Lochs are 4 miles south of Elgin on the A941 Rothes road. There are two lochs covering an area of ½ square mile and they are in a woodland setting to the east of the main road. Four boats are available for anglers and bank fishing is not allowed. The District Council stocks the loch with up to 2000 rainbow trout each season and their average weight is just over 1lb. It also puts in a few fish at 3–5lb. Most outings should send you home with a basket of two or three fish and most seasons produce trout of up to 4lb. Fish are taken all over the lochs and the traditional loch fly patterns all do well. A new boat house and jetty have been provided and Millbuies is an excellent, well-managed fishery. Like Loch of the Blairs (above) and Glenlatterach (below), it is a credit to the enterprise of the District Council and an asset to the area.

GLENLATTERACH RESERVOIR 28/188525

Permission: Department of Recreation, Moray District Council, District Headquarters, Elgin, Morayshire.
Tel: Elgin (0343) 543451

The Glenlatterach Reservoir is 7 miles to the south of Elgin. Approach

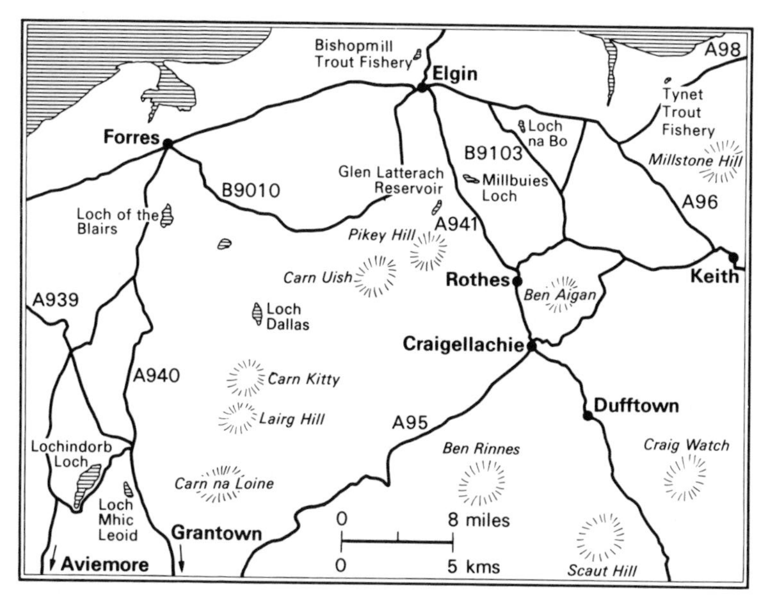

23 Morayshire

via the A941 at Whitewreath and turn right opposite the entrance to the Millbuie Lochs. The water is 3/4 mile long by 150 yards wide, and is easily accessible. It contains brown trout which average 12oz. There is bank fishing only. Fish are taken all round and they rise to standard loch fly patterns. Results in 1991 indicate that the average weight of fish in Glenlatterach is improving and Glenlatterach is the closest this area has to a west-coast hill loch, with hard-fighting brown trout.

LOCH-NA-BO 28/283600

Permission: D. Kinloch, Gardener's Cottage, Loch-na-Bo, Lhanbryde, Elgin.

Tel: Lhanbryde (034384) 2214

This loch is near Elgin, 1/2 mile east of Lhanbryde, and is approached via the A96 Fochabers road. Na-Bo is some 35 acres in extent and only boat fishing is allowed. Trout average 8oz and baskets of three or four fish can be expected. This is a popular loch, so advance booking is advisable.

TYNET TROUT FISHERY 28/393618

Permission: The Manager, Tynet Trout Farm, Buckie, Banffshire.
Tel: Clochan (05427) 295

This is a 1¼-acre pond adjacent to the A98 Buckie–Fochabers road. It is within the confines of the trout farm and fishing is for rainbow trout. There is a bag limit of five fish per rod and the average weight is 1lb. Most flies catch fish.

LOCH MHIC LEOID (Loch McLeod) 27/009347

Permission: The Strathspey Estate Office. The Square, Grantown-on-Spey, Morayshire.
Tel: Grantown-on-Spey (0479) 2529

Loch McLeod is a small loch of 4 acres, stocked with both brown and rainbow trout. It lies to the north of Grantown on the A939 Forres road and a good track leads from the road to the loch. Fishing is from the bank only, and during 1991 the average weight of trout caught was 1lb. The heaviest brown trout weighed 2lb, and the heaviest rainbow trout weighed 1lb 8oz. There is a bag limit of three fish per rod. A pleasant little loch, easily accessible and offering great sport. Standard loch fly patterns work well.

23 Angling joy, Scottish wild brown trout

LOCH LOCHINDORB 27/970360

Permission: J. Scott, Head Keeper, Lochindorb Lodge, Glenferness, Nairn.
Tel: Glenferness (03095) 270

Approach Lochindorb either from the B9007 Carrbridge–Ferness road or the A939 Grantown–Forres road. This is a shallow loch, 2 miles long by 3/4 mile wide. A windy place at times. It was the lair of the infamous Wolf of Badenloch during the Middle Ages and his ruined castle, with its water dungeon, dominates the loch from a small island. Lochindorb is full of hard-fighting, little trout and is one of my favourite lochs in the area, ideal for beginner or expert alike. Even in high winds the trout still rise like express trains through the waves. Use standard pattern loch flies and expect 12 fish to weigh about 5lb 8oz. But beware, there are also a few monsters – perhaps waiting just for you. A wonderful loch and a delight to fish.

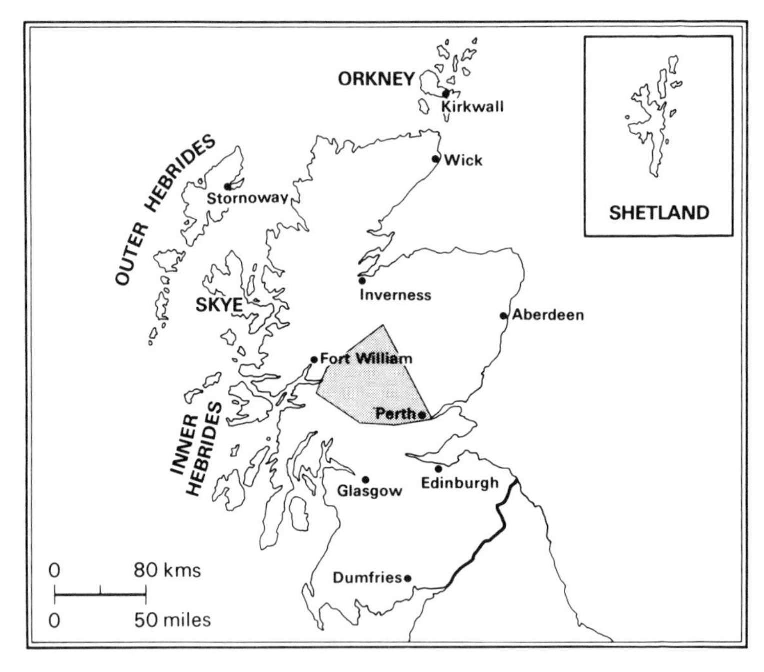

24 Perthshire

7 Perthshire

Perthshire is a county of contrasts and offers the visiting angler every conceivable type of loch in almost every conceivable type of setting. They all have one thing in common, however: they all contain good-quality, hard-fighting trout. One of the reasons for this commendable state of affairs is, I think, the excellent Pitlochry Angling Association, for the waters it controls are carefully managed and regularly stocked. Perthshire is such a lovely place to fish and from the desolate wilderness of Rannoch Moor to the calm and serenity of Butterstone, there is a loch to suit everyone. I first visited Perthshire as a boy and from scout camps near Dunkeld we would wander into the hills, sleeping out under the stars by the shores of Rotmell and Loch Ordie. Our camp was on the banks of the Tay, to the north of Dunkeld, and I have worked out that the new motorway passes right over the spot where our tents were pitched. I always think of Perthshire as a wonderland of rowan, pine and heather-clad hills, huge, sparkling rivers and sudden, breathtakingly beautiful little hill lochs and the smell of wood smoke in the autumn air. Perthshire has just about everything any trout fisherman could desire – and more.

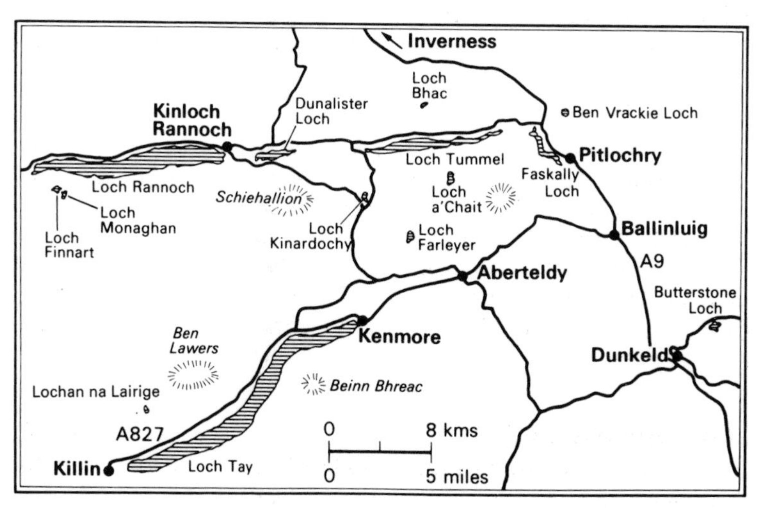

25 Rannoch and Pitlochry

LOCH TAY

Sheet 51

Permission: J. Lewis, Fishing Tackle Shop, Main Street, Killin, Perthshire.
Tel: Killin (05672) 362/241
Ben Lawers Hotel, Aberfeldy, Perthshire – boat for hire, with gillie.
Tel: Killin (05672) 436
Kenmore Hotel, Kenmore, Perthshire.
Tel: Kenmore (08873) 205
Facilities for disabled anglers: contact Mr Stephen Brown, The Ardeonaig Hotel, South Loch Tay, Perthshire.
Tel: Killin (05672) 400
Highland Lodges Limited, Milton Morewish, by Killin, Perthshire.
Tel: Killin (05672) 323
Croft-na-Caber, Kenmore, Perthshire.
Tel: Kenmore (08873) 236

Loch Tay is 16½ miles long by more than ¾ mile wide. Its main interest for anglers is as a salmon fishery but it does contain good trout as well, with fish of over 5lb sometimes being caught. The average weight of brown trout is 8oz and in recent years rainbow trout have established themselves in the loch. While they also average 8oz, rainbows of 4lb or more are taken regularly and recently a huge rainbow of 18lb was landed. The west and east end are best for brown trout, in the shallows, while the middle of the loch produces the best sport with rainbow trout.

LOCHAN NA LAIRIGE

51/600400

Permission: J. Lewis, Fishing Tackle Shop, Main Street, Killin, Perthshire.
Tel: Killin (05672) 362/241

Approach from the A827 and turn north at Edramucky on the minor road to Bridge of Balgie. Na Lairige lies to the west of the road and is easily accessible. The trout are not large but give a good account of themselves and rise well, particularly to small black flies. If they are 'off', then why not have a quick canter up Ben Lawers (1214m) to pass the time, or, for a less strenuous outing, follow the nature trail that begins by the visitor centre and mountain rescue post. Fish or no, a magnificent place to be.

LOCHAN NAN CAT

51/645426

Permission: J. Lewis, Fishing Tackle Shop, Main Street, Killin, Perthshire.
Tel: Killin (05672) 362/241

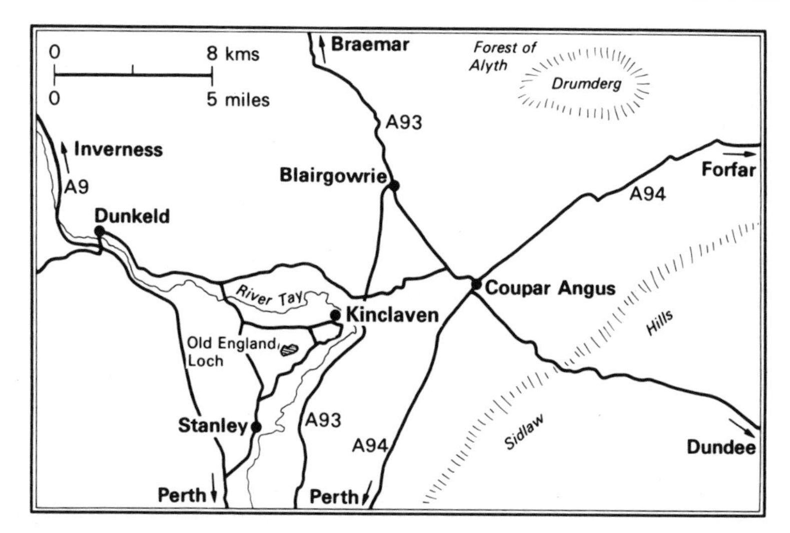

26 Blairgowrie

The approach to Nan Cat is from Lawers Village on the A827. Follow the track north on the east side of Lawers Burn, past East Mealour, into the hills. Lochan nan Cat lies at the end of a stiff walk of about 1½ hours, and is cradled in a hollow below the summit of Ben Lawers and Meall Garbh, at an altitude of almost 2500 feet. The loch contains large numbers of small brown trout which are more than ready to take anything offered. A good place to spend a day in utterly splendid surroundings.

LOCHAN BREACHLAICH 51/621315

Permission: J. Lewis, Fishing Tackle Shop, Main Street, Killin, Perthshire.
Tel: Killin (05672) 362/241

Approach Breachlaich along the minor road that turns south after the Falls of Dochart on the A827. This track follows the south shore of Loch Tay and at Cloichran (615342) you will find the outlet burn from the loch. Keep to the east side of the burn and hike up to Breachlaich – this is a walk of about 40 minutes. The loch contains traditional wild brown trout which average 8oz and they rise to the usual standard pattern loch flies. Breachlaich is a wild, lonely place to fish and well worth the effort involved in reaching it.

LOCH IUBHAIR 51/422266
LOCH DOCHART 51/405256

Permission: Mr R. Taylor, Portnellan Lodge House, Crianlarich, Perthshire.
Tel: Crianlarich (08383) 284

These lochs form part of the River Dochart and lie adjacent to the A85. Fishing is for salmon and brown trout, and groups of anglers are welcome, by advance booking, with boats, fishing tackle, outboard motors and gillies available by arrangement.

LOCH LYON 51/420410

Permission: The Keeper's Cottage, Lubreoch, Glen Lyon, Perthshire.
Tel: Innerwick (08876) 244

Loch Lyon lies at the head of Glen Lyon and is now part of a hydro-electric scheme. Approach via Fortingall, past the famous Fortingall Yew, reputed to be the oldest tree in Europe. The Keeper's Cottage is at the dam, at the end of the road. There is a track along the north shore of Lyon which soon takes you out into the wilderness, far from the madding crowd. Trout are not particularly large, although there are *ferox* in the depths, and fishing is by fly only – using all the standard patterns.

LOCH AN DAIMH 51/480460

Permission: R. Mason, Croc-na-keys, Glen Lyon, Perthshire.
Tel: Innerwick (08876) 244

Approach from Fortingall, but phone first, for when the weather is very wild the loch is closed. Turn north at Gallin, just past Meggernie Castle, and follow the narrow, twisting road up the hill to the dam. Bank fishing only, from the north shore, from the dam round to the first island. Traditional highland wild brown trout – and the odd larger specimen. Use standard pattern loch flies.

LOCH OF BUTTERSTONE 52/060450

Permission: R. Knight, Lochend Cottage, Butterstone, Dunkeld, Perthshire.
Tel: Butterstone (03504) 238
(NB: This telephone number will be changing to (0350) 724238 in mid-1992)
Facilities for disabled anglers: As above

24 Clan Sandison at lunch, Butterstone

Butterstone is an easily accessible, well-managed fishery in lovely surroundings. It lies to the north-east of Dunkeld on the A923 Blairgowrie road. The loch is stocked throughout the season and contains brown and rainbow trout. The fishing day is divided into two sessions: 9.00am–5.00pm and 5.30pm until dusk. Bank fishing is not allowed. There is a bag limit of six fish per rod and trout average 1lb 8oz. Catches of three or four fish are normal and blank days infrequent. We all have them though, and Butterstone is no exception, but generally speaking this loch is kinder than most to us poor duffers. The heaviest trout taken recently weighed 7lb 8oz. Most anglers tend to use reservoir lures, but standard loch fly patterns work just as well and the old favourites, Black Pennell, Grouse & Claret, and Soldier Palmer, will produce good results. The loch fishes well all over and on arriving the visitor will be advised where to fish. Butterstone has other fishers and you may be rewarded with the sight of an osprey showing you how it should be done, or a heron stalking the banks. A lovely loch and highly recommended.

MILL DAM 52/031454

Permission: Top Shop, Atholl Street, Dunkeld, Perthshire.
Tel: Dunkeld (03502) 556

This is a small, stocked fishery to the north of Butterstone, approached through Drumbuie Wood. It holds rainbow trout and brown trout which average 1lb, and rise to traditional flies and reservoir lures. Pleasant surroundings and a well-managed little fishery.

LOCH FREUCHIE — 52/865376

Permission: Top Shop, Atholl Street, Dunkeld, Perthshire.
Tel: Dunkeld (03502) 556

Loch Freuchie lies to the west of Amulree in Glen Quaich. The setting is very attractive and both boat and bank fishing are available. Trout average 8–12oz with a few larger fish being taken from time to time. Freuchie is a shallow loch, being no more than 35 feet deep, and fish rise and are taken all round. The most productive areas, however, are in the shallows, towards the west end, where the inlet burn enters the loch. Use standard pattern loch flies.

LOCH FASKALLY — 52/935580

Permission: P. Williamson, The Boathouse, Loch Faskally, Pitlochry, Perthshire.
Tel: Pitlochry (0796) 2919/2612

In spite of its proximity to Pitlochry and the thousands of visitors that arrive each year, Loch Faskally is very popular with anglers. Up to 75 bank and 54 boat permits are available each day and it is also possible to hire outboard motors. Many excellent trout are caught and fish of over 10lb have been landed. The average weight is 12oz and standard loch fly patterns will do. For the angler with an hour or two to spare, Faskally will make you very welcome and is in a very lovely setting.

LOCH A'CHOIRS (Ben Vrackie Loch) — 43/948627

Permission: D. Seaton, Gamekeeper's House, Balsmund, Pitlochry, Perthshire.
Tel: Pitlochry (0796) 2273

Ben Vrackie Loch lies to the north of Pitlochry. It is a small loch which involves a steep climb but there are spectacular views to the south as you climb. Fishing is from the bank only and there are six daily permits available for visitors. Trout average 8oz and standard loch fly patterns will bring good results. Just the place to work up an appetite before dinner – or to clear the head from the night before.

LOCH BHAC 43/823623

Permission: Airdanair Hotel, Atholl Road, Pitlochry.
Tel: Pitlochry (0796) 2266
Mitchells of Pitlochry, Game Fishing Specialists, 23 Atholl Road, Pitlochry (opposite the Tourist Information Office).
Tel: Pitlochry (0796) 2613

There are two boats on Loch Bhac and 12 bank fishing permits are available daily to visitors. The loch lies to the west of Pitlochry in the Allean Forest and covers an area of over 500 yards by 200 yards. This is really a hill loch, lying at an altitude of 1000 feet, and it is managed by the Pitlochry Angling Club. The club stocks the loch with brown trout, rainbow trout and brook trout. Fish rise and are taken all over, particularly where feeder burns enter in the south-east and south-west corners. Fish average 12oz–1lb and there is a bag limit of six fish per rod. Trout of up to 7lb have been taken and this is a first-class water where the fish fight very hard. Offer standard pattern loch flies.

LOCH TUMMEL 52/820595 – 43/885603

Permission: Forestry Commission Exhibition Centre, Queen's View, Loch Tummel, Killiecrankie, Perthshire.
Tel: Killiecrankie (079687) 223
Port-an-Eilean Hotel, Strathtummel, by Pitlochry.
Tel: Tummel Bridge (08824) 233
Queen's View Hotel, Strathtummel, by Pitlochry.
Tel: Killiecrankie (079687) 291

Loch Tummel, on 'The Road to the Isles', is 7 miles long by 1 mile wide. It is easily accessible from roads which run along both north and south shores. Tummel contains brown trout, pike and perch and both boat and bank fishing are available. Trout average 8oz but much larger fish are sometimes taken and fish of over 4lb have been caught. Loch Tummel is a very popular area with visitors and campers but it is always possible to find a secluded corner somewhere, and on its day Tummel can give great sport. Fish the shallows round the islands at the eastern end and at the bay below the 'Duns'. Depending upon wind direction, the south shore between Kynachan and Donlellan can be very rewarding. However, trout can be caught over most of the loch and there are a multitude of interesting bays and points to try.

LOCH A'CHAIT 52/846560

Permission: Capt. and Mrs N. A. H. McKerrow, Lick Foss, Strathtummel, Perthshire.
Tel: Tummel Bridge (08824) 208

This small loch lies at an altitude of over 1500 feet and is approached from the road which runs along the south shore of Loch Tummel. About 1 mile past the Mains of Duntanlich there is a feeder burn which passes under the road. Follow this burn into the hills and you will come to the loch after about 2 miles – and a little short of breath. Fishing is from the bank only and the average weight of trout is 8oz. Best flies include all the standard patterns. My wife and I had one of our most memorable days out here, taking fish up up to 1lb, thanks to the courtesy of the then owner, Major Whitson. A wonderful, glorious walk amidst superb scenery.

LOCH KINARDOCHY 52/777550

Permission: Airdanair Hotel, Atholl Road, Pitlochry, Perthshire.
Tel: Pitlochry (0796) 2266
Mitchells of Pitlochry, Game Fishing Specialists, 23 Atholl Road, Pitlochry (opposite the Tourist Information Centre).
Tel: Pitlochry (0796) 2613
Facilities for disabled anglers: As above

This loch lies between Tummel and Aberfeldy and is approached via the B846. Fishing is from the two boats only. Its exposed position can make Kinardochy a wild place to fish. However, it is easily accessible and there is a good hut and mooring bay. There is almost no natural spawning, so the Pitlochry Angling Club stocks the loch each year and stock fish quickly reach 8oz during their first year. The average weight is 12oz and fish of up to 3lb 8oz are sometimes taken. Trout rise and are caught all over this shallow loch and it is very popular with local anglers, so book early. Use standard pattern loch flies.

LOCH FARLEYER 52/810520

Permission: Major Neil Ramsey, Farleyer, Aberfeldy, Perthshire.
Tel: Aberfeldy (0887) 20523

Loch Farleyer is a delightful hill loch to the north of Aberfeldy at an altitude of 1000 feet. There is a good track out to the loch from Camserney on the B846 and fishing is managed and controlled very strictly. This loch has been stocked with brown trout and Loch Leven trout and the average weight is 8oz. Baskets of five to eight fish are normal and all the standard pattern loch flies produce results. Trout are caught all over the loch but the most productive areas are in the vicinity of the two feeder burns which enter on the north corner and the small bay on the eastern shore.

DUNALASTAIR LOCH 42/700585

Permission: Dunalastair Hotel, Kinloch Rannoch, Perthshire.
Tel: Kinloch Rannoch (08822) 323
E. M. Beattie, 2 Schiehallion Place, Kinloch Rannoch, Perthshire.
Tel: Kinloch Rannoch (08822) 261
Bookings via Mr Ken Robertson.
Tel: Kinloch Rannoch (08822) 354

Dunalastair is a large, flooded area between Tummel and Rannoch, 1½ miles long by ½ mile wide. It is a shallow loch and it is quite possible to run aground in the middle because of tree stumps lurking just below the surface. It is a very beautiful place to fish with Schiehallion (1083m) dominating the southern horizon and Beinn a'Chuallaich (891m) to the north. The slopes of the hills are gently wooded and wildlife abounds. So do some rather large trout – but they are hard to catch. Fish of up to 6lb have been taken and the largest trout caught during 1991 weighed 4lb 4oz. The average weight is 2lb. Boat fishing only and there are up to six available for visiting anglers. Flies to use include Black Pennell, Silver Invicta and Alexandra.

LOCH RANNOCH 42/600580

Permission: Dunalastair Hotel, Kinloch Rannoch, Perthshire.
Tel: Kinloch Rannoch (08822) 323
The Bunrannoch Hotel, Kinloch Rannoch, Perthshire.
Tel: Kinloch Rannoch (08822) 367
The Country Store, Kinloch Rannoch, Perthshire.
Tel: Kinloch Rannoch (08822) 306

Loch Rannoch is 10 miles long by ¾ mile wide and is renowned for the steady stream of monster trout produced over the years: 1867 – 22lb, 1904 – 21lb, 1905 – 23lb 8oz, 1912 – 18lb 8oz. Even today, large fish are still taken and during 1991 trout of 16lb, 12lb 8oz, 12lb, 10lb 8oz and 8lb were taken. However, don't get too excited, because the average weight is more like 8–12oz. The larger fish are taken by trolling and are, of course, the exception rather than the rule. But a day on Loch Rannoch should produce a nice basket of about 10 trout, although much larger baskets are frequently taken and you could always run into the odd much bigger fish. Use standard pattern loch flies (Wickham's Fancy does well) and the best area to fish is at the western end of the loch between Finnart and Eilan Mor. Loch Rannoch is one of my favourite lochs and the Rannoch Conservation Association works hard to keep it that way, regularly patrolling the loch to ensure fair play. We are all in its debt.

LOCH EIGHEACH 42/450570

Permission: John Brown, The Square, Kinloch Rannoch, Perthshire.
Tel: Kinloch Rannoch (08822) 268

Loch Eigheach lies to the west of Loch Rannoch and is 1¾ miles long by 1 mile wide. Fishing is from the bank only and the loch is approached via the B846 out to Rannoch Station. This is wild, desolate country and the loch is full of small brown trout which average three to the pound. But John Brown, the Secretary of the Rannoch & District Angling Club, tells me that during 1991 two fish weighing 7lb each were caught – so treat every rise with respect. Eigheach has many delightful little islands and there are numerous inviting little bays and corners where trout may be caught. Grouse & Claret, Grouse & Green and Black Pennell do well. An ideal loch for beginners, and one where you might just fill the glass case as well.

LOCH LAIDON 41/360502-42/415570

Permission: N. Thexton, Gaur Cottage, Rannoch Station, Perthshire.
Tel: Bridge of Gaur (08823) 248
Moor of Rannoch Hotel, Rannoch Station, Perthshire.
Tel: Bridge of Gaur (08823) 238

Absolutely splendid and a very special place, Loch Laidon is a long, narrow loch which runs for 5½ miles over Rannoch Moor. It is linked

25 Glorious Loch Rannoch

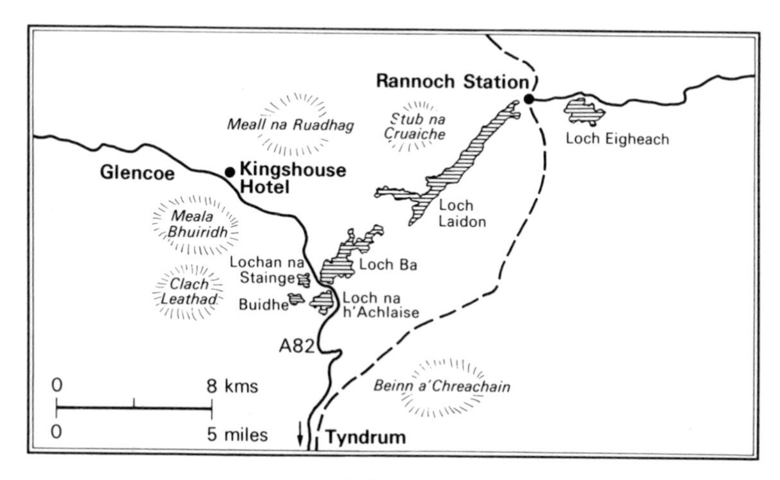

27 Rannoch

to Loch Ba in Argyll near to the A82 Glencoe road and ends in the north-east at Rannoch Station. The loch is surrounded by majestic peaks and desolate moorlands and is a paradise for fishermen and nature lovers. Both boat and bank fishing are available and the loch is a seemingly unending succession of bays and points, full of bright little trout. The average weight is 6oz, with the odd much larger fish being taken from time to time. Baskets of 20–30 small trout are common, but a few years ago my wife and I saw one of the largest trout we have ever encountered, slowly rising over a small black fly, close to the islands at the west end of the loch. This fish most certainly weighed more than 10lb. Use all the standard pattern loch flies to try and tempt them. This is one of Scotland's great wilderness areas, a priceless asset and a wonderful place to fish.

LOCH BA 41/330510 – 50/320495

Permission: The King's House Hotel, Glencoe, Argyllshire.
Tel: Kingshouse (08556) 259

Loch Ba, on Rannoch Moor, is a wild scattering of islands and bays to the east of the Glencoe–Tyndrum road. The loch wanders over the moor for 2 miles before joining Loch Laidon via the Abhainn Ba Burn. Ba is easily accessible, being adjacent to the main road, but a few minutes' dedicated walking takes you well out of view of passers-by. The trout average 8oz and large baskets are often taken. But Ba holds bigger fish as well: have a look at the trout in the King's House Hotel – it weighed an impressive 11lb – and fish of up to 5lb are still caught today. Standard pattern loch flies work well and this is a lovely loch to fish, in impressive surroundings.

LOCHAN NA H'ACHLAISE 50/310480
LOCH BUIDHE 50/298483
LOCHAN NA STAINGE 50/303490

Permission: The King's House Hotel, Glencoe, Argyllshire.
Tel: Kingshouse (08556) 259

These lochs lie close to the main Glencoe–Tyndrum road and are the most southerly of the Rannoch Moor lochs. The lochs are all shallow, varying from 30 feet in h'Achlaise to 3–4 feet in Buidhe. They are easily accessible and contain large numbers of small trout which rise well to standard pattern loch flies. A 1-lb fish is a monster for these waters but the lovely setting makes up for it and therefore these little lochs are well worth a visit.

LOCH ERROCHTY 42/690650

Permission: Highland Guns & Tackle Shop, Blair Atholl, Perthshire.
Tel: Blair Atholl (079681) 303

Loch Errochty is 3 miles long by over ½ mile wide and fishing is from the bank only. Approach from the B847 at Calvine, to the north of

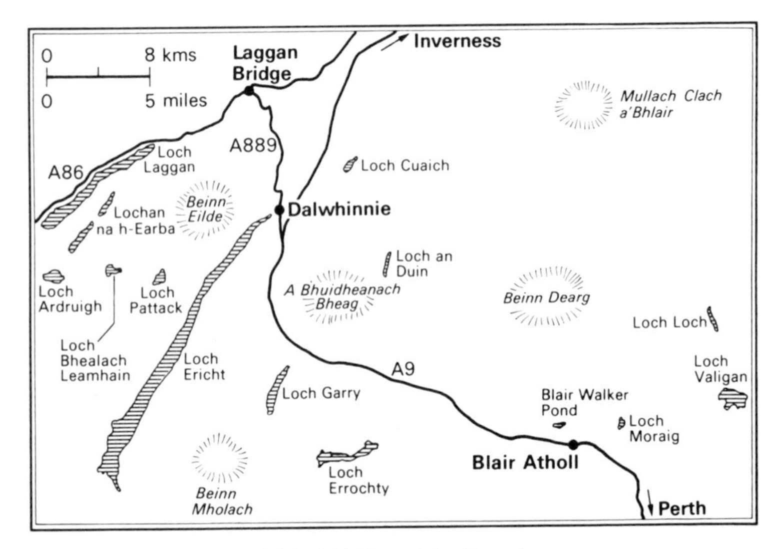

28 Loch Ericht and the Grampians

Pitlochry. This is a hydro-electric loch but nonetheless attractive, and the western end is the most productive area. There is a track running the full length of both shores and the loch contains brown trout and pike. The average weight is around 8oz and good baskets are caught. Use standard pattern loch flies – there is always the chance of the occasional much larger trout grabbing them.

BLAIR WALKER POND 43/867671

Permission: Highland Guns & Tackle Shop, Blair Atholl, Perthshire.
Tel: Blair Atholl (079681) 303

This pond is within the grounds of Blair Castle and is easily accessible. Fishing is from the bank only and there is a bag limit of three fish per rod. Four permits are available daily and the loch is stocked with trout which average 12oz.

LOCH MORAIG 43/907667

Permission: Major A. D. Gordon, Lude House, Blair Atholl, Perthshire.
Tel: Blair Atholl (079681) 240

This is an easily accessible loch lying to the north of Blair Atholl. Fishing is available from mid April until 12 August, from 9.00am until 5.00pm. Moraig is a shallow loch 350 yards long by 300 yards wide and there are two boats available. Trout are taken all round the loch but the west shore is a particularly productive area. The average weight of fish is 8oz–1lb, with the odd heavier fish from time to time. Standard loch fly patterns work well and it is always a privilege to fish amidst such wonderful surroundings.

LOCH VALIGAN 43/975694

Permission: Major A. D. Gordon, Lude House, Blair Atholl, Perthshire.
Tel: Blair Atholl (079681) 240

Fishing on Loch Valigan is from the bank only and the walk out is 4 glorious miles. Permits are issued each day, but after 1 July Valigan is closed for fishing. This is a classic hill loch with plenty of small, hard-fighting trout, and it lies at an altitude of 1800 feet. A wonderful place to fish, deep among the magnificent mountains of Atholl, peaceful and remote.

LOCH LOCH 43/989745

Permission: The Atholl Estate Office, Blair Atholl, Perthshire.

Tel: Blair Atholl (079681) 355
Highland Guns & Tackle Shop, Blair Atholl, Perthshire.
Tel: Blair Atholl (079681) 303

Fishing Loch Loch involves a long walk into the mountains, via Glen Tilt, and access is restricted after 1 August because of grouse shooting and stalking. Scottish estates depend on revenue from these activities in order to maintain standards of all game sports and are deserving of every angler's support in their efforts. Loch Loch is a dramatic water, 1¼ miles long by 250 yards wide. Carn nan Gabhar (1121m) towers to the west and the crags of Braigh Feith Chiubhaschain climb from the water's edge to the east. Trout average 8oz, although larger fish lurk in the 80-foot depths of this lovely loch. Small black flies produce best results and Loch Loch is a marvellous place to spend a day.

LOCH TILT 43/993828

Permission: The Atholl Estate Office, Blair Atholl, Perthshire.
Tel: Blair Atholl (079681) 355

Follow in famous footsteps, up Glen Tilt to this most wonderful little loch, deep in the heart of the Atholl Forest. Mary, Queen of Scots travelled this way in the 16th century to attend a great deer hunt. Queen Victoria and Prince Albert were greatly 'amused' by the lovely Glen; the acerbic Welshman, Thomas Pennent, was not. Anglers will find great sport in Loch Tilt with traditional highland wild brown trout. But the real joy is just being there.

LOCH GARRY 42/630700

Permission: Airdanair Hotel, Atholl Road, Pitlochry.
Tel: Pitlochry (0796) 2266

Loch Garry is 3 miles long by some 500 yards wide. Its northern end may be glimpsed from the A9 Inverness road and fishing is from the bank only. Loch Garry is a dark, deep loch, surrounded by mountains rising to 1000 feet from the water's edge. Apart from *ferox*, the loch contains trout and Arctic char and the average weight of trout is 8oz. In the right conditions good baskets are taken. And you don't have to cast very far out to be amongst the fish.

LOCH ERICHT 42/500640-630840

Permission: The Grampian Lodge, Dalwhinnie, Inverness-shire.
Tel: Dalwhinnie (05282) 210

The Loch Ericht Hotel, Dalwhinnie, Inverness-shire.
Tel: Dalwhinnie (05282) 257
John Brown, The Square, Kinloch Rannoch, Perthshire.
Tel: Kinloch Rannoch (08822) 268

Most anglers have a quick look at Ericht as they speed northwards on the new road from Perth to Inverness. It lies to the west of the small village of Dalwhinnie, and what you see from the road is but the northern end of a loch which is 15 miles long. It runs south-westwards towards Rannoch Moor through some of the most magnificent scenery in all of Scotland and on either shore mighty peaks line the water's edge: Ben Alder (1148m), Meall Liath (911m) and Meal Cruaidh (897m) to the north-west, while the wild slopes of the Dalnaspidal Forest crowd the south-east shore. Trout average 8–12oz and the loch also contains huge *ferox*, rarely fished for, whose weight often reaches double figures. Boats are available from the hotels at the north end, while bank fishing is best at the south end. Best fishing is in McCook's Bay, at the south end below Ben Alder and Cluny's Cave – where Bonnie Prince Charlie and five companions, including Cluny McPhearson, hid after the Battle of Culloden. There are some very large fish in Loch Ericht. Use standard pattern loch flies to tempt them – and have the glass case ready.

LOCH PATTACK 42/54079
LOCH A'BHEALAICH LEANMHAIN 42/500796
LOCHAN NA H'EARBA 42/480830
LOCH ARDRUIGH 42/455808

Permission: Osprey Fishing Centre, The Aviemore Centre, Aviemore.
Tel: Aviemore (0479) 810767

These lochs all lie between Loch Ericht and Loch Laggan in a remote, dramatic setting. The Osprey Fishing School offer an inclusive fishing/camping holiday by Landrover and foot which includes fishing them all, and Loch Laggan. The trout are typical hill-loch fish and range from 8oz to over 2lb. The first camp is set up at Loch Pattack, which is the best loch, particularly around the south shore where the Allt a' Chaoil-reidhe enters. Thereafter the party walk on to the other lochs with goods and chattels following in the vehicle. No further than 2 miles is traversed at a time, so you won't be left behind. A well-organized outing and great fishing. Worth considering.

LOCH LAGGAN 41/374809-42/536897

Permission: Laggan Estates, Estate Office, Loch Laggan.
Tel: Dalwhinnie (05282) 304

Fishing on Loch Laggan is from the north shore only, but access is easy since the A86 Kingussie–Spean Bridge road runs along the shore for the whole length of the loch. This water is 12 miles long by ½ mile wide, and there are many good bays and points for bank anglers. Boats are also available, as are some really delightful self-catering properties. Laggan trout are dour, averaging about 8–12oz, but there are some very much larger fish as well, including *ferox*. Great skill and standard pattern loch flies should be used to tempt them.

LOCH CUAICH — 42/693877

Permission: The Keeper's House, Cuaich, Dalwhinnie, Inverness-shire.
Tel: Dalwhinnie (05282) 254

This is a small loch to the east of the A9 Perth–Inverness road. It is approached from the A9 some 2 miles north from Dalwhinnie. Access is via the Keeper's House only, and both boat and bank fishing are available. There is one boat and eight bank-fishing permits are issued daily. The loch is not available to anglers between 12 August and 15 September.

TROSSACHS LOCHS

LOCH EARN — 51/640240

Permission: The Post Office, St Fillans, Loch Earn, Perthshire.
Tel: St Fillans (076485) 309
The Post Office, Lochearnhead, Perthshire.
Tel: Lochearnhead (05673) 201
Boats from: J. R. Wills, Rose Cottage, St Fillans.

Loch Earn is one of the most popular lochs in Scotland and is a venue for all kinds of water sports. Approach from the A85. Most anglers seem to prefer bank fishing but boats are available. The loch is stocked every year and contains both brown and rainbow trout which average 12oz in weight. There are much larger fish and trout of up to 5lb are taken most seasons. Best flies include Blae & Black, Greenwell's Glory, Grouse & Claret and Woodcock & Yellow. St Fillans is the most favoured fishing end but further down the loch, where the feeder burn enters at Ardvorlich, is also a good area to try. Fish the shallows and small bays and expect a basket of up to eight trout.

LOCH VOIL — 57/510200
LOCH DOINE — 57/470190

Permission: Mrs Catriona Oldham, Muirlaggan, Balquhidder, Lochearnhead, Perthshire.

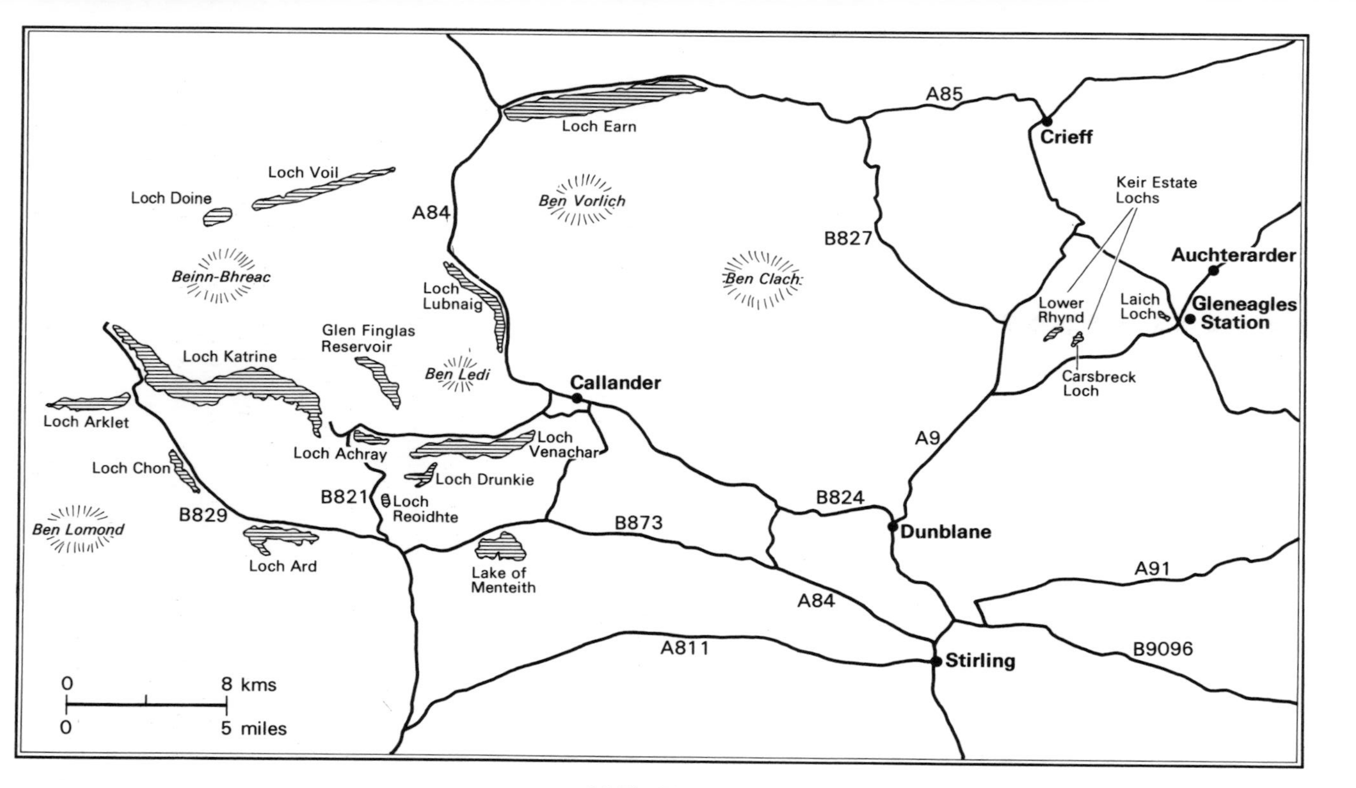

29 The Trossachs

Tel: Strathyre (08774) 219
Rob and Jean Lewis, Mouachyle Mhor, Balquhidder, Lochearnhead, Perthshire (excellent accommodation and food).
Tel: Strathyre (08774) 622

Loch Voil, Loch Doine and the Braes of Balquhidder are MacGregor country, forever linked with the exploits of Rob Roy MacGregor, Scotland's Robin Hood. The Braes extend northwards in a vast array of peaks and corries, culminating in Ben More (1174m), while to the south are the tree-lined slopes of Ceann na Baintighearna (694m) and Creag Mhor (657m), with Ben Vorlich (983m) towering to the east. This is magnificent countryside and Voil is one of Scotland's most lovely lochs. It is also one of the few remaining unspoiled natural lochs in the area and contains salmon, sea trout, brown trout and Arctic char. Both boat and bank fishing are available. Wading can be difficult and requires great care. Trout in Voil and Doine average 8–12oz and in 1990 a basket of 16 trout weighed 10lb. Trolling brings up the larger gentlemen and *ferox* of 11lb have been taken. In 1987 five salmon were taken by Mr Allan in two hours of fishing, weighing between 7lb and 18lb – a total basket weight of 64lb. 1988 also produced good sport with salmon, including a fish of 17lb and in 1989 a sea trout of 7lb 8oz was landed. Great sport was had in 1991 with brown trout, including fish of up to 4lb. All the standard loch fly patterns produce results: Blae & Black, Black Spider, Black Pennell, Grouse & Claret, Grouse & Green, Cinnamon & Gold and Kate McLaren. Dapping is well worth while. Voil and Doine are Scotland at its most beautiful.

LOCH LUBNAIG 57/570140

Permission: Mr Winters, Muirlaggan Farm, Strathyre.

Loch Lubnaig lies to the west of the A84 Callander–Lochearnhead road. This road runs along the east shore and makes access easy, Loch Lubnaig is a popular fishing venue. It contains salmon and brown trout and the best fishing area is at the shallow northern end. This large, sheltered bay often produces good baskets of 8-oz trout but, as with most of the deep Trossachs lochs, much larger trout are frequently taken. Lubnaig has produced fish of 4–6lb. Blae & Black, Black Pennell and Greenwell's Glory all do well on this lovely loch, surrounded by majestic peaks with forest-covered lower slopes. Autumn particularly is a riot of colour and Lubnaig is always worth visiting, regardless of size of trout or weight of baskets.

LOCH VENACHAR 57/570055

Permission: J. Bayne, Tackle Shop, Main Street, Callander, Perthshire.

Tel: (0877) 30218
Stirling District Council, Municipal Buildings, Corn Exchange Road, Stirling.
Tel: Stirling (0786) 70000, Ext. 152
Facilities for disabled anglers: As above

Loch Venachar is to the west of Callander and is 4 miles long by ¾ mile wide. The A821 is adjacent to the north shore, where boats are available for visiting anglers. The loch contains brown trout and sea trout with the occasional salmon, and the best fishing area is to the western end of the loch where the Black Water enters from Loch Achray. Standard loch fly patterns work well and the trout average 8–12oz, with much larger fish being taken from time to time. Venachar is in a lovely setting. A warm spring day with the snow still on the mountains makes a lasting impression – and there are also some days when fish do likewise.

GLEN FINGLAS RESERVOIR 57/525090

Permission: Strathclyde Regional Council, Department of Water, 419 Balmore Road, Glasgow.
Tel: Glasgow (041) 355 5333

Glen Finglas is 1¾ miles long with a 'dog-leg' of ½ mile to the north-west. Approach from Brig o'Turk on the A821. The reservoir is stocked by the council and trout average 12oz. Fly fishing only from rowing boats supplied by the Department. No outboard motors. An average day – for an average angler – should produce a basket of four fish, and trout of up to 2lb are sometimes taken. This is grand fishing in a grand setting, easily accessible and well managed. The best area to fish is down the east shore and in the bay where the feeder burn enters. Standard loch fly patterns work well.

LOCH ACHRAY 57/515065

Permission: Loch Achray Hotel, The Trossachs, by Callander, Perthshire.
Tel: Trossachs (08776) 229
Forestry Commission, David Marshall Lodge, Aberfoyle, Perthshire.
Tel: Aberfoyle (08772) 258
Facilities for disabled anglers: As above

Loch Achray is 1¼ miles long by over 600 yards wide and lies between Loch Katrine and Loch Venachar. It is in a lovely woodland setting and is a most attractive loch to fish. The loch is 100 feet deep at its deepest point, but in other areas little more than 4 feet deep. It contains brown trout, pike and perch. Bank fishing only. The best place to fish is from the north bank, especially where the Black Water leaves at the east end. Trout average 8oz but a few larger specimens are occasionally taken. For access to the south shore, approach from the A821 and the Loch Achray Hotel.

LOCH KATRINE 57/490075-56/382135

Permission: Strathclyde Regional Council, Department of Water, 419 Balmore Road, Glasgow.
Tel: Glasgow (041) 355 5333

Loch Katrine has attracted visitors to its tree-clad, heather-bedecked banks for hundreds of years and is one of the most famous lochs in all of Scotland. Katrine used to flow east to the River Forth, until, in the mid-nineteenth century, it was diverted to supply Glasgow with water. Happily this alteration has detracted little from the charm and character of the loch. Katrine is 8 miles long and on average 1 mile wide. It is approached from the A821 Aberfoyle road, or from Loch Venachar to the east. The Regional Council stocks the loch and fishing is by fly only, from rowing boats supplied by the Department. No outboard motors are allowed. The average weight of trout is about 12oz and this is an improving fishery, thanks largely to sympathetic management by the Department of Water.

Trout of over 3lb are not infrequently taken and an average day should produce a basket of three or four fish. The most favoured fishing area is the western end of the loch, from Glengyle (the birthplace of Rob Roy) down to Black Island bay below Portnellan. Fish the shallows all round the west end with Grouse & Claret, Peter Ross and Silver Butcher. Crossing the fingers also helps.

LOCH ARKLET 56/380090

Permission: Strathclyde Regional Council, Department of Water, 419 Balmore Road, Glasgow.
Tel: Glasgow (041) 355 5333

Loch Arklet lies between Loch Katrine and Loch Lomond and is a long, narrow water of 2½ miles by 650 yards. On either side of the loch tower the heights of Ben Lomond (974m), Ben Venue (727m) and Beinn a'Choin (769m), and their shadows can often make Arklet a dark, forbidding place to fish. The Regional Council stocks the loch and trout average 8oz. Fly fishing only, from rowing boats supplied by the Department. The best area to fish is in the vicinity of the Duke's Boathouse and Corrieheichan Bay. Trout of up to 2lb have been caught using Grouse & Claret, Peter Ross and Silver Butcher.

LOCH DRUNKIE 57/545044

Permission: Forestry Commission, David Marshall Lodge, Aberfoyle, Perthshire.
Tel: Aberfoyle (08772) 258
Facilities for disabled anglers: As above

Drunkie is in the Achray Forest and may be approached by vehicle (on payment) via a forest road. Drunkie is to the north of Aberfoyle and drains into Loch Venachar. The loch consists of a main section lying north/south, with a narrow neck running east/west. Another long, narrow bay runs south-west alongside the forest from the southern bay. Drunkie can be dour and fishing is from the bank only. Trout average 12oz and there are also pike in the loch. Try standard pattern loch flies.

LOCH REOIDHTE 57/522035

Permission: Forestry Commission, David Marshall Lodge, Aberfoyle, Perthshire.
Tel: Aberfoyle (08772) 258
Facilities for disabled anglers: As above

This small loch is situated to the east of the A821 and the Duke's Pass, just to the north of Aberfoyle. The loch is stocked with both brown and rainbow trout and fishing is from the bank only. Standard loch fly patterns work well and trout average 12oz, with rainbow trout being slightly heavier. The one ticket also gives permission to fish Drunkie and Achray.

LOCH ARD 57/465051

Permission: The Alskeith Hotel, Kinlochard, by Aberfoyle, Perthshire.
Tel: Kinlochard (08777) 266
J. R. Ferguson, Newsagent, Main Street, Aberfoyle, Perthshire.
Water Bailiff: P. McMillian.
Tel: Kinlochard (08777) 339
Facilities for disabled anglers: As above

Loch Ard is to the west of Aberfoyle on the B829 Stronaclachar road and is 3 miles long by 1 mile wide across the western bay. There are several boats available for visitors and the loch is now regularly stocked with brown trout which average 12oz. Fish of up to 4lb are sometimes caught. Ard has been sadly damaged in recent years by ill-planned blanket afforestation, but great efforts are being made to re-establish a trout population in this once excellent fishery.

LOCH CHON 56/420050

Permission: Mr McNair, Frenich Farm, Aberfoyle, Perthshire.
Tel: Inversnaid (087786) 243

Loch Chon lies 8 miles to the west of Aberfoyle. The wooded slopes of Beinn Dubh (511m) are to the west, with Ben Lomond in the distance. The loch is 1¾ miles long by some 600 yards wide. Both boat and bank fishing are available, and the average weight of fish is 8–12oz. Larger fish can be caught but you will have to troll for them. Pike are netted from the loch by the Forestry Commission. Use standard loch fly patterns.

LAKE OF MENTEITH 57/580000

Permission: Lake of Menteith Fisheries, Port of Menteith, Perthshire.
Tel: Port of Menteith (08775) 664

The Lake of Menteith is a lovely, gentle water, surrounded by good farming land and fine forests. It has many historical associations and each year visitors make their way across the loch to the island of Inchmahome and the ruined Augustinian monastery. The lake is about 1 mile from north to south and 1½ miles from east to west. It is a well-managed, highly organized trout fishery with 22 boats available for visiting anglers, who may use their own outboard motors if they wish. Bank fishing is not allowed. The average weight of trout is 1lb 4oz and the loch is regularly stocked with brown trout, rainbow trout and some brook trout. Each year several very large fish are introduced, weighing up to 15lb. Best flies to use to tempt them include Black Pennell, Peter Ross, Greenwell's Glory, Butchers and Grouse & Claret. Anglers will be advised on arrival of the 'fly of the moment' and also about where to fish. But, generally speaking, trout may be caught all over this fine loch. There is a boat limit of 21 fish.

LAICH LOCH 58/919113

Permission: The Sports Manager, Gleneagles Hotel, Auchterarder, Perthshire.
Tel: Auchterarder (0764) 2231

Laich Loch lies within the grounds of Gleneagles Hotel and fishing is reserved for residents. The loch is stocked with brown and rainbow trout and there is one boat available for guests. The average weight of fish is over 1lb and all the standard patterns work well. If you think that you deserve a special treat, and can persuade your better half to accompany you, there are few more restful places to fish.

CARSBRECK LOCH 58/868093
LOWER RHYND 58/857098
UPPER RHYND 58/863100

Permission: Blackford Farms Limited, The Farmhouse, Burnside of Balhadie, Dunblane, Perthshire.
Tel: Dunblane (078682) 4000

These small lochs lie to the north of the A9 between Blackford Village and Dunblane. They are easily accessible and regularly stocked with brown trout which average 12oz in weight, with the odd fish of up to 4lb. Carsbreck is the most productive water and there are seven boats available for visiting anglers. The other lochs contain smaller fish but they also give good sport and are great fun to fish. Use Greenwell's Glory, Olives and Black Pennell.

SANDYKNOWES FISHERY 58/140185

Permission: Marjorie Brien, Sandyknowes Fishery, Rhynd Road, Bridge of Earn, Perthshire.
Tel: Perth (0738) 810303
Facilities for disabled anglers: As above

A small, stocked fishery lying close to the M90, screened from passing traffic by woodlands. Easily accessible and well-managed, with good-quality trout which average around 1lb 8oz – and the usual 'monsters'. Try standard pattern loch flies.

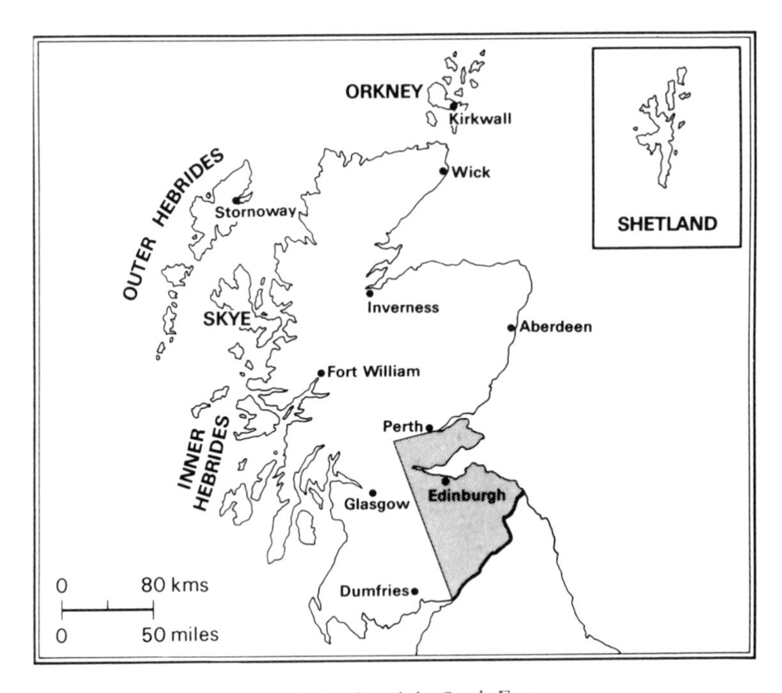

30 Edinburgh and the South-East

8 Edinburgh and the South-East

My first attempts at fishing took place in the centre of Edinburgh, on the Water of Leith and the lochs of the King's Park. As the years passed I travelled further afield and soon discovered the many lochs and rivers which surround the city. The visiting angler has the best of all worlds in Edinburgh: excellent trout fishing on such waters as Loch Leven, Gladhouse and Portmore, and all the delights of Scotland's capital. When I was a boy, crossing the Firth at Queensferry was a real adventure and it could take up to four hours. Now, thanks to the road bridge, there are over one hundred trout lochs all within an easy drive of the city. Most of these waters are carefully managed and stocked. Consequently, although they may lack some of the scenic beauty of the more northern waters, they contain larger trout and are somewhat less unpredictable. There are many, however, that are really remote and if you really want to get away from it all, climb up by the Grey Mare's Tail waterfall and fish Loch Skeen, near Moffat – they don't come much more remote. Edinburgh is ringed with hills: to the south, east and west are the Pentlands, Lammermuir and Moorfoot Hills, while over the Firth of Forth in Fife lie the Ochil Hills. All contain good trout waters which are readily available to the visiting angler. One small word of warning, however: take great care if wading round some of the reservoirs, for the margins can become soft and dangerous owing to fluctuations in the water level, as I have learned from bitter experience. My own favourite waters are Portmore, Gladhouse and Coldingham – and, of course, lovely Loch Leven – but there are many more excellent trout lochs in the region. I know that you will enjoy any time you spend in and around 'Auld Reekie'.

LOCHS OF FIFE

GLENFARG RESERVOIR 58/105110

Permission: Fife Regional Council, Water Division, Flemmington Road, Glenrothes, Fife.
Tel: Glenrothes (0592) 756541

Glenfarg Reservoir is 600 feet up in the Ochil Hills and is approached via Glenfarg Village between Perth and Kinross. Five boats are available and bank fishing is not allowed. This is a very pleasant water,

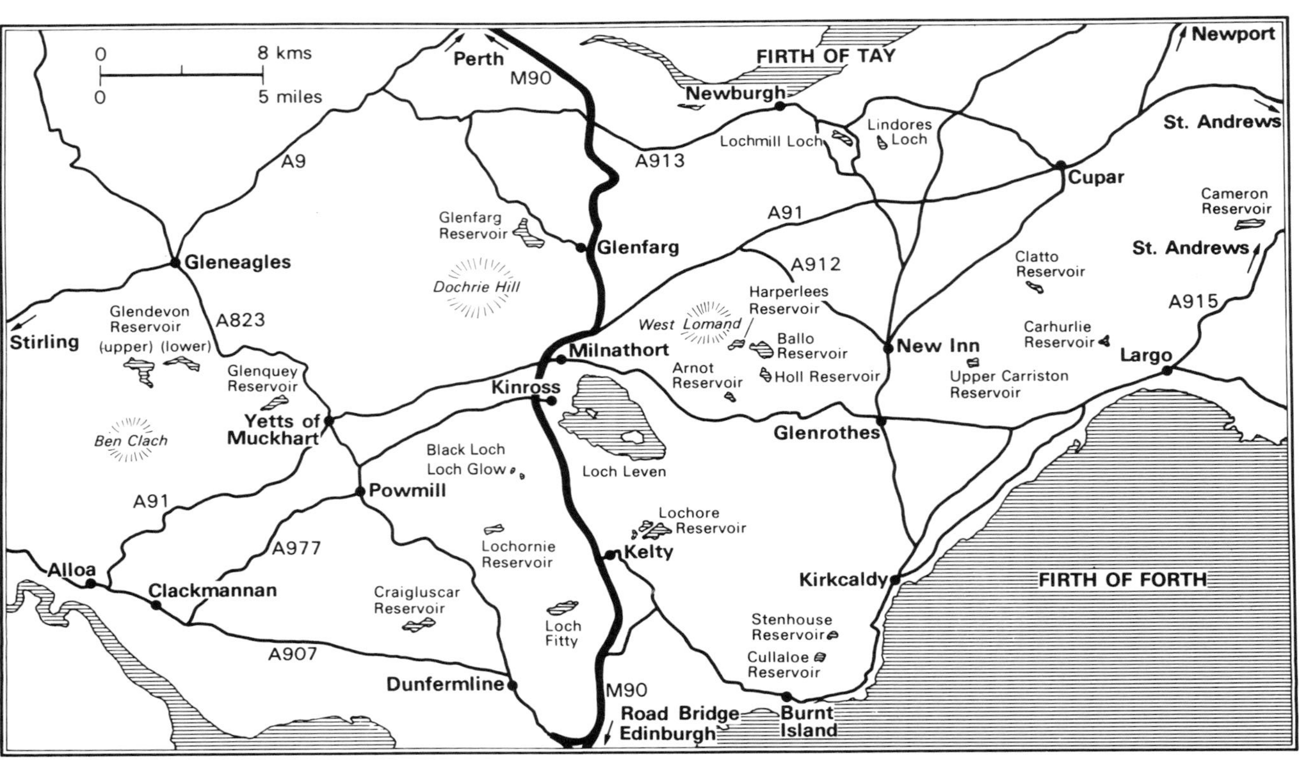
0 8 kms
0 5 miles
Perth
M90
FIRTH OF TAY
Newburgh
Newport
St. Andrews
Lindores Loch
Lochmill Loch
A9
A913
Cupar
Cameron Reservoir
A91
Glenfarg Reservoir
Glenfarg
St. Andrews
Clatto Reservoir
Gleneagles
A912
Dochrie Hill
Harperlees Reservoir
A915
Glendevon Reservoir (upper) (lower)
A823
West Lomand
Carhurlie Reservoir
Stirling
New Inn
Ballo Reservoir
Largo
Milnathort
Glenquey Reservoir
Arnot Reservoir
Holl Reservoir
Upper Carriston Reservoir
Kinross
Yetts of Muckhart
Ben Clach
Glenrothes
Black Loch
Loch Glow
Loch Leven
Powmill
A91
Lochore Reservoir
A977
Lochornie Reservoir
Kelty
Alloa
Kirkcaldy
FIRTH OF FORTH
Clackmannan
Craigluscar Reservoir
Loch Fitty
Stenhouse Reservoir
A907
Cullaloe Reservoir
Dunfermline
M90
Road Bridge
Edinburgh
Burnt Island

31 Fife

stocked with brown trout, average 12oz. The reservoir fishes best during May and June, although larger fish are usually taken towards the end of the season, and they can weigh as much as 4lb. Best flies are Black Pennell, Greenwell's Glory and Butchers. The northern end, where the reservoir divides into two bays, is the best fishing area, particularly the longer bay running directly north.

CASTLEHILL RESERVOIR 58/995036

Permission: Fife Regional Council, Water Division, Flemmington Road, Glenrothes, Fife.
Tel: Glenrothes (0592) 756541

A small, roadside reservoir stocked with brown trout which average 10oz. A somewhat public place to fish and not particularly attractive.

GLENQUEY RESERVOIR 58/976022

Permission: Fife Regional Council, Water Division, Flemmington Road, Glenrothes, Fife.
Tel: Glenrothes (0592) 756541

This is a small reservoir high up in the Ochil Hills between Auchlinsky and Whitewhisp Hill (634m) to the south and north. Glenquey is triangular in shape and the fishing is managed by the Devon Angling Association which issues five daily permits to visitors. Approach from the A823 Yetts of Muchart–Glendevon road and turn left at Burnfoot. Glenquey is stocked with brown trout which average 10–12oz, with the occasional fish of up to 4lb 8oz. Best flies to use include Olives, Black Spider, Grouse & Claret and Greenwell's Glory. Book in advance.

UPPER GLENDEVON RESERVOIR 58/910045
LOWER GLENDEVON RESERVOIR 58/935048

Permission: Fife Regional Council, Water Division, Flemmington Road, Glenrothes, Fife.
Tel: Glenrothes (0592) 756541

Fishing on these two reservoirs is managed by the Regional Council. Approach from A823 Yetts of Muchart–Auchterarder road. The entrance is just to the north of Glenhead Farm. Boats are available on both reservoirs but bank fishing is only allowed on Lower Glendevon. These are hill lochs and lie at an altitude of 1000 feet. Upper Glendevon is a bit bleak and subject to considerable changes in the water level. Lower Glendevon is a much more attractive water. Use standard pattern loch flies – there are good brown trout waiting to grab.

26 Lower Glendevon Reservoir, Kinross

CRAIGLUSCAR RESERVOIR 58/065905

Permission: The Club Hut, Craigluscar Reservoir, Dunfermline.
Tel: Dunfermline (0383) 732891
John Stewart, The Club Secretary, 44 Rumbling Well, Dunfermline.
Tel: Dunfermline (0383) 729835

Fishing on Craigluscar is managed by the Dunfermline Artisans Angling Club and the reservoir lies to the north-west of the town, 2 miles along the A823. The club has been looking after this water since 1911 and brown trout of 12oz–1lb are stocked once each year. Rainbow trout are stocked throughout the season. Trout of up to 7lb 9oz have been caught and fish of 4–5lb are not infrequently taken. The club imposes a bag limit of 6 fish per rod and fishing is from the bank only. Owing to an abundance of natural fly life anglers have to work hard for their fish, but it is considered to be well worth the effort. Nymphs work extremely well, as do Black Pennell, Black Zulu and Black Spider during the early part of the season, and Wickham's Fancy, Dunkeld, Invicta and Kingfisher Butcher during the 'back end'. This is a very well-managed and exciting loch to fish and worthy of your close attention.

LOCH FITTY 58/120915

Permission: Game Fisheries Limited, The Fishing Lodge, Loch Fitty, Kingseat, Dunfermline, Fife.
Tel: Dunfermline (0383) 620666

Loch Fitty lies 3 miles to the north-east of Dunfermline and covers 160 acres. It is a shallow, natural loch, at one time mainly used for coarse fishing but now developed into a most excellent trout fishery. Loch Fitty produces very good results and trout average 1lb 3oz. The best trout caught weighed 9lb and each season fish of 3–5lb class are frequently taken. The loch is stocked during the season with more than 20,000 brown and rainbow trout, along with a number of 5–7-lb salmon and grilse. There are 20 clinker-built boats all fitted with outboard engines available for anglers. Bank fishing is also allowed. Trout are caught all over the loch and gillies will be happy to advise the visitor where to fish and, more importantly, what flies to use. Lures which always do well include Ace of Spades, Sweeney Todd and Viva. Flies that produce results are Black Pennell, Grouse & Claret, Montana Nymphs, Wickham's Fancy and Soldier Palmer, all tied on size 12 hooks. There is a small restaurant and tackle shop on the site. The loch is well-managed and visitors and anglers are well received and attended to.

LOCH LEVEN 58/150010

Permission: The Fishery Manager, The Pier, Kinross.
Tel: Kinross (0577) 63407
Facilities for disabled anglers: As above

I was lucky in that the first loch I ever fished was Loch Leven, in 1952. That was in the days of no outboard motors and two boatmen, when most seasons produced upwards of 40,000 fish. Now poor Loch Leven is beset with problems and controversy, with hardly a good word to be said for it. The last time I passed, on a very windy day in July 1991, I was absolutely astonished to see that the whole loch was bright green, presumably as a result of chemical-farming residue on the bottom being stirred up by the wind. Fish are notoriously dour and hard to catch, and anglers complain bitterly about paying high prices for, frequently, little sport. Trout rarely rise to the surface, and anglers increasingly have to resort to reservoir-type lures to catch them. Happily all is not doom and gloom – the loch is being restocked annually with 150–180,000 5½-inch trout, reared from native stock. In time this might restore the loch to its former glory, but the principal cause for the decline – intensive chemical farming and pollution – remains unresolved.

Nevertheless Loch Leven can still produce spectacular sport, and the trout average 1lb 6oz. The largest trout ever caught was taken on 15 August 1991 and weighed 8lb 3oz; but a rise of trout on Loch Leven today is now as rare an event as it was commonplace in the 1950s and 1960s. The loch covers 3500 acres and there are seven islands, the largest being St Serfs in the south-east, on which are the remains of monastery buildings dating back to the fourteenth century. The other major island is Castle Island, where Mary, Queen of Scots was imprisoned. In spite of all the problems, Loch Leven is still one of the finest and most famous trout lochs in the world. I wish those responsible for its management nothing but well. They have in their care a vital part of Scotland's angling heritage, and it would be wonderful if they could revitalize this outstanding fishery. And tragic if they should fail.

HEATHERYFORD 58/105021

Permission: The Kinross Trout Fishery, Heatheryford, Kinross.
Tel: Kinross (0577) 64212
Facilities for disabled anglers: As above

Heatheryford lies close to the M90 west of Loch Leven and reached via Junction 6. Immediately after leaving the motorway, follow the track south over the South Queich burn, down to the parking place and licensed restaurant. There are four ponds extending to approximately 10 acres and the fishery is well stocked with brown and rainbow trout. The fishing day is divided into three sessions: 9.00am-1.00pm; 1.30pm-5.30pm and 6.00pm-9.30pm. Bank fishing only, with trout of up to and over 6lb.

BALLO RESERVOIR 58/225050
HOLL RESERVOIR 58/227036

Permission: Fife Regional Council, Water Division, Flemmington Road, Glenrothes, Fife.
Tel: Glenrothes (0592) 756541

Fishing on these reservoirs is managed by the Regional Council and is from boats only. There are two sessions: 10.00am-4.00pm and 4.00pm-10.00pm. Young persons under 16 must be accompanied by an adult. These reservoirs are to the west of Leslie and are stocked with brown trout which average 12oz. On their day, they offer great sport.

ARNOT RESERVOIR 58/207024

Permission: W. Ferguson, Little Arnot, Leslie, Fife.
Tel: Scotlandwell (059284) 325

Fishing on this 40-acre reservoir is by private arrangement only. Arnot is a most attractive and productive little fishery where the average weight of trout is well over 1lb. It is advisable to book well in advance, and use standard pattern loch flies.

HARPERLEES RESERVOIR 58/213053

Permission: Constables Jewellers, 39a High Street, Kirkcaldy, Fife.
Tel: Kirkcaldy (0592) 60770

Harperlees Reservoir covers 44 acres and lies on the eastern slopes of the Lomond Hills. Approach from the A911 west of Leslie and drive past Holl Reservoir to Harperlees. Fishing is managed by the Fife Technical Teachers' Angling Association and the loch is stocked with brown trout. The average weight is 12oz and two or three fish would represent an average basket. Trout of up to 2lb 8oz are caught, and since the water is very clear a good wind helps to disguise murderous intent from the well-educated inhabitants below the surface. Boat fishing only. At times this is an infuriating place to fish, but it is in lovely surroundings and well worth a visit. Best flies include Black Pennell, Blae & Black and Greenwell's Glory.

LOCH ORE 58/160955

Permission: Park Centre, Lochore Meadows Country Park, Crosshill, Nr Lochgelly, Fife.
Tel: Ballingry (0592) 860086
Facilities for disabled anglers: As above

Loch Ore was the site of an open-cast mining operation and has been developed into the largest freshwater loch in Fife. Surrounded by a most attractive Country Park, Lochore is a well-organized venture which offers a wide variety of activities catering for most outdoor pursuits. The loch is stocked with both brown and rainbow trout and their average weight is 12oz. Fish of up to 5lb have been caught and you might expect a basket of 14 fish to weigh 8lb 12oz. Bank fishing is allowed but best results come from the boats. Flies to use include Black Spider, Black Pennell, Grouse & Claret, Woodcock & Yellow, Wickham's Fancy and Kingfisher Butcher. Loch Ore is rich in wildlife and there is a cafeteria, picnic area, golf course and sailing. At times very busy, but a valuable asset and a credit to the enterprise of the Regional Council.

UPPER CARRISTON RESERVOIR 59/327037

Permission: J. Caldwell, Newsagent and Fishing Tackle, Main Street, Methilhill, Leven, Fife.
Tel: Buckhaven (0592) 712215
Facilities for disabled anglers: As above

Upper Carriston is situated between Glenrothes and Markinch and is a pleasant water, fringed by woods. Fishing is managed by the Methilhaven and District Angling Club and is all from the bank, with a maximum of 20 anglers fishing. There is a bag limit of six fish per rod and the reservoir contains brown trout with an average weight of 1lb–1lb 8oz. The heaviest fish caught during 1991 weighed 3lb 8oz. The best fishing areas are along the north dam wall and round the east bay. Flies to use include Greenwell's Glory, Dunkeld, Black Pennell, Wickham's Fancy and nymphs. There is good natural feeding in the reservoir and the growth rate of fish is exceptional. The club stock the water twice a year and Sunday fishing is also allowed. However, Upper Carriston is not for beginners, rather for the angler who likes a challenge. Evening fishing during the early months of the season can produce first-class results. At times the trout rise as though there were going to be no flies tomorrow. Persuading them to take what you happen to be offering is the only problem – isn't it always?

STENHOUSE RESERVOIR 66/210877

Permission: John McCracken, Newsagent, East Porte, Burntisland, Fife.
Tel: Burntisland (0592) 872292

Stenhouse lies adjacent to the A909 to the north of Burntisland and is a very pleasant loch with good trout. It is 900 yards long by 200 yards wide and fishing is managed by the Burntisland Angling Club. The club stocks the reservoir each year and the average weight of trout is an impressive 1lb 8oz. Trout of 2lb–2lb 8oz are unremarkable and fish of 4lb–4lb 8oz are occasionally caught. The heaviest trout to come from this excellent water weighed 8lb. There is a bag limit of six fish per rod and the loch fishes best in the evenings during the spring, and during the day later in the season. Flies to use include all the standard pattern loch flies and this is an easily accessible water offering first-class sport in attractive surroundings.

LOCH GLOW 58/088958
BLACK LOCH 58/077963

Permission: Local tackle shops in Dunfermline, Cowdenbeath, Kinross and Leslie; also, at Lochornie Cottage, which is 1 mile south from the lochs. For further details, contact: John Mill, 12 Kingseat Road, Dunfermline, Fife.
Tel: Dunfermline (0383) 722128

Loch Glow is the principal water at 140 acres, fed from its smaller neighbour, Black Loch. The waters are managed by the Civil Service Sports Association Angling Section, and stocked three or four times each year with brown trout. Fish are stocked at 10-11 inches, with some yearling Loch Leven trout among them, and their average weight is 12–14oz.

The Black Loch regularly produces fish of over 3lb and the heaviest fish taken weighed 7lb 2oz. Flies to try include Invicta, Connemara Black, Kingfisher Butcher, Wickham's Fancy and Greenwell's Glory. The fishing is probably the best value for money in Fife and well worth trying.

CARHURLIE RESERVOIR 59/395050

Permission: Davesports, 14 Bridge Street, Leven, Fife.
Tel: Leven (0333) 25115

Carhurlie is a small reservoir to the north of Largo in the 'Wee Kingdom' of Fife. Approach from the north by turning left off the A916 Cupar–Methill road at Montravie, or from the A921 Methill–Largo road by turning left at Sillerhole. The reservoir is 500 yards long by about 250 yards wide and is in the shape of a 'Y'. There is no bank fishing, and only one boat available, so you have the loch to yourself for the day. The reservoir contains brown trout but they have the reputation of being hard to catch. The average weight is 8–10oz and the best time to fish is in the evenings. An average basket should account for two or three fish, and trout of over 2lb are rare. Flies to try include Wickham's Fancy, Greenwell's Glory, Black Spider, Black Pennell and Butchers, all in size 14 dressings. There are good hatches of flies in the summer months, and this is a secluded, pleasant water to fish.

CLATTO RESERVOIR 59/360079

Permission: By application at the Waterman's Cottage at the reservoir.
Tel: Cupar (0334) 52595

Clatto Reservoir lies between the A916 Kennoway–Cupar road to the south and the A92 Glenrothes–Cupar road to the north. The reservoir is 25 acres in extent and is a very pleasant, sheltered place to fish. The fishing is well managed by the Clatto & Stratheden Angling Club which has a boat available for hire to visiting anglers. Fishing from the bank is also allowed and can be just as productive as from the boat. The average weight of fish in Clatto is about 1lb and fish of around 3lb are frequently taken. For starters, try a cast with Black Pennell, Invicta or small buzzers. Clatto fishes best during May, June and September.

CAMERON RESERVOIR 59/470112

Permission: St Andrew's Angling Club, Cameron Reservoir, St Andrew's, Fife.
Tel: The Fishing Hut, Peat Inn (033484) 236
Facilities for disabled anglers: As above

This reservoir is ¾ mile long by 250 yards wide and is easily accessible from the A915 via a minor road at Cameron school. The reservoir is stocked with brown trout and their average weight is just under 1lb. The St Andrews Angling Club manages this excellent water and imposes a bag limit of nine fish per rod per day. Both boat and bank fishing are available but outboard motors are not allowed. Limit bags are not uncommon, although the average basket is more likely to be three or four fish. Best flies are Wickham's Fancy, Greenwell's Glory, Black Spider, Dunkeld, Grouse & Claret and, of course, the Cameron Demon – gold body, jungle cock eye and blue hackle, rather like an Alexandra – invented by Mr D. Hutchison, Hon. Sec. of the Clatto and Stratheden Angling Club. Cameron Reservoir tends to become weedy after July, when boats always do better than bank fishers. There are 12 boats available. This is a shallow water with good natural feeding and excellent-quality trout.

LINDORES LOCH 59/265165

Permission: F. G. Hamilton, 18 Strathview Place, Comrie, Perthshire.
Tel: Comrie (07647) 8221

Lindores Loch is 2 miles to the south-east of Newburgh and covers an area ¾ mile long by 350 yards wide. It is a pleasant, well-managed fishery, containing rainbow trout and some brown trout. There are also pike in the loch but these are controlled by regular netting. Some escape, however, and a pike of 29lb has been caught here. There are seven boats available for anglers but outboard motors are not allowed, nor is bank fishing. The average weight of fish is 1lb 8oz and a reasonable day should net you up to four trout. Recently a basket of six trout weighed 19lb 8oz. Trout of 5lb are sometimes caught and the best flies to use include Dunkeld, Black Pennell, Teal & Green, Wickham's Fancy and Grouse & Claret. For reservoir lures, try Sweeney Todd, Whisky Fly, and Muddlers. Easily accessible and can be great sport.

LOCHMILL LOCH 58/225163

Permission: Gina Crawford, Albert Bar, Newburgh, Fife.
Tel: Newburgh (03374) 439

Lochmill Loch is a small loch to the south of Newburgh and may be approached via the minor road which joins the A983 Auchtermuchty–Cupar road to the south, or from Woodruffe Road in the town. The loch is 700 yards long by 200 yards wide and fishing is controlled by the Newburgh Angling Club, which was formed in 1943. This is an easily accessible water and one boat is available for visitors. The loch has been stocked over the years with Loch Leven trout and rainbow trout, but the present policy is to stock only with brown trout. There is excellent natural feeding in Lochmill and the average weight of trout is around 12oz, with fish of over 2lb often being taken. Fishing is best in the small bays at the western end of the loch. Flies to try include Blae & Black, Soldier Palmer, Greenwell's Glory, March Brown and Black Spider.

LOTHIAN LOCHS

BEECRAIGS LOCH 65/010744

Permission: Park Centre, Beecraigs Country Park, Linlithgow.
Tel: Linlithgow (0506) 844516
Facilities for disabled anglers: As above

Beecraigs is a small, well-managed and very popular reservoir to the south of Linlithgow. It is stocked with good-quality rainbow trout, tiger trout and occasional brook trout. In 1990 14,313 trout were caught. Their average weight was 1lb 10oz and more than 20 fish of over 10lb were caught each month. The heaviest trout taken weighed 13lb 8oz. From August 1991 fish are being stocked at an average weight of 2lb and during the 1991 season trout of 4–6lb were being caught every week. Between May and August there is a 'night-shift', for those so afflicted, which lasts from 11.00pm until 7.00am the following morning. Beecraigs is easily accessible and well equipped, not only with trout but also with a good tackle shop, lodge and toilets. Use standard pattern loch flies. Book well in advance.

LINLITHGOW LOCH 65/000775

Permission: Forth Area Federation of Anglers, Linlithgow Loch Bookings, P.O. Box 7, Linlithgow, West Lothian.
Tel: (0831) 288921 (mobile telephone)

This is an easily accessible loch in a dramatic setting dominated by the Palace of Linlithgow. The loch is stocked with both brown trout and rainbow trout and fish of up to 9lb have been caught. Trout of 3–5lb are frequently taken and the average weight is about 1lb 8oz. During 1991 the heaviest rainbow caught weighed 7lb 12oz, while the heaviest brown trout weighed 4lb 10oz. The natural feeding in the loch is very good and stocked fish grow quickly. Unfortunately trout tend to be bottom feeders, so most anglers launch their attack using reservoir type lures. Both boat and bank fishing are allowed and there is a bag limit of eight fish per rod per day. This is an excellent, well-managed fishery and well worth a visit.

BOWDEN SPRINGS 65/977737

Permission: W. Martin, Bowden Springs Fishery, Caribber, Linlithgow, West Lothian.
Tel: Linlithgow (0506) 847269
Facilities for disabled anglers: As above

These are spring-fed 5- and 2-acre lochs, 2 miles south-west from Linlithgow on the A706. Excellent natural feeding – and excellent trout fishing – in an attractive, completely private setting. There is easy access to all parts of both lochs for bank fishing and two punts are available on the larger water. The average depth is 6 feet and the lochs are regularly stocked with brown trout and rainbow trout ranging from 1lb 8oz up to 8lb. An average year produces around 100 fish in excess of 4lb. The fishing day is divided into two sessions, with a bag limit of four fish per session. Bowden Springs also specializes in Corporate Entertainment, offering exclusive use of all facilities, which include a comfortable fishing lodge and full catering, from snacks to buffets and barbecues.

EDINBURGH RESERVOIRS

BONALY RESERVOIR 66/210662

Permission: Not required

This was a favourite walking-tour stopping-off place for me many years ago, and is a very attractive little water in the Pentland Hills. It has a good stock of small brown trout and is hard to pass by, particularly when there is always the odd chance of a much larger fish – trout of up to 8lb have been taken in the past. Easily accessible and ideal for a couple of hours' respite from the hustle and bustle of the city.

CLUBIEDEAN RESERVOIR 66/200668

Permission: Pentland Hills Ranger Service, Pentland Hills Country Park, Boghall Farm, Midlothian.
Tel: Edinburgh (031) 445 3383
Facilities for disabled anglers: As above

Clubidean covers 12 acres and is near Colinton on the outskirts of Edinburgh. This reservoir is regularly stocked and produces excellent

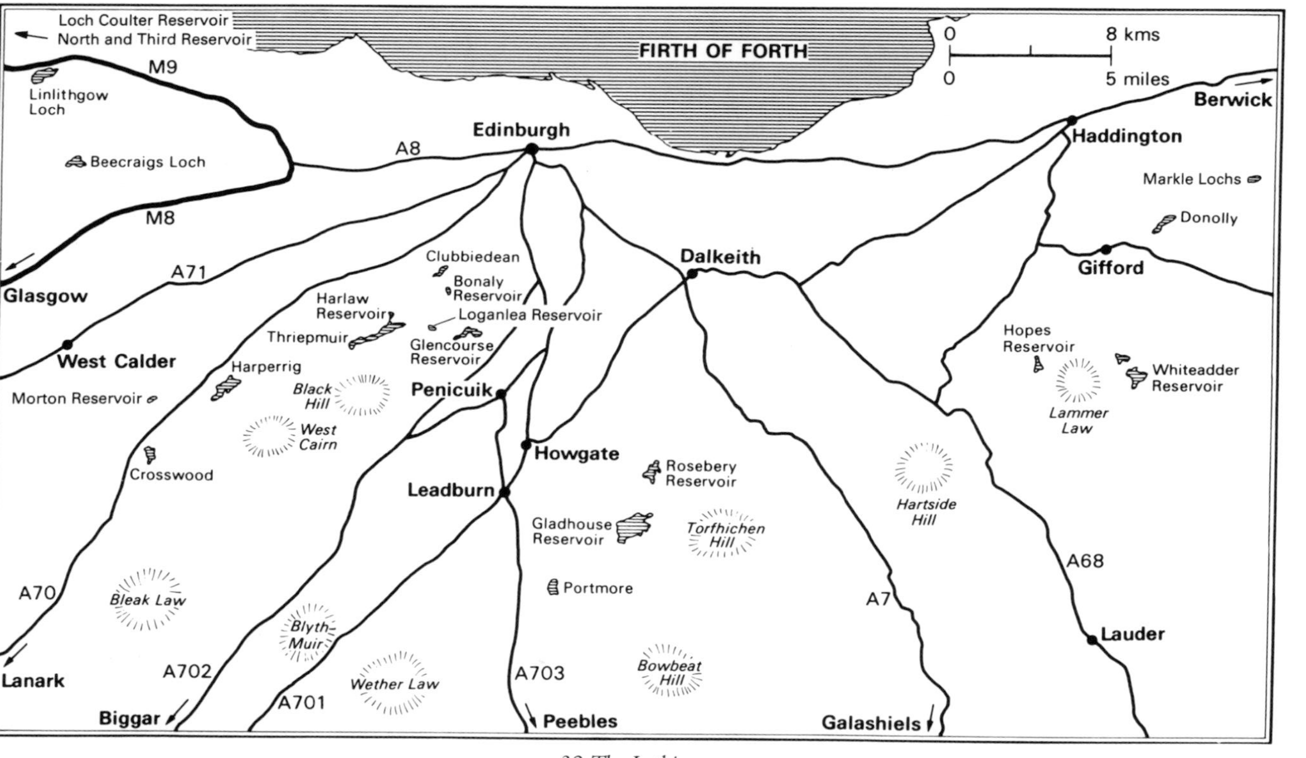

32 The Lothians

results with trout averaging about 14oz. Bank fishing is not allowed and there are three boats available, bookable up to one month in advance. Two casting platforms have been constructed for the use of disabled anglers.

GLENCORSE RESERVOIR 66/215638

Permission: Pentland Hills Ranger Service, Pentland Hills Country Park, Boghall Farm, Midlothian.
Tel: Edinburgh (031) 445 3383

Glencorse is in a valley in the Pentland Hills, just outside Edinburgh's boundary. This is a popular place for a day out and the valley can become quite busy, with anglers, hill walkers and families out for a stroll. Our parents used to take us, as children, there on Sundays as a special treat, as parents still take their offspring today. Glencorse is in a delightful setting and offers good fishing for brown trout, rainbow trout and brook trout. There is a bag limit of six fish per rod per day and some really excellent fish are caught. Average weight is around 10oz. Listen for the Glencorse bell. When the reservoir was formed a church was 'drowned' and on windy days, or when some disaster is looming, the bell tolls. Some say that the bell was removed, before the valley was flooded – but I still hear it.

LOGANLEA RESERVOIR 66/195624

Permission: Steven McGeachie, 20 Avon Grove, Penicuik, Midlothian.
Tel: Penicuik (0968) 75684

Drive on past Glencorse Reservoir (above), and you will eventually arrive at Loganlea, at the end of the road, sheltering between Black Hill and Carnethy Hill. This small loch has been stocked recently and offers great sport in peaceful surroundings. Ideal for an evening's fishing, easily accessible and great fun. Use standard pattern loch flies.

CROSSWOOD RESERVOIR 65/060575

Permission: Pentland Hills Ranger Service, Pentland Hills Country Park, Boghall Farm, Midlothian.
Tel: Edinburgh (031) 445 3383

This is a delightful reservoir of some 30 acres, within easy reach of the city, 6 miles south from Livingston. Stocked with brown, rainbow and brook trout, Crosswood is very popular and there is a bag limit of six fish per rod per day. Three boats for anglers, no bank fishing. Use standard pattern loch flies and book in advance.

WEST WATER 65/117524

Permission: Pentland Hills Ranger Service, Pentland Hills Country Park, Boghall Farm, Midlothian.
Tel: Edinburgh (031) 445 3383
Slipperfield Estate, Romano Inn, Romano Bridge, Peebleshire.
Tel: Romano Bridge (0968) 60781

West Water is a relatively new fishery which lies in the Pentland Hills to the west of West Linton. The loch extends to 93 acres, in an SSSI (Site of Special Scientific Interest) and visitors must avoid disturbing wildlife. There is a locked gate immediately before the parking area and boat house, and the keys for this gate may be obtained at Bells Shop in West Linton. The loch has a maximum depth of 90 feet and is stocked with good-quality brown trout which average 12oz. Boat fishing only using standard pattern loch flies.

GLADHOUSE RESERVOIR 66/300535

Permission: Pentland Hills Ranger Service, Pentland Hills Country Park, Boghall Farm, Midlothian.
Tel: Edinburgh (031) 445 3383
Facilities for disabled anglers: As above

Gladhouse has always had an excellent reputation for the quality of trout fishing and for at least 30 years an average of 1500 fish have been caught each season. The reservoir covers an area of 400 acres and is delightfully situated to the south of Edinburgh. The Regional Council makes four boats available for anglers, one of which has a modified seat to accommodate disabled anglers. Bank fishing is not allowed. During the busy months the fishing day is divided into two sessions: 8.00am-4.00pm and 4.30pm until one hour after dusk. Sunday fishing is allowed from 11.00am until one hour after sunset.

Gladhouse is also a nature reserve and an important resting place for geese during the winter. The boat house at the reservoir has a full list of all the different species which visit Gladhouse and it makes interesting reading. Anglers must avoid disturbing nesting birds and should note that landing on the south island is not permitted. Landing on the north island, where there is an old shelter and toilets, is permitted. During the early 1960s, while visiting Gladhouse one spring, I witnessed the remarkable sight of some 50,000 seagulls resting on the loch – at least that was my rough estimate. The best areas to fish on Gladhouse are round the islands and along the south-west shore. There is no bank fishing, so be prepared for some hard oar-work because Gladhouse can be very wild and windy. Fish of 3lb are sometimes caught but the average weight is about 12oz. Standard loch

27 Gladhouse Reservoir

pattern flies all work well but a good cast to start off with might be Black Pennell, Grouse & Claret and Cinnamon & Gold. Expect a basket of five trout to weigh about 4lb and a catch for the day of up to six fish. Yes, it can be dour like anywhere else, but good baskets are taken each year and catches of 10 fish are frequently recorded. Gladhouse is really a hill loch, lying at an altitude of some 900 feet, and is one of my favourite Lothian waters. Highly recommended.

HARLAW RESERVOIR 66/180650

Permission: Pentland Hills Ranger Service, Pentland Hills Country Park, Boghall Farm, Midlothian.
Tel: Edinburgh (031) 445 3383

Harlaw Reservoir is adjacent to Threipmuir and is easily accessible from either Balerno or Currie, to the south of Edinburgh. The reservoir was stocked by the Regional Council in 1979 and again in 1980 and holds both brown trout and rainbow trout. Bank fishing for trout averaging 12oz, with the odd fish of up to 4lb. Wading can be dangerous here because the water is deep close to the shore, so stay firmly on terra firma. The council plans improvement works on the reservoir during 1992. Standard pattern loch flies will produce results.

HARPERRIG RESERVOIR 65/095610

Permission: Pentland Hills Ranger Service, Pentland Hills Country Park,

Boghall Farm, Midlothian.
Tel: Edinburgh (031) 445 3383

Harperrig is a wild, windy loch out on the Lang Whang, the local name for the moorland A70 road from Edinburgh to Lanark. It is nevertheless a very popular fishing venue and each year produces good numbers of high-quality trout. The average weight is about 8oz but they fight hard and give a good account of themselves. There are four boats available for anglers and all of the shoreline is used for bank fishing. Take care if you are wading, since variations in the water level tend to make the margins soft – particularly the sands at the north-west corner. However, don't be put off, but do take care. Standard pattern loch flies work well here, as does dry fly in calm conditions – if and when they occur.

ROSEBERY RESERVOIR 66/308565

Permission: Pentland Hills Ranger Service, Pentland Hills Country Park, Boghall Farm, Midlothian.
Tel: Edinburgh (031) 445 3383

I first fished Rosebery Reservoir in a howling gale in 1957 and still remember the difficulty of rowing the heavy boat round the first headland. I also remember it as a lovely loch and it still is. It covers an area of 52 acres and there are two boats available for anglers. The loch is stocked by the Regional Council and trout average approximately 12oz, with the odd much larger fish being taken from time to time. Boats may be booked up to one month in advance and because Rosebery is a very popular fishing venue you would be well advised to do so. Use the standard pattern loch flies and watch out for action – and the wind.

MORTON RESERVOIR 65/075635

Permission: Morton Fisheries, Morton Reservoir, Mid Calder, West Lothian.
Tel: Mid Calder (0506) 882293

A well-managed brown trout and rainbow trout fishery lying to the north of Harperrig Reservoir. Fly fishing only, and a bag limit of three fish per rod per session. Sunday fishing is allowed, there are nine boats available and bank fishing is also allowed. Fishing is from early March until mid-October, with two sessions operating from May until August. The largest rainbow trout caught during 1991 weighed 9lb 1oz and the average weight of fish is 1lb 8oz. Book well in advance.

THREIPMUIR RESERVOIR 66/175640

Permission: The Factor, Dalmeny Estate Office, South Queensferry, West Lothian.
Tel: South Queensferry (031) 331 4840
Alexander Flemming, 42 Main Street, Balerno, Edinburgh.
Tel: Edinburgh (031) 449 3833

Season permits are available on Threipmuir by ballot and to be included anglers should write to the Factor at the above address by 1 March. A limited number of day tickets for fly fishing from the bank are available from Alexander Flemming in the village. Threipmuir covers an area of 246 acres and opinions vary wildly concerning it – from magnificent to very, very dour. It is, however, a lovely water and easily accessible. Boat fishing is controlled by the Threipmuir Angling Club. The loch is stocked with both brown and rainbow trout and there is a bag limit of six fish per rod per day. The bank-fishing area is from the boat house to Black Springs and anglers must use thigh waders – no chest waders are allowed. The eastern end of the reservoir is an SSSI (Site of Special Scientific Interest) and visitors must take great care not to disturb wildlife. The average weight for this water is 12oz but each season several fish of between 3lb and 3lb 8oz are caught. Two fish would be considered an average basket and any more a red-letter day. But the

28 Victorian Hopes

quality of trout is very good indeed and they fight hard. The best fishing areas are in the vicinity of Black Springs and around the margins. Threipmuir fishes best from the bank during the early months of the season, and during August and September when evening fishing is most likely to produce results.

HOPES RESERVOIR 66/547620

Permission: Lothian Regional Council, Department of Water Supply Services, Alderston House, Haddington, East Lothian.
Tel: Haddington: (062082) 4131

This is a very lovely little reservoir covering 35 acres and lying high in the Lammermuir Hills, to the south of Haddington. The average size of trout is not large, only 8oz, but great sport can be had and good baskets are regularly taken. There are larger fish, and trout of over 1lb are caught most seasons. The reservoir is well established and the buildings and dam blend easily with the surrounding scenery. Everything is meticulously neat and tidy. It is a nice place to spend a day, and if the fish are not rising there are super hills to explore until they do.

DONOLLY RESERVOIR 67/577688

Permission: Lothian Regional Council, Department of Water Supply Services, Alderston House, Haddington, East Lothian.
Tel: Haddington: (062082) 4131

Donolly is a small, remote water near Gifford, at the foot of the Lammermuir Hills. It is a very pleasant place to fish and there are two boats available for anglers. Bank fishing is not allowed. This reservoir is not fished as much as the other Regional Council waters but the average weight of fish is respectable and it is well worth a visit. The reservoir was drained in 1991 but is being refilled and restocked for the 1992 season. Use standard pattern loch flies.

WHITEADDER RESERVOIR 67/655635

Permission: Mr Kerr, The Water Keeper's House, Hungry Snout, Whiteadder Reservoir, East Lothian.
Tel: Longformacus (03617) 362
Facilities for disabled anglers: As above

Whiteadder Reservoir covers 193 acres to the south-east of Gifford. It lies between Starleton Edge and Penshiel Hill, near to Cranshaws on the B6355. The reservoir was built in 1969 and there are three boats available for anglers. Bank fishing is not allowed, and a drogue is essential on this exposed, often wild loch. Trout average 8oz but fish of over 2lb are also caught. There is a good boat house for shelter in stormy weather and boats may be booked up to one month in advance. Use standard pattern loch flies.

WATCH WATER RESERVOIR 67/660564

Permission: W. F. Renton, Watch Water Reservoir, Longformacus, Duns.
Tel: Longformacus (03617) 333 or Berwick-Upon-Tweed (0289) 306028

Approach from Longformacus, south from the village past the Rathburne Hotel and Rawburn. The reservoir extends to 119 acres and is 76 feet deep at the deepest point. It is surrounded by the Lammermuir Hills: Sting Law, Twin Law, Dunside Hill, Scar Law, and Whinrig Hill, and is one of the most remote and attractive of the Lothian stocked fisheries. The owners are planting hardwoods by the loch, in order to improve the natural habitat. There are two boats, as well as bank fishing, and it is a strictly fly-only water. Bookings must be made in advance and all situations are catered for, including the provision of tackle, flies, and even soup and a roll if required. The loch has been stocked with both brown and rainbow trout and fish average 1lb 12oz. The heaviest rainbow caught recently weighed 9lb 3oz; the heaviest brown trout weighed 5lb. This is away-from-it-all fishing amidst stunning Border scenery where visitors are well received and well looked after.

MALTINGS FISHERY 67/653769

Permission: Dunbar Trout Farm, South Belton, Dunbar, East Lothian.
Tel: Dunbar (0368) 63244
Facilities for disabled anglers: As above

Fly fishing on a 2-acre stocked loch 4 miles south from Dunbar on the B6370. Open all year round, bank fishing only, book in advance.

FRUID RESERVOIR 78/100190

Permission: Pentland Hills Ranger Service, Pentland Hills Country Park, Boghall Farm, Midlothian.
Tel: Edinburgh (031) 445 3383

Fruid is a wild, remote loch, surrounded by hills and covering 290 acres. The road from Tweedsmuir stops at the dam, where there are two boats available for anglers. Fish the shallows at the southern end where Fruid Water enters, and in the vicinity of Catchope and Priesthope along the south shore. Fishing is for wild brown trout, using standard pattern loch flies, and spinning and worm fishing are also allowed.

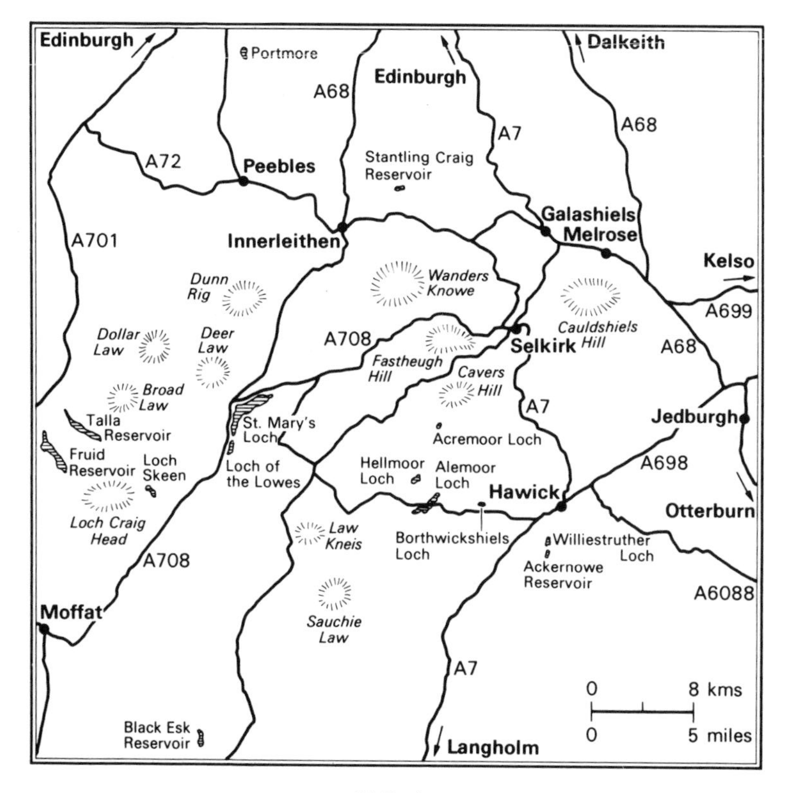

33 Borders

TALLA RESERVOIR 72/110220

Permission: Pentland Hills Ranger Service, Pentland Hills Country Park, Boghall Farm, Midlothian.
Tel: Edinburgh (031) 445 3383

Talla Reservoir covers some 300 acres and can be very windy. Approach from Tweedsmuir. The loch has a good native population of brown trout and both boat and bank fishing are available. Permits can be obtained at the reservoir, from the Water Superintendent. The average weight of trout is 8–10oz but fish of over 2lb are also caught. Best places to fish are where the main feeder burn enters at the south end of the loch, where it is shallow. It is a long row down, so you may prefer to bank fish, approaching via the convenient road along the north shore of the reservoir. Bank fishing is best early in the season, when a good basket should account for about seven fish. A bit intimidating, but a wonderful place to fish.

29 Talla Reservoir

MEGGET RESERVOIR 73/215228

Permission: Pentland Hills Ranger Service, Pentland Hills Country Park, Boghall Farm, Midlothian.
Tel: Edinburgh (031) 445 3383

Recently formed, and lying to the west of St Mary's Loch, Megget has established itself as a very popular and productive fishery. It is stocked with brown, rainbow and brook trout. Boats are available but outboard motors are not allowed. Pack a drogue or take along a strong young friend. There are excellent facilities at the reservoir, including a well-equipped and well-maintained boat house with kitchen and toilets. Use standard pattern loch flies.

ST MARY'S LOCH 73/250230
LOCH OF THE LOWES 79/237195

Permission: Tibbie Shiels Inn, St Mary's Loch, Yarrow, Selkirk.
Tel: Cappercleuch (0750) 42231

These two lochs, which lie to the south of Innerleithen, are separated by a narrow neck of land. They contain brown trout, pike and perch and are stocked occasionally. St Mary's Loch is 3 miles long, 1/2 mile wide and, at its deepest, 150 feet. The most productive areas to fish are around the shallow bays: Megget Bay, Bowerhope Bay and Tibbie Shiels Bay. Another good area is along the March Woods. Most anglers, when fishing from a boat, 'keep the bottom in sight'. Bank fishing is also allowed and can be good as well. But St Mary's has a reputation for being dour and fish are often very hard to catch. Trout average about 8oz, but baskets of six fish weighing 7lb are taken, and there are much larger fish in the loch, including pike of up to 20lb. Flies to use are Black Pennell, Black Spider, Black Gnat, Blue Zulu, March Brown and Kingfisher Butcher.

The adjacent Loch of the Lowes is, if anything, even more dour than St Mary's, but the fish are larger and if you do get one it will probably be over 1lb. Use the same flies as for St Mary's and the best fishing place is the roadside bank.

These lochs are in a lovely area, the land of Sir Walter Scott, James Hogg – The Ettrick Shepherd – and Thomas Todd Stoddart, who often fished with Hogg on St Mary's Loch. There are other activities on the loch, such as sailing, but plenty of room for all.

LOCH SKEEN 79/170165

Permission: Not required

Skeen is a beautiful loch, 6 miles to the north of Moffat on the A708.

This is superb countryside and some of the wildest in all of Scotland. The only problem with Skeen is getting there. The loch lies above the Grey Mare's Tail waterfall, which plunges spectacularly 200 feet down to the road. The quickest way to the loch is by the track up the side of this waterfall, but do be careful for it can be dangerous, particularly in stormy weather. An easier but longer way in is to approach from further up the glen. Skeen lies at an altitude of 1700 feet and is full of small, hard-fighting trout. The average weight is 6–8oz but from time to time fish of up to 2lb are caught. Bank fishing only and the far end of the loch is the best fishing area (it always is). Ten trout would weigh about 5lb and all the standard pattern loch flies produce results. It is not so much the trout that make Skeen such a desirable place to fish, rather it is the remote, magnificent surroundings. Waders are a great help when fishing Skeen. Lugging them there is not.

LOCH COULTER RESERVOIR 57/765860

Permission: Andrew Patterson, 6 Wheatlands Avenue, Bonnybridge, Stirlingshire.
Tel: Bonnybridge (032481) 2643

Coulter lies to the west of the intersection of the M80 and M9 at Bannockburn House and is managed by the Larbert and Stenhousemuir Angling Club. This is a stocked fishery offering good sport with both brown and rainbow trout in an attractive setting.

NORTH AND THIRD RESERVOIR 57/755890

Permission: George Holdsworth, Greathill, Cambusbarron, Stirling.
Tel: Stirling (0786) 71967

North and Third is an excellent fishery offering sport with stocked brown and rainbow trout in a delightful setting. The loch covers 108 acres and there are 20 boats available, and bank fishing. Fishing is open seven days a week from 15 March until 31 October. The best brown trout in recent years weighed 6lb 12oz, and the heaviest rainbow weighed 9lb 8oz.

MARKLE FISHERIES 67/579774

Permission: Markle Fisheries Limited, East Linton, East Lothian.
Tel: East Linton (0620) 860155
Facilities for disabled anglers: As above

A new fishery created and managed by Bob Wallace and now under extensive development by Markle Fisheries Limited. Markle fish have an

30 Looking natural, Portmore Loch

astonishingly good growth rate and trout of up to 20lb have been caught. There are at present two lochs covering 8 acres and trout are reared on site, using a 'ranch-farming' technique, and consequently Markle fish are fully finned, properly coloured and fighting fit. There is a comfortable clubhouse with bar and food, as well as a tackle shop and ancillary services. During 1991 nine trout weighing over 15lb were caught. The minimum stocking size is 2lb, the average weight is 3lb 4oz and the heaviest fish stocked recently weighed 25lb 8oz. It is still there, waiting perhaps just for your fly.

SELM MUIR FISHERIES 65/088651

Permission: Selm Muir Fisheries, Mid Calder, West Lothian.
Tel: Mid Calder (0506) 882593

Selm Muir is a 3-acre stocked fishery sheltered by mature woodlands, south from East Calder. Approach from Ormiston and Latch Farm and expect good sport with both brown trout and rainbow trout. Fishing is from 9.00am-9.00pm only. Book in advance.

PORTMORE LOCH 73/260500

Permission: Steven McGeachie, 20 Avon Grove, Penicuik, Midlothian.
Tel: Penicuik (0968) 75684

Portmore covers 104 acres and lies 14 miles south of Edinburgh.

Approach via the A703 Edinburgh–Peebles road. This is one of the most lovely lochs in the Borders and one of my 'special' places, where I first fished more than 30 years ago. Portmore lies on the western slopes of the Moorfoot Hills, below Dundreich Hill, and is thus relatively sheltered from high winds. There are small woods of proper trees, rather than factory-forestry, and on a warm spring evening there are few more pleasant places to fish. The loch is regularly stocked and well-managed and each season produces large numbers of brown and rainbow trout weighing over 4lb, with several more of up to 8lb. The heaviest brown trout ever taken from the loch was caught by Ewen Murray during 1991 and was a magnificent wild fish of 8lb 13oz. Whenever I think of loch fishing in the south of Scotland, Portmore is one of the first on my list – rain or shine, fishless or otherwise.

STANTLING CRAIG RESERVOIR 73/430395

Permission: Tweed Valley Hotel, Walkerburn, Peebleshire.
Tel: Walkerburn (089687) 636; Fax: (089687) 639

Stantling Craig is a small reservoir on the south-east slopes of the Moorfoot Hills. Fishing has been managed by the Tweed Valley Hotel since 1972 and Charles Miller, the owner of the hotel, has carefully improved the spawning facilities for the native stock. Trout average 10oz and rise well to standard pattern loch flies. Bank fishing only, by fly. Easily accessible and a super place to fish.

LINDEAN RESERVOIR 73/500292

Permission: P. & E. Scott, 6 High Street, Selkirk.
Tel: Selkirk (0750) 20749

Lindean lies to the north-east of Selkirk by Bell Hill and is stocked annually with brown trout, and with rainbow trout throughout the season. There is a bag limit of 12 trout per boat per session, and the fishing day is divided into two sessions. Two boats are available and the average weight of rainbow trout is 1lb 8oz, and of brown trout 1lb 4oz. During 1991 two brown trout of over 5lb were caught, as well as a rainbow trout of 4lb. Fish rise and are caught all over the loch, but the most productive area is in the vicinity of the island at the east end. Standard pattern loch flies are fine.

ACREMOOR LOCH 73/407210

Permission: Hawick and District Angling Club, 5 Sandbed, Hawick, Roxburghshire.
Tel: Hawick (0450) 73771

Porteous & Newcombe, Howgate, Hawick, Roxburghshire.
Pet Store, 1 Union Street, Hawick, Roxburghshire.
Tel: Hawick (0450) 73543
Lindsays Grocers, Denholm, Roxburghshire.
Horse & Hounds Inn, Bonchester, Hawick, Roxburghshire.
Tel: Bonchester Bridge (045086) 645

Acremoor is one of the best lochs in the Hawick area and lies to the north of town, below Belmanshaws (353m). Approach via the A7 at Ashkirk Village and follow the farm track out to Longhope Farm. There is a track from the farm and the walk takes about half an hour. The loch has been well stocked in recent years and contains brown trout with an average weight of about 14oz–1lb, but Acremoor has a reputation for much heavier fish. Trout of between 2 and 3lb are not uncommon and fish of over 5lb have been caught. Bank fishing only. A first-class loch in a delightful setting. Take along Greenwell's Glory, Wickham's Fancy, Olives and Butchers.

HELLMOOR LOCH 79/385170

Permission: Hawick and District Angling Club, 5 Sandbed, Hawick, Roxburghshire.
Tel: Hawick (0450) 73771
Porteous & Newcombe, Howgate, Hawick, Roxburghshire.
Pet Store, 1 Union Street, Hawick, Roxburghshire.
Tel: Hawick (0450) 73543
Lindsays Grocers, Denholm, Roxburghshire.
Horse & Hounds Inn, Bonchester, Hawick, Roxburghshire.
Tel: Bonchester Bridge (045086) 645

Hellmoor covers 25 acres and lies at the end of the forestry road to the north of Alemoor Loch. Approach from the B711. Keys for the gate should be obtained from the club premises (a deposit will be required) and must be returned the same day. This is a beautiful loch and the Hawick Angling Club has stocked it with brown trout. Hellmoor also contains pike and a monster of 28lb has been caught. Brown trout average about 1lb and fight hard, and fish of over 4lb have been taken. Expect three or four fish for your day and always try a March Brown.

ACKERNOWE RESERVOIR 79/495106

Permission: Hawick and District Angling Club, 5 Sandbed, Hawick, Roxburghshire.
Tel: Hawick (0450) 73771
Porteous & Newcombe, Howgate, Hawick, Roxburghshire.

Pet Store, 1 Union Street, Hawick, Roxburghshire.
Tel: Hawick (0450) 73543
Lindsays Grocers, Denholm, Roxburghshire.
Horse & Hounds Inn, Bonchester, Hawick, Roxburghshire.
Tel: Bonchester Bridge (045086) 645

Ackernowe lies ½ mile to the south of Williestruther Loch, just outside Hawick. There is one boat on the loch and bank fishing is allowed. The water has been stocked by the Hawick Angling Club with rainbow trout of up to 3lb, and smaller brown trout. Flies that catch them, or should, are March Brown, Olives and Black Spider. The best fishing area on the loch is at the north end, where trout of up to 5lb have been caught. Easily accessible and a pleasant loch to fish.

WILLIESTRUTHER LOCH 79/492115

Permission: Hawick and District Angling Club, 5 Sandbed, Hawick, Roxburghshire.
Tel: Hawick (0450) 73771
Porteous & Newcombe, Howgate, Hawick, Roxburghshire.
Pet Store, 1 Union Street, Hawick, Roxburghshire.
Tel: Hawick (0450) 73543
Lindsays Grocers, Denholm, Roxburghshire.
Horse & Hounds Inn, Bonchester, Hawick, Roxburghshire.
Tel: Bonchester Bridge (045086) 645

Williestruther Loch is a small water to the south of Hawick. Fishing is from the bank only and no boats are allowed. The Hawick Angling Club has stocked the loch with brown trout and the average weight of fish is about 1lb. The weed problem of recent years has also been successfully resolved by the members of this hard-working club, and Williestruther is the ideal place for a few casts after dinner. Standard pattern loch flies will do fine.

ALEMOOR LOCH 79/400155

Permission: Hawick and District Angling Club, 5 Sandbed, Hawick, Roxburghshire.
Tel: Hawick (0450) 73771
Porteous & Newcombe, Howgate, Hawick, Roxburghshire.
Pet Store, 1 Union Street, Hawick, Roxburghshire.
Tel: Hawick (0450) 73543
Lindsays Grocers, Denholm, Roxburghshire.
Horse & Hounds Inn, Bonchester, Hawick, Roxburghshire.
Tel: Bonchester Bridge (045086) 645

Concern has been expressed recently about high aluminium levels in Alemoor Loch and about £750,000 would have to be spent by the council in order to bring the water quality up to new EC standards. In the meantime, the Hawick Angling Club has stocked the loch with brown trout, but it also contains a good population of pike. Bank fishing only, and best in the evenings. Use March Brown, Greenwell's Glory and Silver Butcher. Dour, but worth a cast – trout of up to 5lb have been caught.

BLACK ESK RESERVOIR 79/205965

Permission: For details of fishing available to the public, contact R. R. D'Souza, Sandyford Cottage, Boreland, Lockerbie, Dumfries and Galloway. Visitors may obtain permits at Sandyford, which is on the way up to the reservoir, or at the Hart Manor Hotel (tel: 03873 73217).

This reservoir lies in the Eskdale Moor Forest between Eskdalemuir in the north and Lockerbie to the south. Access is from the B723 at Sandyford, approximately 10 miles north-east of Lockerbie. This is a popular area with visitors and one of great natural beauty. The Black Esk Reservoir is 1 mile long by 500 yards wide and several feeder burns enter from Cairn Knowe and Kilburn Hill. Bank fishing only. The loch has a high population of wild fish – and some land-locked sea trout. Because of the vast numbers of fish, there is no bag limit and both fly fishing and spinning are allowed. Their average weight is 8–10oz and you should use standard pattern loch flies to catch them. No guarantee is given as to the condition and safety of the banks or foreshores and permit holders use the facility at their own risk.

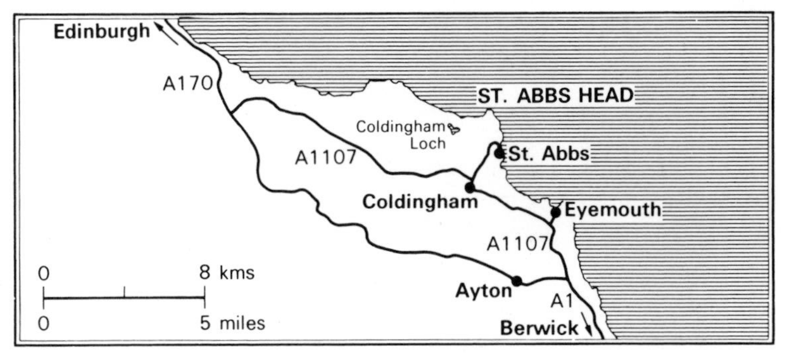

34 Duns and Dunbar

31 Philip Reid, Edinburgh angler, shows what can be done

COLDINGHAM LOCH 67/896685

Permission: Dr E. J. Wise, West Loch House, Coldingham. Berwickshire.
Tel: Coldingham (08907) 71270

This is a beautifully situated little loch and one of the oldest and best managed fisheries in Scotland. It was the first place to introduce rainbow trout, in the late 1940s. The loch is 22 acres in extent and contains both brown and rainbow trout. There is a good boat house and boats can be booked either for the full day, when the bag limit is five fish per rod, or for a morning or evening only, when there is a bag limit of three fish per rod. Trout rise and are caught all over the loch and no one area is better than any other. The average weight is 1lb 8oz. Coldingham has always had a reputation for large fish and trout of 7lb are not infrequently taken. Flies to use include Black Pennell, Greenwell's Glory, Wickham's Fancy, Black Spider, Soldier Palmer and various buzzers. On arrival visitors will be given the best available advice regarding flies and where to use them. Be warned, however: Coldingham can be very dour at times. Dr Wise has a number of well-furnished, comfortable, self-catering cottages, scattered throughout the estate in idyllic settings. My favourite is the boat house, overhanging the loch itself. What angler could ask for more?

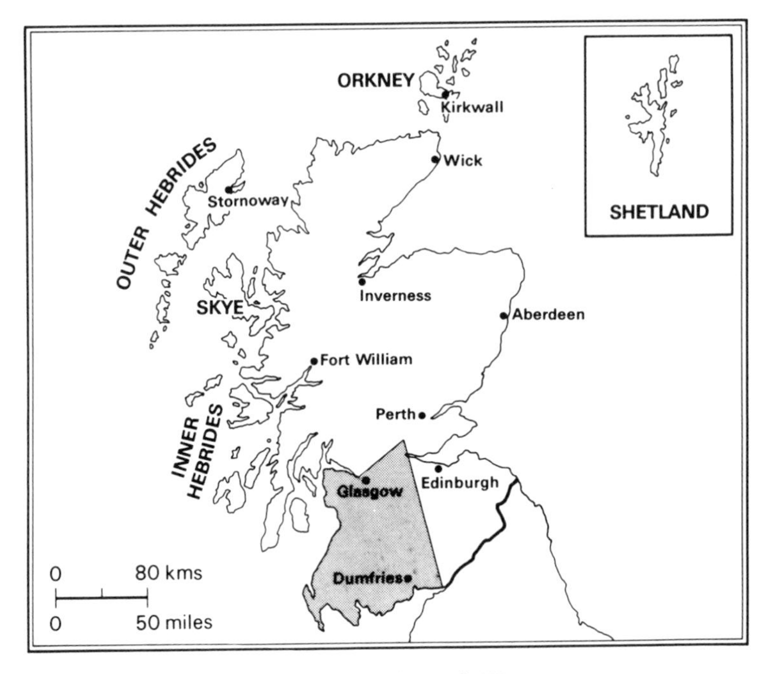

35 Glasgow and the South-West

9 Glasgow and the South-West

There are hundreds of trout lochs within easy reach of Glasgow, and no other major industrial centre in Europe can offer such a diversity of fine sport. Glorious Loch Lomond is a short drive north, where, in spite of its popularity, you will always find a quiet corner. Wander deep into the Galloway Forest Park to fish Loch Dee or Bradan, climb the boulder-scattered screes of Merrick, the highest mountain in the south of Scotland, and you will hardly see another soul all day. Visit scenic little Morton Castle Loch near Thornhill, or the wild moorlands to the north of Stranraer in Wigtownshire, fishing to suit everyone amidst wonderful scenery. You are never very far from the 'shades' of Scotland's greatest poet, Robert Burns. From Ellisland Farm, near Dumfries, to the Auld Kirk at Alloway, immortalized in his wonderful poem 'Tam O'Shanter', the presence of the great man dominates the country. But if I were forced to choose one area it would have to be the Galloway Forest Park, where there is an abundance of everything which makes fishing my favourite pastime: forest tracks and secret places, wild, beautiful hills and moorlands, perfect peace and superb trout fishing.

LOCH LOMOND Sheet 56

Permission: The Boatyard, Balmaha, Drymen, Glasgow.
Tel: Balmaha (036087) 214
Inverbeg Inn, Luss, Dumbartonshire.
Tel: Luss (043686) 678
Ardlui Hotel, Ardlui, Loch Lomond, Arrochar, Dumbartonshire.
Tel: Inveruglas (03014) 243
Rowardennan Hotel, Drymen, Glasgow.
Tel: Balmaha (03687) 273
R. A. Clement & Co., 224 Ingram Street, Glasgow.
Tel: Glasgow (041) 2210068
Facilities for disabled anglers: Contact above

The main interest here for the angler is salmon and sea trout and most visitors fish for them. Loch Lomond is, however, a good trout loch and well worth a visit. Such a vast water makes it difficult to give more than a very brief outline of the fishing opportunities, but I think that

36 Kilsyth

most people who know the loch would agree with me that you can walk down to the shore at almost any point and catch trout. The western shoreline is the most easily accessible, and consequently the most busy. But if you want to really get away from it all, explore the east shore. The West Highland Way runs the full length of the east shore, giving reasonably easy access, but you will have to hoof it up the track to reach the best places. It is all very beautiful, and Loch Lomond is probably one of the most famous waters in the world. The trout are also very lovely: well shaped and golden, with bright red spots. They average 8oz, although, as you would imagine, very much larger fish lurk in the depths. The north end of the loch is the most productive trout fishing area and all the standard loch fly patterns attract fish. In spite of being so close to Glasgow, and the increasing presence of a multitude of other water activities – sailing, wind surfing and the like, there is room for everyone. Much of this activity takes place at the south end of the loch, so trout fishers in the north, particularly from the east bank, may still find peace and quiet.

MOUNT DAM/WHITEFIELD POND 64/644774

Permission: Caurnie Pets & Tackle, Kitkintilloch.
Tel: Glasgow (041) 7764458

These two waters lie in the Campsie Fells midway between Lennoxtown and Milton of Campsie. Fishing is from the bank only and the lochs are stocked with brown trout with an average weight of 12oz. Mount Dam is considered to be the most productive of the two and baskets of up to five trout are often taken. Standard loch fly patterns work well, as does a Grey Duster. A lovely area to fish, redolent of the past with its old castles, ancient forts and wild hills.

BANTON LOCH 64/740785

Permission: From members of the committee of the Kilsyth Fish Protection Association in attendance at the loch.
R. Brown, Clozium Motor Sales & Service, Stirling Road, Kilsyth, Glasgow.
Tel: Kilsyth (0236)822003
Coachman Hotel, Park Foot Street, Kilsyth, Glasgow.
Tel: Kilsyth (0236) 821649

Banton Loch lies 1 mile of Kilsyth and is over ½ mile long by 250 yards wide. It is managed by the Kilsyth Fish Protection Association, whose Secretary is S. Gillies, 13 Findly Street, Kilsyth. The club stocks the loch with brown trout and both boat and bank fishing are available to visitors. The average weight of fish is about 8–10oz, but several trout of 1lb and more are taken each season and fish of up to 2lb 8oz have been caught. Boats should be booked from the Coachman Hotel and there are five available. Two sessions operate, from 8.00am–5.00pm and from 5.00pm until midnight. Fishing is good all round the loch and the trout seem to prefer dark flies. This a well-managed, well-organized loch and worth a visit.

SPRINGFIELD RESERVOIR 72/904520

Permission: Clyde Valley Tackle Shop, 28 Kirkton Street, Carluke, Lanarkshire.
Tel: Carluke (0555) 72183

Springfield Reservoir lies to the east of Carluke in Lanarkshire and is 700 yards long by nearly 300 yards wide. Fishing is managed by the

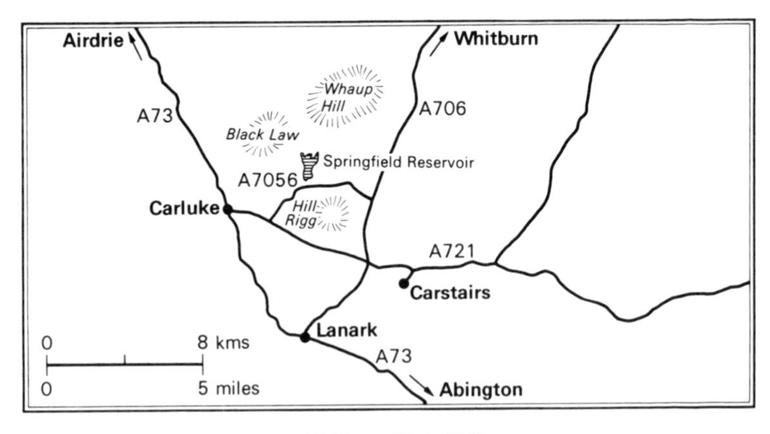

37 Upper Clyde Valley

United Clyde Angling Protection Association, whose address is 20 Cunningham Street, Motherwell. The reservoir contains brown trout and is easily accessible, being adjacent to the B7056, 2½ miles out of town, at Easterseat.

CARRON VALLEY RESERVOIR 57/690840

Permission: Director of Finance, Central Regional Council, Woodlands, Stirling.
Tel: Stirling (0786) 443000

Carron Valley Reservoir lies to the south of the B818 between Denny and Fintry. It is 3 miles long by ¾ mile wide, covers an area of 965 acres and is almost surrounded by the Carron Valley Forest. The lovely Fintry Hills lie to the north and the Campsie Fells to the south, and Carron Valley is a most pleasant loch to fish. It is stocked from time to time and fishing is from boats only, of which there are 12 available for visitors. There is a generous bag limit of 30 fish per boat per day, but before you get too excited I hasten to add that the average basket is about six trout. Nevertheless, they average 1lb and fight very hard indeed. This is a loch for small flies, I think, and the best patterns to use are Black Pennell, Woodcock & Yellow, Grouse & Claret, Greenwell's Glory and Butchers. Fish are caught all round the loch but one of the best areas is the tree-fringed south shoreline. Heavier fish are also caught, so look out for the odd 2-lb trout, and concentrate. Carron Valley can be very windy and an outboard motor is really essential. They may be hired at the loch. Carron Valley is a very popular fishing venue, so you are advised to book well in advance.

GARTMORN DAM FISHERY 58/915942

Permission: Clackmannan District Council, Leisure Services Department, Alloa, Clackmannanshire.
Tel: Alloa (0259) 213131
Gartmorn Dam Country Park Visitors Centre, Alloa, Clackmannanshire.
Tel: Alloa (0259) 214319

Gartmorn lies north-east of Alloa and is approached via the A908 or from the A907 in the south, and from the B9140 in the north. The loch covers an area of 167 acres and is 175 feet deep. Fishing is for stocked brown trout, by fly or spinning and six boats and bank fishing are available. The area round the island, including the north shore, is a nature reserve where fishing is not allowed. Nor is fishing allowed in the east bay and boat fishing is not allowed in the south-east bay. These restrictions aside, expect good-quality trout in beautiful surroundings.

SWAN'S WATER FISHERY 57/782899

Permission: Swans Water Fishery, Sauchieburn, Stirling.
Tel: Stirling (0786) 814405

Swans Water is surrounded by the famous battlefields of Bannockburn and Sauchieburn, and battles still rage today, between man and fish. It is stocked with hard-fighting rainbow trout of around 1lb on which there is no close season. Use standard pattern loch flies.

WHINHILL RESERVOIR 63/277746

Permission: Findlay & Co., 58 Lynedoch Street, Greenock, Renfrewshire.
Tel: Greenock (0475) 24056
J. Rankin, Water House, Loch Thom Reservoir, Greenock.

Whinhill is a small brown-trout reservoir to the south of Greenock and fishing is managed by the Greenock and District Angling Club. Approach from the hill road to Largs, which leaves the B7054 near the golf course.

LOCH THOM 63/260720
GRYFE RESERVOIR 63/280719

Permission: Findlay & Co., 58 Lynedoch Street, Greenock, Renfrewshire.
Tel: Greenock (0475) 24056
J. Rankin, Water House, Loch Thom Reservoir, Greenock, Renfrewshire.

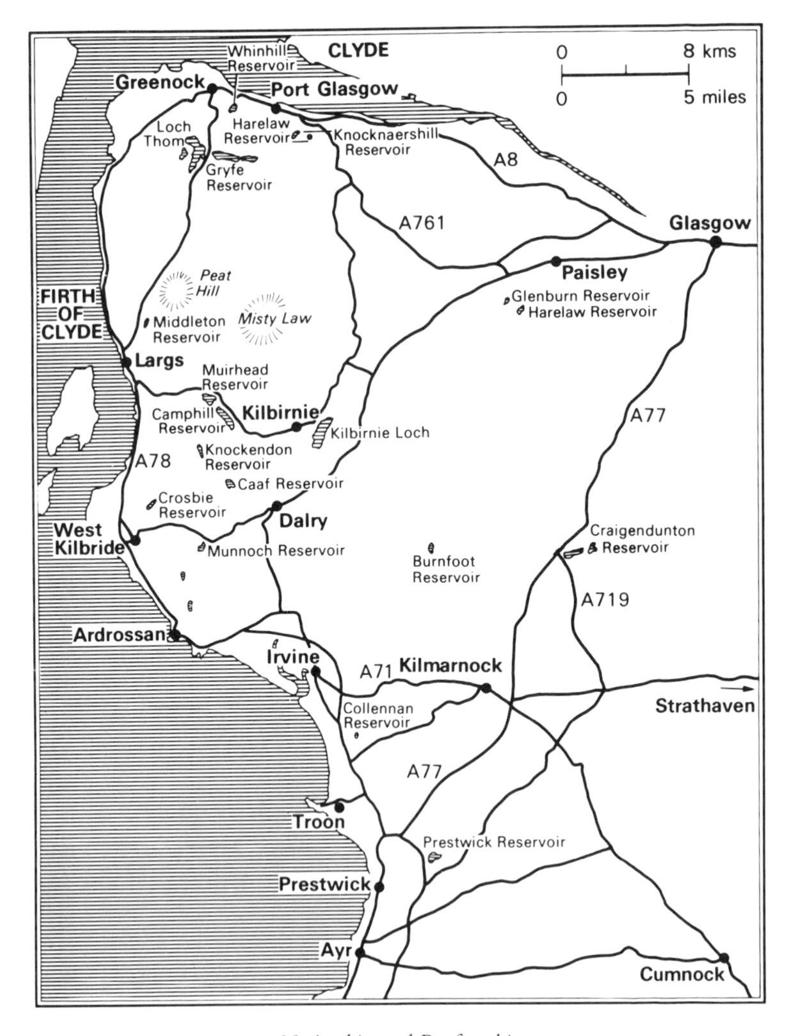

38 Ayrshire and Renfrewshire

Loch Thom and the Gryfe Reservoir are the largest trout waters in the area and lie in the Renfrewshire Hills above Greenock. In spite of the fact that they are close to major urban centres, they remain secluded and remote. They are easily accessible and a welcome facility for local anglers. Fishing is controlled by three separate angling clubs: Loch Thom and the Compensation Reservoirs Nos 6, 7 and 8 by Greenock and District Angling Club, whose Secretary is B. Paterson, 56 Pentland

Court, Greenock; Gryfe Reservoir No. 1 by the Dunrod Angling Club, through T. Rae, 36 Margaret Street, Greenock; and Gryfe No. 2 by the Port Glasgow Angling Club, through P. Graham, 12 Skye Road, Port Glasgow. Permits are also issued by A. Caskie, Garvocks Farm and Mrs A. Baird, Cornalees Farm. I suggest that the visitor would be best advised to contact Findlay & Co. who will give directions and advice.

HARELAW RESERVOIR 63/310733

Permission: P. Graham, 12 Skye Road, Port Glasgow.
Tel: Port Glasgow (0475) 43143

Fishing is controlled by the Port Glasgow Angling Club on this small reservoir lying adjacent to the B788 on Burnhead Moor. It is stocked with brown trout and is easily accessible.

KNOCKNAERSHILL RESERVOIR 63/307733

Permission: P. Graham, 12 Skye Road, Port Glasgow.
Tel: Port Glasgow (0475) 43143

Another Port Glasgow Angling Club water, this lies close to Harelaw Reservoir (above) and is approached by the same route. Fishing is for brown trout which average 8–10oz.

HARELAW RESERVOIR 64/585596

Permission: J. Cuthbertson, 68 Bellfield Crescent, Barrhead, Glasgow.

The St Mirin Angling Club manage this reservoir and membership of the club is restricted to 70 members. There are generally a few memberships vacant and you should contact the Secretary, whose name is given above. Harelaw is to the south of the B774 Barrhead–Paisley road and the club has a good boat house with lighting and cooking facilities. The loch is stocked with 500 two-year-old brown trout each season and their average weight is 12oz. A catch of two or three fish would be considered good for this fishery and trout of 2 or 3lb are caught occasionally. The fish are always in excellent condition. Try Black Pennell, Greenwell's Glory and Silver Butcher.

GLENBURN RESERVOIR 64/475600

Permission: The Lower Clyde Water Board, 19 Underwood Road, Paisley, Renfrewshire.
Tel: Paisley (041887) 5161

Glenburn lies to the south of Paisley in the Fereneze Hills and may be approached through the Glenburn housing estate from either the B774 or the B775. This small reservoir is stocked occasionally with brown trout and their average weight is 12oz. Fishing is all from the bank and the south and west banks produce the best results. An average basket would consist of two fish and the best flies to use are Greenwell's Glory and Olive Duns. Summer evenings are the best times to fish.

DUNWAY RESERVOIR 63/554494

Permission: A. L. Watt, 5 Craignethan Road, Giffnock, Glasgow.
Tel: Giffnock (041639) 1824
Facilities for disabled anglers: Contact above; 50 per cent discount for disabled anglers.

Dunway is a large reservoir lying to the south of Eaglesham and is approached via the B764 Eaglesham–Kilmarnock road. A track leads up to the dam and the reservoir has been well stocked with good-quality brown trout. Use standard pattern loch flies.

BLACK LOCH 63/498514

Permission: A. L. Watt, 5 Craignethan Road, Giffnock, Glasgow.
Tel: Giffnock (041639) 1824
Facilities for disabled anglers: As above

The Black Loch lies to the south of Newton Mearns and is approached from the A77, turning right on the minor road just before St Martin's. Park at Nether Cairn. The loch is stocked with brown trout which average 1lb and fish rise to all the standard pattern loch flies.

CRAIGENDUNTON RESERVOIR 64/526457

Permission: McCririck & Sons, 38 John Finnie Street, Kilmarnock, Ayrshire.
Tel: (0563) 25577
Andrew Magill, 31 Raith Road, Fenwick, Kilmarnock, Ayrshire.
Tel: Kilmarnock (05606) 382
Facilities for disabled anglers: As above

There are two reservoirs here, in a delightful woodland setting amidst the Whitelee Forest. The lochs are stocked with brown trout and their average weight is 12oz. The main part of the reservoir is 700 yards long by 200 yards wide and the best fishing area is along the south shore. Bank fishing only. Average catches are three to six fish and trout of up to 4lb have been taken. Blae & Black, Teal & Green and Greenwell's Glory do most of the damage and fishing is generally good throughout the season. Approach via the A719 Glaston road at Amlaird. The road up to the reservoir is 2½ miles long. A secluded, pleasant place to spend the day.

BURNFOOT RESERVOIR 64/453450-70/450448

Permission: McCririck & Sons, 38 John Finnie Street, Kilmarnock, Ayrshire.
Tel: (0563) 25577
Andrew Magill, 31 Raith Road, Fenwick, Kilmarnock, Ayrshire.
Tel: Kilmarnock (05606) 382

This is a small reservoir to the west of the A77 Kilmarnock–Glasgow road. It is stocked with brown trout and their average weight is 12oz. Fishing is from the bank only and there is a bag limit of six fish per rod. Trout rise and are caught all over the loch and the best flies to use include Greenwell's Glory, Black Pennell, Teal & Red and Teal & Green. An average day should bring you three to six trout and fish of up to 3lb are also sometimes taken. Evenings are the most productive time.

CROSBIE RESERVOIR 63/219505

Permission: P. M. Shepherd, Dunruadh, Bowfield Road, West Kilbride, Ayrshire.
Tel: West Kilbride (0294) 822182
Also from tackle shops in Largs.

Crosbie Reservoir is a small brown-trout water to the north of West Kilbride, below Caldron Hill (392m), and fishing is strictly fly-only with fly rod and reel. Approach via the B781 West Kilbride–Dalry road, just north of the town, and follow the minor road for a few hundred yards to the north. The road up to the reservoir is then on your right. Fishing on Crosbie is managed by the Largs Angling Club. Best flies to use are size 12–14 dressings of Black Pennell, Blae & Black, Invicta and Butchers.

MIDDLETON RESERVOIR 63/215625

Permission: P. M. Shepherd, Dunruadh, Bowfield Road, West Kilbride, Ayrshire.
Tel: West Kilbride (0294) 822182
Also from tackle shops in Largs.

Fishing is managed by the Largs Angling Club and this reservoir is to the east of the Largs–Loch Thom hill road. The loch is stocked with brown trout. Best flies to use are size 14 dressings of Grouse & Claret, Greenwell's Glory, Black Spider and Invicta.

KILBIRNIE LOCH 63/330549

Permission: Ian Johnstone, 12 Grahamston Avenue, Glengarnock, Ayrshire.
Tel: Kilbirnie (0505) 682154
Facilities for disabled anglers: Contact above

Kilbirnie Loch is stocked every year with brown trout and, recently, also with rainbow trout of between 1lb 8oz and 4lb. The loch fishes best from March until June and there are now two boats available for anglers, as well as bank fishing. The east shoreline is the most productive area and during 1990 two splendid brown trout were taken: 9lb 10oz and 6lb 10oz. Great sport is offered by this improving little fishery.

MUIRHEAD RESERVOIR 63/255570
CAMPHILL RESERVOIR 63/270555

Permission: The Lower Clyde Water Board, 19 Underwood Road, Paisley, Renfrewshire.
Tel: Paisley (041887) 5161

These reservoirs lie to the south of the A760 Largs–Kilbirnie road and are easily accessible. They have been stocked with brown trout and fishing is managed by the Largs Angling Club.

MUNNOCH RESERVOIR 63/252477

Permission: Starks Newsagents, Dockhead Street, Saltcoats, Ayrshire.

Munnoch Reservoir is at the junction of the B781 and B780 and is 450 yards by 230 yards. The reservoir contains brown trout which rise to standard pattern loch flies and fishing is controlled by the Munnoch Angling Club.

KNOCKENDON RESERVOIR 70/243523

Permission: Starks Newsagents, Dockhead Street, Saltcoats, Ayrshire.
J. M. Currie, Sports Goods, 32 High Street, Irvine, Ayrshire.
Tel: Irvine (0294) 786703
Facilities for disabled anglers: Contact above

This reservoir has been stocked with brown and rainbow trout and 1991 was the first season, so anglers are still 'experimenting'. Approach via the

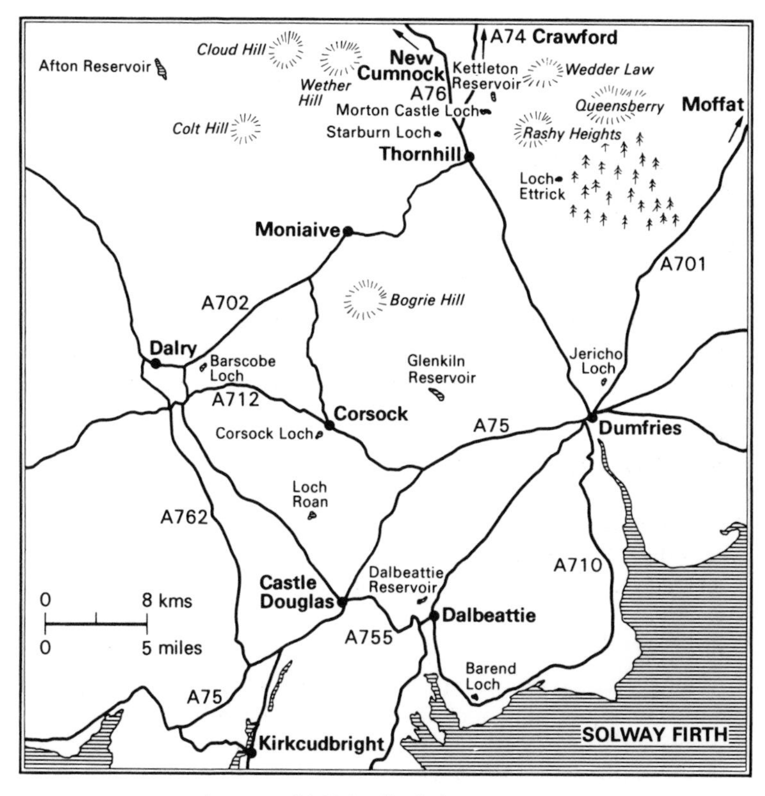

39 Kirkcudbrightshire

same road as for Caff (below) and continue on to Knockendon House. Immediately after the house, there is a track on your right which leads up to the reservoir. Wild, windy country, surrounded by hills and moorlands: Wardlaw, Baidland and Cock Law. Standard pattern loch flies?

CAAF RESERVOIR 70/395272

Permission: Andrew Miller, Dalry Garnock Angling Club, 'Collie-Mor', 59 St Andrews Gardens, Dalry, Ayrshire.
Tel: Dalry (0294) 3308

This is a long, narrow reservoir to the south of the minor road between Glenside on the A78, and to the west of Giffordland on the B789 Ardrossan–Dalry road. Fishing is managed by the Dalry Angling Club and the loch has been stocked with both brown and rainbow trout.

BUSBIE MUIR RESERVOIR 63/242465
MILL GLEN RESERVOIR 63/238448

Permission: James D. Dodds, President, The Kilwinning and Eglinton Angling Club 23 Anderson Terrace, Ardrossan, Ayrshire.
Tel: Ardrossan (0294) 61107

These reservoirs are easily accessible and lie adjacent to the B780 Ardrossan–Dalry road. Fishing is by fly only for stocked brown trout and the trout average 12oz. Standard pattern loch flies tempt them.

PRESTWICK RESERVOIR 70/395272

Permission: Kirk's Sportshop, Ayr, Ayrshire.
Newalls Newsagents, Monkton, Ayrshire.
Wheatsheaf Inn, Monkton, Ayrshire.
C. Hendrie, Prestwick Angling Club, 12 Glenpark Avenue, Prestwick, Ayrshire.
Tel: Prestwick (0292) 70203

Prestwick Reservoir is a 12-acre fishery which lies 3 miles east of Prestwick Airport. The loch is well managed and properly policed, and is considered to be the best trout water in Ayrshire. The club stocks every month with 11- to 12-inch rainbow trout and their average weight is around 1lb 4oz. The season is from 15 March until 15 November and there is a bag limit of six fish per rod per day. Fish of 4lb and 6lb fish have been caught recently.

SNIPE LOCH 70/385174

Permission: From members of the Drongan Youth Group Angling Club, and at the loch.

An excellent 4½-acre stocked fishery close to the B742 Coylton–Dalrymple road by Cloncaird. Rainbow trout are stocked on a weekly basis, with fish averaging 1lb, and there are trout of up to 10lb. Standard pattern loch flies fool them – sometimes.

COLLENNAN RESERVOIR 70/350332

Permission: VG Store, Deveron Road, Brassie, Troon, Ayrshire.
Tel: Troon (0292 312975

This small reservoir lies to the east of the A78, between Loans and the B746 Brassie turn-off. Collennan is stocked each year with fingerling brown trout and weekly, throughout the season, with 120 rainbow trout of between 1lb 8oz and 2lb. Fishing is from the bank only and there is a bag limit of four fish per rod per day. Trout of over 4lb are taken frequently and the heaviest trout caught in recent years (1989) was a rainbow which weighed 6lb 14oz. The south-east shore is the most productive fishing area. Traditional fly patterns do well, but dark flies seem to produce the best results. Try Black Pennell, Black & Peacock Spider, Connemara Black and sedge imitations. There is excellent natural feeding in the loch so the trout are highly selective about what they grab, but an average basket should be two or three fish. Club members go to considerable lengths to protect and preserve their fishing and the loch is under continual surveillance including patrols using two-way radios. This is a delightful, well-managed water and a great asset to the area.

32 Morton Castle Loch

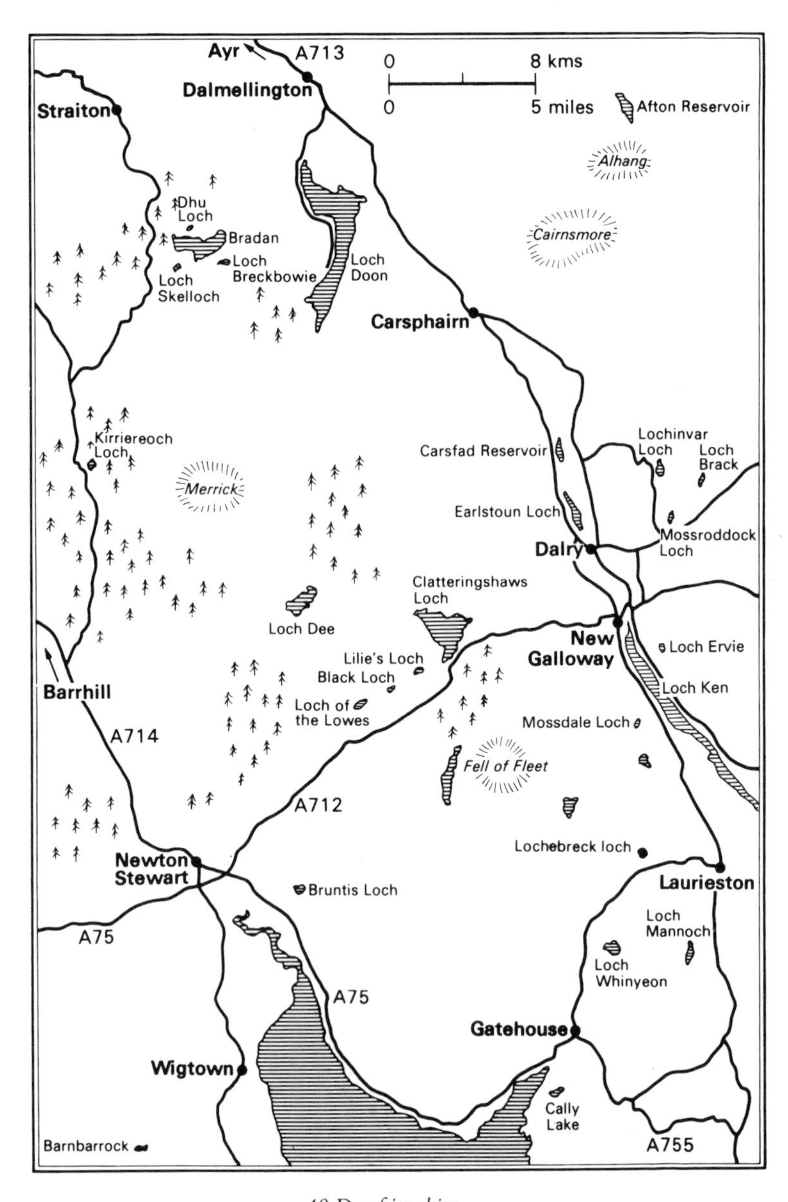

40 Dumfries-shire

MORTON CASTLE LOCH 78/890993

Permission: Buccleuch Estates Limited, Estate Office, Drumlanrig Mains, Thornhill, Dumfries and Galloway.
Tel. and Fax: Marrburn (08486) 283

This small loch covers an area of 8 acres and lies to the north of Thornhill. The loch is dominated by the ruins of Morton Castle, which stands on a hill overlooking the water. There is one boat on the loch and bank fishing is not allowed, so you have the loch to yourself for the day – apart from time to time when the estate gives permission to local Scouts to camp there. The loch has been stocked with brown trout and rainbow trout and their average weight is 1lb. There is a bag limit of four fish per rod per day, for up to a maximum of three rods. The estate can also provide first-class accommodation in self-catering cottages and lodges. Morton Castle Loch is one of the most scenic and lovely little waters in the south-west and really deserves your close attention. Book well in advance.

STARBURN LOCH 78/851980

Permission: Buccleuch Estates Limited,, Estate Office, Drumlanrig Mains, Thornhill, Dumfries and Galloway.
Tel. and Fax: Marrburn (08486) 283

Starburn is a small, sheltered loch covering an area of 4 acres. It lies to the north of Thornhill and the season is from 1 April until 11 August. The loch is in an attractive, mixed-woodland setting and has beautiful water-lilies growing round the edge. Starburn is stocked with both brown and rainbow trout and their average weight is 1lb. Fishing is from the boat only and there is a bag limit of four fish per rod per day for up to a maximum of three rods. Starburn Loch fishes best during the early months of the season and standard pattern loch flies will do fine. A perfect place to fish and the estate can also provide excellent accommodation.

AFTON RESERVOIR 77/635040

Permission: Stanley Stores, Unit 9, Glaisnock Shopping Centre, Cummnock, Ayrshire.
Tel: Cummnock (0290) 22467
And from committee members of the New Cummnock Anglers' Association.

Fishing on Afton Reservoir is managed by the New Cummnock Anglers' Association and the reservoir is approached via Afton Road in Afton Bridgend on the A76. This is very lovely countryside and the quality of the scenery is matched by the quality of the fishing. The water contains both brown and brook trout and an average basket from Afton should amount to five to seven fish – although baskets of 10–15 trout are common – and the average weight of fish is 8–12oz. The reservoir is stocked at least once every 18 months with about 1000 trout. Both boat and bank fishing are available, and the most productive fishing area is at the top end of the loch where Montraw Burn and Afton Water enter. Two further feeder burns come in on the south-west shore and this is also a good fishing area. Afton is almost completely surrounded by forest, with Carsphairn (797m) and the scar of Gairy Cairnsmor to the south and Cairshairn Forest covering the slopes to the west. A beautiful loch offering good sport.

LOCH ETTRICK 78/897005

Permission: Gilchristland Estate, Closeburn, Thornhill, Dumfries and Galloway.
Tel: Thornhill (0848) 30827
W. Stitt, Gilchristland Cottages, Closeburn, Thornhill, Dumfries and Galloway.
Tel: Thornhill (0848) 31364
Closeburn Post Office.
Tel: Thornhill (0848)31230

Loch Ettrick, which covers 19 acres, is situated in attractive country adjacent to the Forest of Ae. It is readily accessible from the C6 which runs along its southern edge. It is approached from the A76 (signpost to Loch Ettrick and Ae) on the east. The loch is regularly stocked with good-quality rainbow trout and there are some indigenous brown trout. The average weight of fish is approximately 1lb and some fish of over 3lb are taken. Good baskets are regularly caught, a maximum of four fish per rod being permitted, and returns are monitored throughout the season. Two boats are available and standard pattern loch flies should be offered.

KETTLETON RESERVOIR 78/897005

Permission: I. R. Milligan, 37 Drumlanrig Street, Thornhill, Dumfries and Galloway.
Tel: Thornhill (0848) 30555

This small reservoir lies to the north of Thornhill between Parr Hill (423m) to the east and Nether Hill (393m) to the west. Bank fishing only and small flies do best. Kettleton is a well-managed fishery and is regularly stocked with rainbow trout of up to 6lb throughout the season. The average weight of fish is about 1lb and the heaviest fish taken recently weighed 7lb 8oz. The reservoir can be very windy, but it is beautifully situated amidst the Lowther Hills.

LOCH DOON 77/490990

Permission: Not required

This is the largest and deepest loch in the area and is 7½ miles long by 1¾ miles wide. The Ayrshire Angling Association manages the fishing and holds its annual competition on the loch. This is usually won with a basket of eight to ten fish weighing 3–4lb. Fish of over 1lb are very rare, although occasionally monsters of up to 17lb are taken, and the loch also contains Arctic char, pike and perch. This is a hydro-electric water and wading calls for great care owing to the unstable nature of parts of the margins. Best areas to fish include Starr Bay in the north-east, Graple Burn – the outfall for Loch Finlas – on the west shore, and where the Carrick Lane enters the loch south of Graples. Another good area is at the south end of the loch round Loch Head Burn. Best flies to use include Black Pennell, Teal & Yellow and Butchers. In spite of being numerous, the trout are not all that ready to give themselves up, but Loch Doon is a pleasant place to fish, popular with local anglers and visitors alike.

DRUMLAMFORD LOCH 76/280775
LOCH MABERRY 76/286750
LOCH DORNAL 76/290760
LOCH GOWER 76/289771
LOCH NAHINIE 76/278771

Permission: A. McKeand, Head Keeper, The Kennels, Barrhill, Girvan, Ayrshire.
Tel: Barhill (046582) 256

Drumlamford is a small, tree-fringed loch to the south of Barrhill and offers excellent sport in lovely surroundings. It is stocked each season with up to 3000 brown trout and there are also brook trout and rainbow trout. The average weight of fish is 1lb 3oz and there is a bag limit of six fish per rod. Fishing is best from the boat and trout rise and are caught all over the loch. Best cast is Blae & Black, Wickham's Fancy and Silver Butcher. Trout of over 2lb are not uncommon and the loch fishes best early in the season. The estate also has fishing available on several other lochs, which contain wild brown trout averaging 8–12oz. Drumlamford is the most popular loch in the area and is easily accessible. Book in advance.

PENWHAPPLE RESERVOIR 76/260970

Permission: Reservoir Superintendent, Penwhapple Reservoir, Girvan, Ayrshire.
Telephone bookings are not accepted.

Penwhapple Reservoir is ¾ mile long by 500 yards wide and lies 5 miles south of Girvan on the B734. The water is stocked each year with up to 1000 11-inch brown trout. During the past 10 years Penwhapple has produced an average of 1200 fish each season, with an average weight of 12oz. Trout of over 2lb are also caught. Bank fishing only for visitors. Catches of 10–15 trout are common but the average basket is usually about four to five fish. Flies to try include Greenwell's Glory, Grouse & Claret, Black Pennell, Wickham's Fancy, Blae & Black and Butchers. Best months are April, May and June. This is a well-managed fishery in pleasant surroundings and worth a visit.

LOCH BRADAN 77/425970

Permission: Forestry Commission, Ayrshire Forest District, Forest Office, Dalmellington Road, Straiton, Maybole, Ayrshire.
Tel: Straiton (06557) 637
R. Heaney, Taliminnoch, Straiton, Maybole, Ayrshire.
Tel: Straiton (06557) 617
Facilities for disabled anglers: Contact above

Loch Bradan is the largest of the lochs to the west of Loch Doon and lies to the south of Straiton on the road to Newton Stewart. Five boats are available for anglers, and buoyancy aids (waistcoat type) are included at no charge, but outboard motors are not allowed. The reservoir is stocked at intervals of approximately 4–6 weeks and the average weight of trout is 8–12oz, with fish of up to 3lb being taken occasionally. There are much larger trout and the heaviest fish caught during 1991 was a brown trout of 5lb. Take care when wading, especially to the east of the dam, where underwater tree stumps can present difficulties. The headland round Craig Dhu is a good area for bank fishing, although fish are caught from the shore round most of the loch. Flies to use include Black Pennell, Peter Ross, Grouse & Claret and Butchers. A weekly ticket is available which also includes fishing on nearby Loch Skelloch.

LOCH SKELLOCH 77/4110962

Permission: Forestry Commission, Ayrshire Forest District, Forest Office, Dalmellington Road, Straiton, Maybole, Ayrshire.
Tel: Straiton (06557) 637
R. Heaney, Taliminnoch, Straiton, Maybole, Ayrshire.
Tel: Straiton (06557) 617

Loch Skelloch lies to the south of Loch Bradan and is approached via a track from Sinclair Bridge on the Straiton–Newton Stewart road. The Water of Girvan passes through Loch Skelloch on it way down the Shalloch of Minnoch from tiny Loch Girvan Eye. One boat is available for anglers and the loch contains hard-fighting brown trout which average 8–12oz. A delightful little loch, in very attractive surroundings. Outboard motors are not allowed. Standard loch fly patterns do well.

THE DUH LOCH 77/422986

Permission: Forestry Commission, Ayrshire Forest District, Forest Office, Dalmellington Road, Straiton, Maybole, Ayrshire.
Tel: Straiton (06557) 637
R. Heaney, Taliminnoch, Straiton, Maybole, Ayrshire.
Tel: Straiton (06557) 617

This lovely small loch is in the forest to the north of Loch Bradan and near to Craig Duh (415m) and is a 200-yard walk from the car park. It is stocked twice each year with brown trout averaging 12oz–1lb. Bank fishing only and small flies work best, particularly olives and sedges, in size 14–16 dressings. The Duh Loch is a 'special' place and very attractive.

LOCH BRECKBOWIE 77/433960

Permission: Forestry Commission, Ayrshire Forest District, Forest Office, Dalmellington Road, Straiton, Maybole, Ayrshire.
Tel: Straiton (06557) 637
R. Heaney, Taliminnoch, Straiton, Maybole, Ayrshire.
Tel: Straiton (06557) 617

Loch Breckbowie lies to the south of Loch Bradan, in the Carrick Forest. The track out to the loch has been marked for the first mile over the moor and there is one boat available for anglers. Bank fishing is also allowed. Breckbowie can be windy but shelter can generally be found round the shore and this is a pleasant loch to fish. Trout average 12oz and the flies to use to tempt them are Black Pennell, Grouse & Claret and Peter Ross.

LOCH DEE 77/470790

Permission: Clatteringshaw Forest Wildlife Centre, New Galloway, Castle Douglas, Kirkcudbrightshire.
Tel: New Galloway (06442) 285
Forestry Commission, Caldons Camp Site, Bragrennan, Newton Stewart, Wigtownshire.
Tel: Bragrennan (067184) 218

Forestry Commission, Creebridge, Newton Stewart, Wigtownshire.
Tel: Newton Stewart (0671) 2420
Forestry Commission, Castle Douglas Forest District, 21 King Street, Castle Douglas, Kirkcudbrightshire.
Tel: Castle Douglas (0556) 3626
Forestry Commission, Talnotry Caravan Park, Newton Stewart, Wigtownshire.
Tel: Newton Stewart (0671) 2170

Loch Dee is remote, yet easily accessible and lies amidst the Galloway Hills surrounded by boulder-strewn granite crags. This is a delightful place to fish and the loch is stocked each year with trout reared from native Loch Dee stock. Their average weight is 1lb 3oz. Access is from Clatteringshaws Loch and visitors will be given detailed directions when obtaining permits. All fishing is from the bank and the most productive areas are the peninsula and around the south-west shore. Several trout of over 3lb are caught each year and the flies that do most damage include Blae & Black, Greenwell's Glory and Wickham's Fancy. A typical basket would be 2 trout weighing 2lb 14oz. However, be prepared: fish of up to 6lb have been caught in Loch Dee.

LILIE'S LOCH 77/517747

Permission: Clatteringshaw Forest Wildlife Centre, New Galloway, Castle Douglas, Kirkcudbrightshire.
Tel: New Galloway (06442) 285
Forestry Commission, Caldons Camp Site, Bragrennan, Newton Stewart, Wigtownshire.
Tel: Bragrennan (067184) 218
Forestry Commission, Creebridge, Newton Stewart, Wigtownshire.
Tel: Newton Stewart (0671) 2420
Forestry Commission, Castle Douglas Forest District, 21 King Street, Castle Douglas, Kirkcudbrightshire.
Tel: Castle Douglas (0556) 3626
Forestry Commission, Talnotry Caravan Park, Newton Stewart, Wigtownshire.
Tel: Newton Stewart (0671) 2170

Lilie's Loch is a small forest loch to the north of the A712 between Clatteringshaws Loch and Murray's Monument. It lies on the line of the Pulran Burn close to the old Edinburgh road. Approach through the forest along a good track – an easy and very pleasant walk. The loch has been stocked and contains brown trout with an average weight of 8–12oz. Bank fishing only and small flies, Blae & Black and Black Spider do best.

LOCH OF THE LOWES 77/469705

Permission: Clatteringshaw Forest Wildlife Centre, New Galloway, Castle Douglas, Kirkcudbrightshire.
Tel: New Galloway (06442) 285
Forestry Commission, Caldons Camp Site, Bragrennan, Newton Stewart, Wigtownshire.
Tel: Bragrennan (067184) 218
Forestry Commission, Creebridge, Newton Stewart, Wigtownshire.
Tel: Newton Stewart (0671) 2420
Forestry Commission, Castle Douglas Forest District, 21 King Street, Castle Douglas, Kirkcudbrightshire.
Tel: Castle Douglas (0556) 3626
Forestry Commission, Talnotry Caravan Park, Newton Stewart, Wigtownshire.
Tel: Newton Stewart (0671) 2170
Facilities for disabled anglers: As above

Loch of the Lowes is 1 mile to the south of the Black Loch (below) and a walk of 500 yards from the car park on the A712, a small forest loch full of good 8-oz trout. There is a limit of five fish per rod and the loch is stocked each year by the Forestry Commission. Fishing is from the bank only and the south bank is the most productive area. The term 'free-rising' really does apply to the trout in these small forest lochs and they are a perfect place to take a newcomer to fly fishing.

THE BLACK LOCH 77/497728

Permission: Clatteringshaw Forest Wildlife Centre, New Galloway, Castle Douglas, Kirkcudbrightshire.
Tel: New Galloway (06442) 285
Forestry Commission, Caldons Camp Site, Bragrennan, Newton Stewart, Wigtownshire.
Tel: Bragrennan (067184) 218
Forestry Commission, Creebridge, Newton Stewart, Wigtownshire.
Tel: Newton Stewart (0671) 2420
Forestry Commission, Castle Douglas Forest District, 21 King Street, Castle Douglas, Kirkcudbrightshire.
Tel: Castle Douglas (0556) 3626
Forestry Commission, Talnotry Caravan Park, Newton Stewart, Wigtownshire.
Tel: Newton Stewart (0671) 2170

This is a delightful forest loch close to the A712 road south of Clatteringshaws Loch. It has been stocked with brown trout and their average weight is 8oz. Fishing is from the bank only and is best from the north bank. Small black flies do best and the trout rise well, with good baskets regularly taken. The permit also includes fishing on Loch Dee, Loch of the Lowes and Lilie's Loch.

BRUNTIS LOCH 83/447654

Permission: R. Marr, 1 St Couan's Place, Newton Stewart, Wigtownshire.
Tel: Newton Stewart (0671) 2193
And from gun and tackle shops in Newton Stewart.

Bruntis Loch lies close to Newton Stewart and is beautifully situated amidst tree-covered Auchannoch Hill. Two miles east of town on the A75, turn left at Craig Hall on to a rough forestry road. The car may be parked at the top of the hill and from this point it is a ½-mile stroll through the forest to the loch.

The loch does not have natural spawning so the Newton Stewart Angling Club, which manages the water, introduce rainbow trout and brown trout twice each year. The average weight of fish is 12oz and there is a bag limit of four fish per rod per day. Fishing is from the bank only and the loch covers 10 acres. The occasional trout of up to 2lb is caught. Pleasant fishing in attractive surroundings.

KIRRIEREOCH LOCH 777/365866

Permission: R. Marr, 1 St Couan's Place, Newton Stewart, Wigtownshire.
Tel: Newton Stewart (0671) 2193

This loch lies between Rowantree Toll and Glentrool village and is approached either from Straiton in the north or from the A714 Newton Stewart–Girvan road to the south at Bargrennan. Fishing is from the bank only and there is a limit of four fish per rod per day. The loch is stocked twice yearly with brown trout and their average weight is 12oz, although several fish of up to 2lb are taken every season. The treeless west bank is the preferred fishing area but trout can be caught all round the loch. Make sure that you have a Mallard & Claret and a Teal & Black in your fly box before you go because these two patterns do very well on this loch. Kirriereoch fishes best in August and September, particularly in the evening – the midges like it, too – and you may expect two to four fish. The trout are of excellent quality, well marked and Loch Leven yellow.

LOCH OCHILTREE 76/315745

Permission: R. Marr, 1 St Couan's Place, Newton Stewart,

Wigtownshire.
Tel: Newton Stewart (0671) 2193

Ochiltree is 6 miles to the north of Newton Stewart between the A714 and B7027. The loch is 3/4 mile long by 1/2 mile wide and fishing is managed by the Newton Stewart Angling Club. The loch is stocked twice each year and contains brown trout. There is a bag limit of four fish per rod per day and both boat and bank fishing are available. Bank fishing is best during the early months of the season but after June the best baskets are taken from the boat. The average weight of trout is 1lb and you may expect to catch two fish. Trout of 5lb have been taken from the loch and fish of 3lb are not uncommon. Can be very windy. Standard pattern loch flies work well.

LOCH OF FYNTALLOCH 76/314740

Permission: R. Marr, 1 St Couan's Place, Newton Stewart, Wigtownshire.
Tel: Newton Stewart (0671) 2193

Fyntalloch lies to the south of Ochiltree and is also managed by the Newton Stewart Angling Club. This loch has both brown and rainbow trout and the club stock it twice yearly. The north end of the loch is the most productive fishing area, and down the west shore, particularly south from the headland. Use standard pattern loch flies.

WEE GLENAMOUR 83/431664

Permission: R. Marr, 1 St Couan's Place, Newton Stewart, Wigtownshire.
Tel: Newton Stewart (0671) 2193

This is a small roadside lochan, close to the A712 Newton Stewart–New Galloway road, stocked twice each year with rainbow and brown trout which average 12oz. Use standard pattern loch flies.

MOSSRODDOCK LOCH 77/632815

Permission: Milton Park Hotel, Dalry, Castle Douglas, Kirkcudbrightshire.
Tel: Dalry (Kirk) (06443) 286

This loch is controlled by the Milton Park Hotel and guests have priority. It is stocked with brown and rainbow trout and lies to the north of the A702 just outside the town. It is easily accessible from the road and visitors should inquire at the hotel for permits.

LOCH BRACK 77/615830

Permission: Milton Park Hotel, Dalry, Castle Douglas, Kirkcudbrightshire.
Tel: Dalry (Kirk) (06443) 286

This is a small loch in the Corriedoo Forest below Tarqhuain Hill. It is 3 miles to the east of the town and may be approached by the A702 via Drummanister. Hotel guests have priority and visitors should inquire at the hotel for further details. The loch is regularly stocked and contains both brown and rainbow trout. The average weight is over 12oz and baskets of five fish are common. Trout of up to 2lb are taken and the best flies to try are standard patterns, Cow Dung and Bluebottle Fly. Best place to fish is down the east bank, though trout rise all over the loch. There are also Arctic char in Loch Brack.

EARLSTOUN LOCH 77/615830

Permission: The Clachan Inn, St John's Town of Dalry, Glenkens, Dumfries and Galloway.
Tel: Dalry (Kirk) (06443) 241

Earlstoun Loch lies adjacent to the A713 north of Dalry. Fishing is managed by the Dalry Angling Association and the loch is stocked each year. Boat fishing only. The loch contains brown trout averaging 8–12oz. Best flies to use are Blae & Black, Grouse & Claret, Greenwell's Glory and Coch-y-Bondhu, and the area to concentrate on is the far side from the road. Earlstoun is one of the 'headponds' in the Loch Doon Water System and is easily accessible.

CARSFAD RESERVOIR 77/607860

Permission: The Clachan Inn, St John's Town of Dalry, Glenkens, Dumfries and Galloway.
Tel: Dalry (Kirk) (06443) 241

Carsfad is the second of the 'headponds' for the Galloway power scheme and fishing is managed by the Dalry Angling Association who regularly stock the loch. The water lies adjacent to the A713 and fishing is allowed only from the west bank. No boats. Trout average 8–10oz and you may hope for a basket of three or four fish.

LOCHINVAR LOCH 77/658854

Permission: Lochinvar Hotel, Dalry, Castle Douglas, Kirkcudbrightshire.
Tel: Dalry (Kirk) (06443) 210
Kenmure Arms Hotel, New Galloway, Castle Douglas,

Kirkcudbrightshire.
Tel: New Galloway (06442) 240
Ken Bridge Hotel, New Galloway, Castle Douglas, Kirkcudbrightshire.
Tel: New Galloway (06442) 211

This is a really delightful loch to the north-east of Dalry and may be approached from the A702 Dalry–Thornhill road. The loch is stocked with both brown and rainbow trout. Boats are available for visitors, and bank fishing is also allowed. The average weight of fish is 12oz and good baskets of trout are frequently taken. The best fishing area is at the north end of the loch and also round Donald's Isle in the south. Lochinvar, with its dramatic ruined castle, is famous for its association with Sir Walter Scott's poem. Standard pattern loch flies work well.

BARSCOBE LOCH 77/670812
Permission: Milton Park Hotel, Dalry, Castle Douglas, Kirkcudbrightshire.
Tel: Dalry (Kirk) 06443) 286

Barscobe Loch is 3 miles east of Dalry and covers 13 acres. It is in a very lovely setting amidst the Galloway Hills and is one of the best lochs in the south-west. The loch is on the estate of Sir Hugh Wontner of Barscobe and the estate is strict about casual access, litter and picnickers.. Barscobe is stocked with brown trout, rainbow trout and brook trout and their average weight is 1lb, although several trout of over 2lb are taken each season. Best fish recently included a rainbow trout of 5lb 12oz and a brown trout which weighed 4lb 8oz. Standard loch pattern flies will produce results and fishing is best from the boat. Some bank fishing may be available. An excellent loch in delightful surroundings and well worth visiting.

CLATTERINGSHAWS LOCH 77/540770
Permission: Clatteringshaws Forest Wildlife Centre, New Galloway, Castle Douglas, Kirkcudbrightshire.
Tel: New Galloway (06442) 285

Clatteringshaws was formed in the 1930s as part of the Loch Doon hydro-electric scheme and is a large, windy water, adjacent to the A712. This is a popular fishing venue, stocked with brown trout and also containing pike and perch. The trout average 8–10oz, with the odd much larger fish taken from time to time. Standard pattern loch flies should produce results. Black flies and Cinnamon & Gold do particularly well.

JERICHO LOCH 78/990810

Permission: M. N. Gordon Pattie & Sons, Queensberry Street, Dumfries.
Tel: Dumfries (0387) 2891
Baird & Stevenson, Locharbriggs, Dumfries.
Tel: Amisfield (0387) 710237
R. M. Currie, Glenclova Caravan Park, Amisfield, Dumfries.
Tel: Dumfries (0387) 710447

Jericho Loch was established as a fishery in 1981 and has gained a reputation for producing excellent trout of good quality. It lies 3 miles to the north of Dumfries on the A701 Moffat road. The loch covers 10 acres and is stocked with brown trout, rainbow trout and brook trout. There is a bag limit of four fish per rod per day and the average weight is just under 2lb. Fish of over 5lb are not uncommon and this is a popular fishing venue, so book in advance. Use standard pattern loch flies.

LOCH MANNOCH 83/665605

Permission: G. M. Thomson & Co., 27 King Street, Castle Douglas, Kirkcudbrightshire.
Tel: Castle Douglas (0556) 2701/2973

This loch is 3 miles north of Twynholm, 27 miles west of Dumfries on the A75. It is part of the Lairdmannoch Estate, a small sporting estate, easily accessible and yet lying amidst beautiful and unspoiled scenery, completely secluded. The loch is long and narrow, being over 1 mile in length, and covers 72 acres. It is absolutely full of small, hard-fighting wild fish which average 9oz, and a trout of over 1lb would be a monster for this water. Nevertheless, they are great fun to catch and rise readily to all the usual standard patterns of loch flies.

LOCH KEN 84/720670

Permission: Kenmure Arms Hotel, New Galloway, Castle Douglas, Kirkcudbrightshire.
Tel: New Galloway (06442) 240
Boats may also be hired from the Loch Ken Holiday Centre.

Loch Ken is part of the Loch Doon hydro-electric scheme and is a long, straggling water, nearly 9 miles in length by up to 1¼ miles wide. Ken is famous for the size of pike it can produce, including one fish caught in 1771 and reputed to have weighed 72lb. It used to be a notable salmon and sea-trout fishery, but, perhaps as a result of the effects of forestry and increasing acidification, the fishery declined to an alarming extent. In recent years, however, an enormous effort has been made to restore the condition of the loch and there is encouraging evidence that fishing on

Loch Ken is improving rapidly. The New Galloway Anglers' Association fishes the loch and some now consider it to be the best loch in the area, sustaining good runs of sea trout and producing brown trout of up to 11lb. The most productive trout fishing area is at the New Galloway end of the loch. Seek advice from the Kenmure Arms Hotel and investigate the loch for yourself.

MOSSDALE LOCH 77/657710

Permission: Cross Keys Hotel, New Galloway, Kirkcudbrightshire.
Tel: New Galloway (06442) 494

Follow the A762 south from New Galloway with Loch Ken on your left and the Cairn Edward Forest on your right. As the forest ends, to the right of the road lies Mossdale Loch. Fishing is from boats only and the loch holds some good brown trout. Standard pattern loch flies get them out – sometimes.

DALBEATTIE RESERVOIR 84/806615

Permission: M. McCowan & Son, 43 High Street, Dalbeattie, Kirkcudbrightshire.
Tel: Dalbeattie (0556) 610270
For further details contact G. W. Garroch, Hon. Sec., Dalbeattie Angling Association, 15 Church Crescent, Dalbeattie DG5 4BAT.
Tel: Dalbeattie (0556) 611373

This reservoir covers 10 acres and is 2 miles to the west of town on the A745 Castle Douglas road. The reservoir has a reputation for being dour and baskets of two or three trout would be considered good. Nevertheless, it is a popular place to fish and in an attractive setting. It contains both brown and rainbow trout and two boats are available, as well as bank fishing. Trout average about 12oz–1lb and the heaviest fish taken during 1991 was a brown trout which weighed 2lb 9oz. Flies to use are Black Pennell, Greenwell's Glory, Grouse & Claret and Peter Ross. Dalbeattie Reservoir fishes best during the early months of the season.

LOCH ROAN 84/744693

Permission: Tommy's Sports Shop, 178 King Street, Castle Douglas, Kirkcudbrightshire.
Tel: Castle Douglas (0556) 2851
Facilities for disabled anglers: Contact above

Loch Roan lies 3 miles to the north of Castle Douglas on the A713 via

Crossmichael and Wallbutt. There are four boats, but bank fishing is not allowed. Roan is stocked with brown and rainbow trout and their average weight is 1lb. There is a limit of eight fish per boat per day and an average day should account for four to six fish. Trout of over 4lb are sometimes taken and all the usual standard pattern loch flies work well. This is a popular loch so book well in advance.

GLENKILN RESERVOIR 84/845780

Permission: Applications for permits should be made to Director of Water and Sewerage, Dumfries and Galloway Regional Council, Marchmount House, Marchmount, Dumfries DG1 1PW.
Tel: Dumfries (0387) 60756

Glenkiln Reservoir lies north of the A75 Dumfries–Castle Douglas road and is approached via Shawhead. Boats are available and bank fishing is allowed, and is free of charge to OAPs resident in the area. Strictly fly fishing only, for stocked rainbow and brown trout which, although dour, are worth catching. Average weight is about 8–10oz and fish of up to 2lb and over are not infrequently taken. The largest trout caught recently weighed 7lb 2oz.

LOCH WHINYEON 83/624608

Permission: M. Brown, Newsagent, High Street, Gatehouse of Fleet, Kirkcudbrightshire.
Tel: Gatehouse (05574) 814222
Other details from E. J. Farrer, Hon. Sec., Kirkcudbright and Gatehouse Angling Association, 32 Boreland Road, Kirkcudbright.
Tel: Kirkcudbright (0557) 30303

Loch Whinyeon is to the north of Gatehouse of Fleet and covers 104 acres. There is a 1-mile walk along a forestry track to get to the loch and visitors should approach from Laghead on the Gatehouse of Fleet–Laurieston minor road. The most productive areas are the small bays in the north-west and south-east corners. The loch is stocked with brown trout, to augment the wild population, and there is one boat available for visitors. Bank fishing is also allowed. The average weight is about 10–12oz, with the odd fish of up to 2lb. Size 12–14 flies do best and all the standard patterns bring results. This is a good loch, very pleasantly situated, and is recommended.

LOCHENBRECK LOCH 83/645655

Permission: M. and E. Brown, 52 High Street, Gatehouse of Fleet,

Kirkcudbrightshire.
Tel: Gatehouse (05574) 222

This is a lovely loch to the west of the minor road from Laurieston to Gatehouse of Fleet. It is a sheltered water, surrounded by forest, with Kenick Hill to the east and Slogarie Clack and Laughenghie Hills to the west and north. This is a well-established fishery, managed by the Kirkcudbright and Gatehouse Angling Association and regularly stocked with both brown and rainbow trout. Their average weight is 12oz and a reasonable day should produce a basket of up to six trout. The largest fish caught recently was a rainbow weighing 8lb 4oz, and the largest brown trout weighed 3lb 10oz. The loch covers 70 acres and the most productive areas are in the bays at the south-east and south-west corners. Small flies work best, particularly Blae & Black, Black Spider and Black Pennell. There is a road to within 200 yards of the loch.

BAREND LOCH 84/880550

Permission: Barend Properties, Sandyhills, Dalbeattie, Kirkcudbrightshire.
Tel: Southwick (038778) 663

This is a small loch of 6 acres and it forms part of a holiday village. The loch is stocked with 500–700 rainbow trout each year and the average weight of fish is 12oz. The best fish to come from the loch weighed 4lb. Fishing is from the bank and there is a bag limit of three fish per rod per day.

SOULSEAT LOCH 82/100590

Permission: J. S. Nimmo, Secretary, Inchparks Schoolhouse, Stranraer, Wigtownshire.
Tel: Stranraer (0776) 44568

This is the most popular loch in the area and it is managed by the Stranraer and District Angling Association. Approach via the A75 Stranraer–Glenluce road. Two boats are available and bank fishing is also allowed. The loch covers 72 acres and holds both brown and rainbow trout. The average weight is 1lb–1lb 8oz and fish of over 5lb have been caught. An easily accessible loch offering excellent sport.

PENWHIRN RESERVOIR 82/125697

Permission: J. S. Nimmo, Secretary, Inchparks Schoolhouse, Stranraer, Wigtownshire.
Tel: Stranraer (0776) 44568

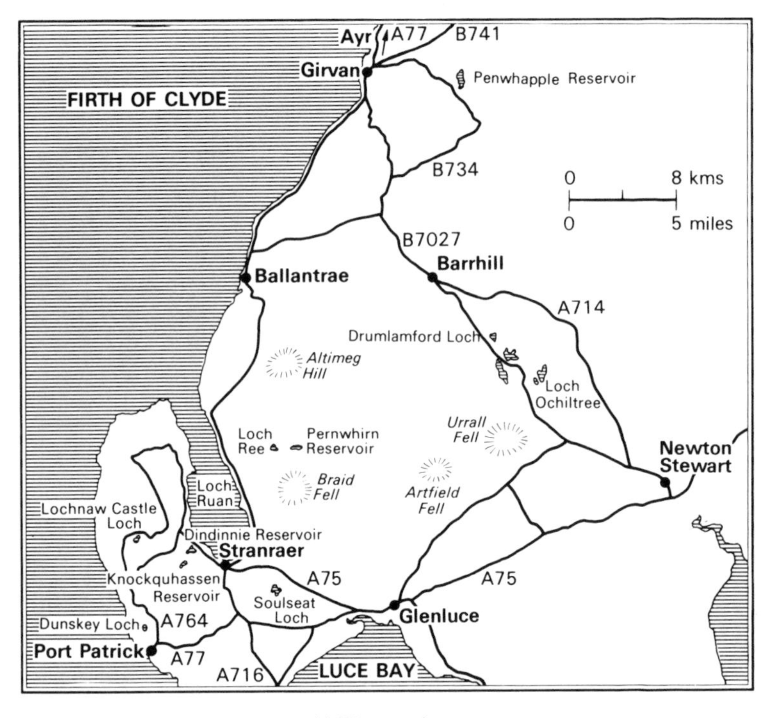

41 Wigtownshire

Penwhirn lies to the north of Stranraer and is at the end of the New Luce road. The loch covers some 150 acres and fishing is from the bank only. The fish are wild brown trout and they rise well to standard pattern loch flies. The north shore fishes best and the loch is in a most attractive setting.

LOCH REE 82/104699

Permission: J. S. Nimmo, Secretary, Inchparks Schoolhouse, Stranraer, Wigtownshire.
Tel: Stranraer (0776) 44568

Loch Ree is a small loch to the west of Penwhirn Reservoir (above) and is approached via the New Luce road. A track follows the south shore of Penwhirn to Awies Farm at the end of the reservoir and Loch Ree is a walk of about 1 mile from this point. Bank fishing only, for hard-fighting, 8–10-oz trout. Remote and beautiful and well worth a visit. Standard pattern loch flies work well.

DINDINNIE RESERVOIR 82/022607

Permission: J. S. Nimmo, Secretary, Inchparks Schoolhouse, Stranraer, Wigtownshire.
Tel: Stranraer (0776) 44568

Fishing on Dindinnie is managed by the Stranraer and District Angling Association and the loch has been stocked with brown trout which average 1lb. Best flies are Black Spider, Black Pennell, Greenwell's Glory and Butchers. Bank fishing only. The south end of the loch, where the feeder burn enters, is a good fishing area although fish are caught from all round the shore. Approach via the Stranraer–Kirkcolm A718 road and turn right at Auchneel. Leave the car at Dindinnie Farm.

KNOCKQUHASSEN RESERVOIR 82/020595

Permission: J. S. Nimmo, Secretary, Inchparks Schoolhouse, Stranraer, Wigtownshire.
Tel: Stranraer (0776) 44568

This reservoir is to the south of Stranraer and is full of little bays and interesting points. The west end fishes best, especially near the small island. Although the trout are not monsters, they give a good account of themselves and fight well. Follow the old Portpatrick road from Stranraer and at the top of Auchtralure Hill turn right to Greenfield Farm. Standard pattern loch flies work well. A windy place to fish, but a very pleasant water.

LOCHNAW CASTLE 82/993630

Permission: Lochnaw Castle Hotel, Leswalt, by Stranraer, Wigtownshire.
Tel: Leswalt (077687) 227

Lochnaw is a small loch of 46 acres within the grounds of Lochnaw Castle Hotel. Guests have priority. Follow the A718–B798 road to Leswalt and then turn left. The hotel is 2 miles further along the B7043. The loch has been stocked with Loch Leven trout and their average weight is 12oz, with the occasional fish of up to 3lb. Use standard pattern loch flies, but always fish with a Black Spider on the cast. Boat fishing only and guests may choose to fish all day or either morning or evening sessions. The most favoured fishing area is round the small island. This is a very lovely loch to fish and the castle stands at the edge of the loch amidst acres of rhododendron bushes and mature beech woods. The estate also has a number of comfortably furnished self-catering cottages, making this the ideal location for a super family and fishing holiday.

33 Tense moments

DUNSKEY LOCH 82/006565

Permission: The Keeper, Dunskey Kennels, Portpatrick, Wigtownshire.
Tel: Portpatrick (077681) 364 or 211

Two small lochs in the grounds of Dunskey Estate, 2 miles from Portpatrick on the A764. Both are sheltered by trees and are stocked with brown trout. The average weight is 1lb but much larger fish of up to 5lb have been caught. Fishing is fly only from boats and there is a bag limit of two fish per rod. Day tickets are available. Special arrangements can be made for visitors staying in the estate's self-catering cottages.

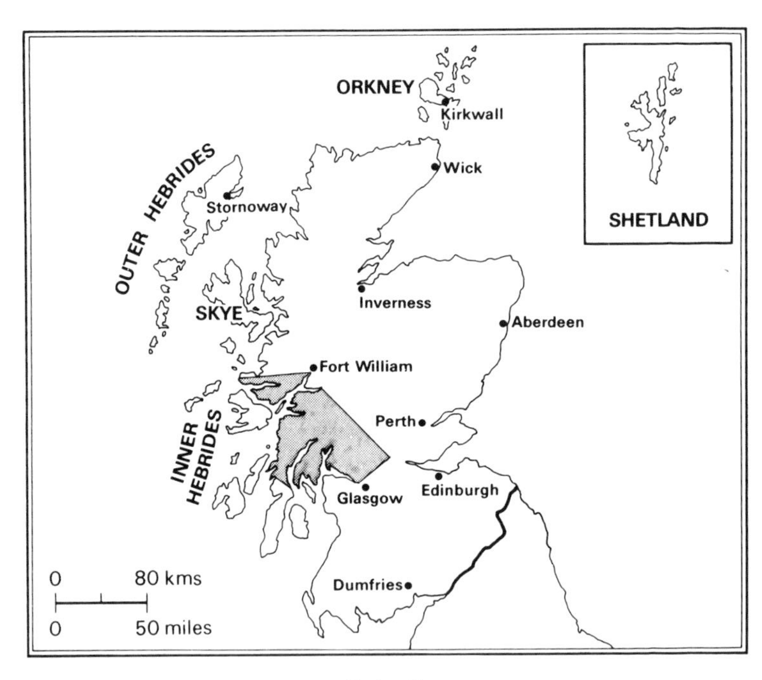
ORKNEY
Kirkwall
SHETLAND
OUTER HEBRIDES
Stornoway
Wick
Inverness
Aberdeen
SKYE
Fort William
INNER HEBRIDES
Perth
Glasgow
Edinburgh
Dumfries
0
80 kms
0
50 miles

42 Argyll

10 Argyll

Loch Awe is the fishing centre of Argyll and one of the most popular lochs in Scotland. It produces good numbers of salmon and very big brown trout, and escaped rainbow trout from local fish farms seem to have established themselves in Loch Awe. In the hills around Awe are dozens of small lochs all containing good trout, and to the north lie the waters controlled by the Oban and Lorn Angling Club. During the winter, when we are comfortably installed before a warm fire, somewhere out in the hills club members will be quietly carrying on the important tasks of stocking and maintaining their waters. They, and so many others like them, deserve our highest praise and support. Their hard work provides us all with pleasure and preserves the quality of sport for the benefit of anglers everywhere. Argyll has a lot to offer the visiting angler, from vast Loch Awe to the intimate beauty of small waters such as the Hospital Lochan by Glencoe. Time spent fishing is seldom wasted, time spent fishing in Argyll is even nicer. Tight lines!

THE HOSPITAL LOCHAN 41/105597

Permission: Mrs S. Mortimer, Sorrybreac Guesthouse, Glencoe.
Tel: Ballachulish (085582) 354
Facilities for disabled anglers: Contact above

The Hospital Lochan lies behind the hospital in the village of Glencoe, with the Pap of Glencoe to the east and Loch Leven to the north. It is a popular place, not only with anglers, but also with photographers, and the lochan regularly appears on calendars and in glossy magazine features. Approach through Glencoe village and the hospital grounds. This is a really delightful loch in a perfect woodland setting, easily accessible and great fun to fish. It is surrounded by trees and bushes, with several small islands, and is sheltered and peaceful. The lochan is stocked and the trout average 12oz, with good baskets being taken, especially during June. Boat fishing, with standard pattern loch flies – and dry fly when it is calm, as it often is on the secluded little loch.

GLEN DUBH RESERVOIR 49/940378

Permission: J. Lyon, Appin View, Barcaldine, Argyll.
Tel: Ledaig (063172) 469

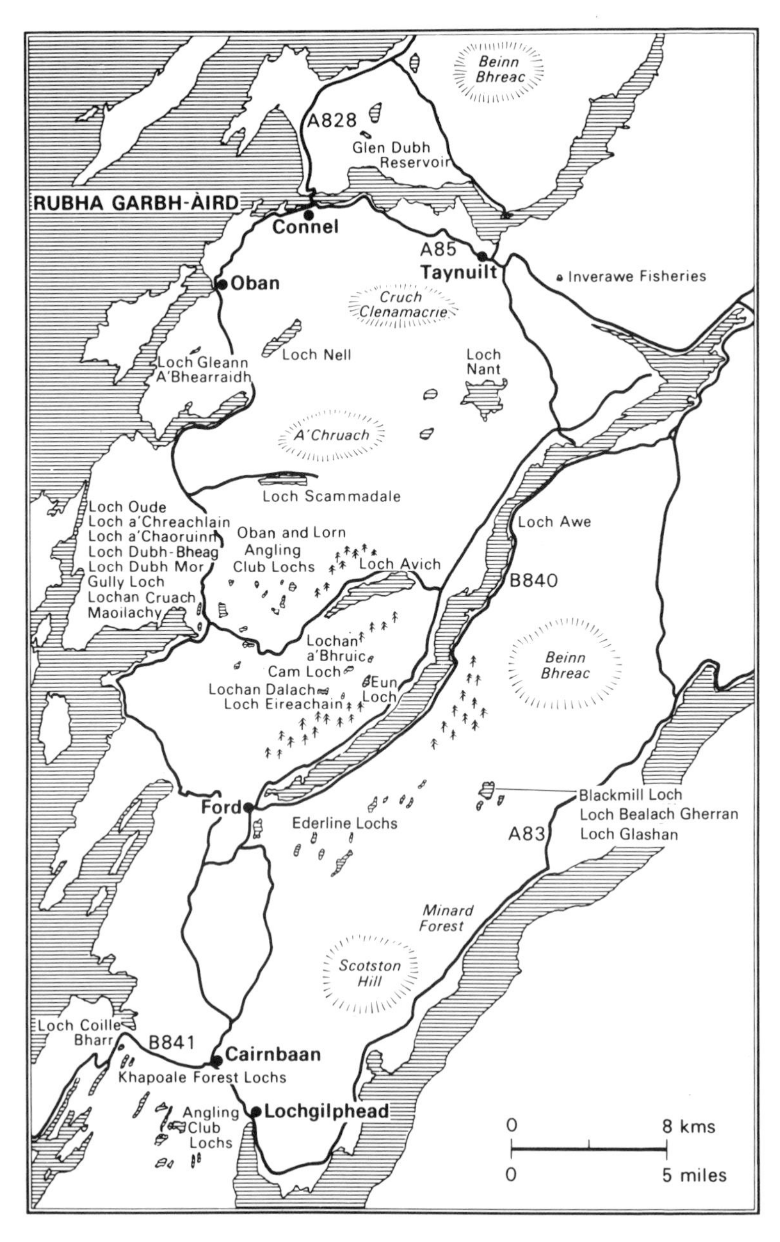

43 Oban and Loch Awe

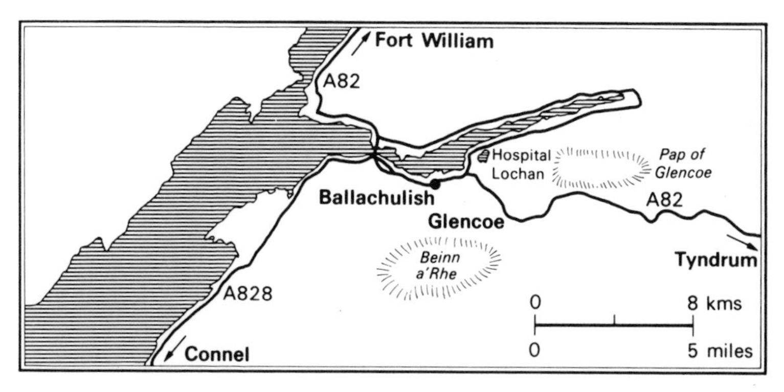

44 Ben Nevis

This small loch lies within the Barcaldine Forest to the north of Connel and there is bank fishing only. Trout average 12oz and the best flies include all the standard patterns. The Forestry Commission stocks Glen Dubh at regular intervals and selective felling of trees has made the fishing more accessible.

LOCH NELL 49/890273

Permission: David Graham, 9-15 Crombie Street, Oban, Argyll.
Tel: Oban (0631) 2069

This is the largest loch in the vicinity of Oban and covers 150 acres. Fishing is available through the excellent Oban and Lorn Angling Club and one boat is reserved for visitors. The day is divided into two sessions: 9.00am–6.00pm and 6.00pm until dusk. The loch drains to the sea by the River Nell and holds salmon, sea trout, brown trout and Arctic char. Salmon average 7–8lb, sea trout 1lb and brown trout 8–10oz. But Loch Nell can produce some very pleasant surprises: a sea trout of 10lb 4oz has been caught (on a size 12 Kingfisher Butcher). The club guide reports that: 'Salmon only reach the loch in significant numbers about the third week of June and fishing continues to improve until the end of September. Large sea trout will be present all season. Arctic char, usually caught accidentally in August, when they come into the shallow water to spawn, are of a better size than the brown trout.'

LOCH A'PHEARSAIN 55/855137

Permission: David Graham, 9-15 Crombie Street, Oban, Argyll.
Tel: Oban (0631) 2069

Loch a'Phearsain is ½ mile long by over 400 yards wide and lies to the east of the A816 near Kilmelford. This shallow loch is in a natural basin, surrounded by hills to the north-east. The loch has been stocked by the angling club and trout average about 8–10oz. All fish under 10 inches must be returned, and the occasional trout of 1lb 8oz–2lb 8oz is sometimes caught. The best fishing areas are in the north-east corner where the feeder burn enters, and in the vicinity of the small island in the southern bay. A'Phearsain also contains Arctic char which average 1lb. Standard pattern loch flies produce results.

OUDIE RESERVOIR 55/850160

Permission: David Graham, 9-15 Crombie Street, Oban, Argyll.
Tel: Oban (0631) 2069

Oudie Reservoir is to the south of Oban, adjacent to the A816. It is easily accessible but in a very pleasant situation with forestry plantations covering the crags and corries of Cnoc nan Larachcloiche (265m) to the west. Fishing is managed by the Oban and Lorn Angling Club and the reservoir is stocked with rainbow trout. The present club policy is to cull all brown trout, in an attempt to improve the average weight of fish. A club boat is sometimes available, otherwise it is bank fishing only, which can be difficult owing to fluctuations in the water level. Brown trout of up to 1lb are not uncommon and trout of over 3lb are also taken – using standard pattern loch flies.

LOCH A'CHAORUINN 55/884137
LOCH DUBH-BHEAG 55/890140
LOCH A'CREACHAIN 55/888143
LOCH DUBH MOR 55/892147
THE GULLY LOCH 55/890145
LOCHAN CRUACH MAOILACHY 55/895139

Permission: David Graham, 9-15 Crombie Street, Oban, Argyll.
Tel: Oban (0631) 2069

This delightful series of small lochs and lochans lies to the north-east of Kilmelford and all the waters are managed by the Oban and Lorn Angling Club. They are linked by small streams and are in a beautiful and peaceful corner of the Kilmelford Forest. All contain good trout which fight well and average 8oz–1lb. The first in the series, Loch a'Chaoruinn, has the largest fish and trout of over 1lb are often caught. As you walk up the glen, a'Creachain and Dubh-bheag come next and are full of bright 8-oz fish. The Gully Loch and Dubh Mor hold fish which average 12oz. The club has a shelter on the east side, between Gull and a'Creachain – it has been known to rain in these parts and the club hut is a very welcome refuge when it does. Standard pattern loch flies work well and this is a lovely area in which to spend a day. Many of these lochs have been stocked over the years by the club and all offer great sport with the chance of a 2-lb trout. All bank fishing, so take care, especially on Loch Dubh-bheag, where there are steep-sided heather banks.

LOCH AN LOSGAINN MOR 55/865120
LOCH AN LOSGAINN BHEAG 55/860127

Permission: David Graham, 9-15 Crombie Street, Oban, Argyll.
Tel: Oban (0631) 2069

The minor road from Kilmelford to Loch Avich is adjacent to the north shore of the loch, making it an easily accessible water. There is a parking place at the west end and fishing is from the bank only. Both lochs have a dour reputation, but Mor holds fish which average 12oz while Beag has some very large trout. Use standard pattern loch flies to try and tempt them.

LOCH A'MHINN 55/865128
LOCH NA CURRAIGH 55/865130

Permission: David Graham, 9-15 Crombie Street, Oban, Argyll.
Tel: Oban (0631) 2069

Fishing is managed by the Oban and Lorn Angling Club and the lochs are stocked with both brown and rainbow trout. The present policy is to cull the brown trout and there is a bag limit of six fish per rod for rainbow trout. Fishing is from the bank only and brown trout average 8oz. The rainbow trout thrive and average 1lb 8oz, with fish of over 3lb frequently taken. Loch na Curraigh is joined to a'Mhinn by a short stream and the same fishing rules apply. Brown trout in a'Mhinn are slightly larger, and rainbow trout average 2lb. Lovely lochs and well worth fishing. Take care, however, when wading in na Curraigh: the south end is very marshy and dangerous.

LOCH NAM BAN 55/872126

Permission: David Graham, 9-15 Crombie Street, Oban, Argyll.
Tel: Oban (0631) 2069

Approach from the Kilmelford–Loch Avich road and walk north from Loch Losgainn Mor. Infrequently fished, and lying in a hollow, where you might just bump into trout of over 2lb. But they are very hard to catch. Use standard pattern loch flies.

LOCH AN DAIMH 55/860111

Permission: David Graham, 9-15 Crombie Street, Oban, Argyll.
Tel: Oban (0631) 2069

This small loch lies to the south of the Kilmelford–Loch Avich road and is managed by the angling club. The loch contains Arctic char and brown trout and the present policy is to cull all brown trout caught in order to improve the overall average weight, which is around 8oz. An ideal loch for beginners, and in a very lovely setting.

LOCH A'CHLACHAIN 55/857116

Permission: David Graham, 9-15 Crombie Street, Oban, Argyll.
Tel: Oban (0631) 2069

This small loch lies to the south-west of Losgainn Mor and is a short walk up the hill. There are good trout here, but they are very hard to catch. An expert's water, but always a challenge and worth a visit.

THE FEINN LOCHS 55/870145

Permission: David Graham, 9-15 Crombie Street, Oban, Argyll.
Tel: Oban (0631) 2069

Reaching these two lochs involves a good walk into the hills and they lie at an altitude of 700 feet on Cruach an Nid. The walk out is well worth while and trout average over 12oz. There is a boat available on Big Feinn but, as on most of the lochs in the area, very good sport can be had from the bank as well. Trout of over 2lb are often taken and the lochs fish best at the beginning of the season, particularly in windy conditions. Try large flies (size 8–10), in the standard patterns, on Big Feinn. Use standard pattern loch flies on Little Feinn.

SOIR LOCHS 49/965230
LOCHAN AIRIGH SHAMHRAIDH 49/954208
LOCH A'BHARRAIN 49/966241

Permission: David Graham, 9-15 Crombie Street, Oban, Argyll.
Tel: Oban (0631) 2069

These remote lochs lie 5 miles out into the hills to the east of the A816 and for the angler who likes walking and wildlife with his fishing, this is the place to head for. Approach from Kilmore, south of Oban, as for Loch Nell, but turn right at the T-junction and continue up the Musdale road for 4 miles where you may park in a quarry. The trout average three to the pound and large baskets are the rule. Use standard pattern lochs flies.

LOCH GLEANN A'BHEARRAIDH 49/846270

Permission: The Barn Bar, Cologin, Leargs, Oban, Argyll.
Tel: Oban (0631) 4501

This is a long, narrow loch 1 mile long by 1/4 mile wide, steep-sided but with a few places where it is possible to bank fish. It lies to the south of Oban and visitors should turn right at the signpost at Leargs, 2 miles from Oban on the A816. There is a good track out to the loch and the walk takes about 30 minutes. The loch contains wild brown trout which average 12oz and the heaviest fish taken during the 1991 season weighed 2lb 8oz. A boat is available. Collect the key for it, and the oars, at the Barn Bar. Use standard pattern loch flies.

LOCH SCAMMADALE 49/890205

Permission: Mary McCorkindale, Glenann, Kilninver, by Oban, Argyll.
Tel: Kilninver (08526) 282

Loch Scammadale lies 9 miles south of Oban and is approached from the A816 by following up the River Euchar in Glenann. The loch is 1 1/2 miles long by 1/3 mile wide and contains salmon, sea trout and brown trout. The loch is over 120 feet deep towards the eastern end and is in a remote and lovely setting. Both boat and bank fishing are available and the most productive fishing area is along the north bank, particularly where the Eas Ruadh burn enters the loch. The average weight of brown trout is 1lb, but success depends very much on weather and water levels. Larger fish are also taken, including sea trout, which average 2lb. Use standard pattern loch flies.

LOCH AWE Sheets 50-55

Permission: David Murray, The Ford Hotel, Argyll.
Tel: Ford (054681) 273
Mrs Mary Ann Stewart, Forest Cabins, Loch Avich, Dalavich, by Taynuilt, Argyll.
Tel: Lochavich (08664) 221
Facilities for disabled anglers: Contact above
Boat hire from W. Flemming.
Tel: Lochavich (08664) 230

Loch Awe is the longest loch in Scotland and would require a book of its own to do it full justice. The loch is nearly 26 miles in length by 3/4 mile wide, and very popular with anglers and country lovers, who make fullest use of the loch's vast area. Sailing, windsurfing and other water activities are enthusiastically pursued, and during the summer visitors crowd the banks. Nevertheless, in spite of all this activity, it is generally possible to find a quiet corner somewhere and Loch Awe is a very beautiful place to spend some time. In recent years it has been at the centre of heated controversy regarding an application for a Protection Order, made by riparian owners, to the Secretary of State for Scotland. Without such a Protection Order, which I hope will shortly be granted, the future for Loch Awe as one of Scotland's most outstanding fisheries is very bleak indeed. Hundreds of 'anglers' descend upon the loch regularly, and use any and every method to catch as many fish as possible. These fishmongers have to be restrained, for the benefit of future generations of true anglers, and a Protection Order is the only sensible way of ensuring the future of this wonderful water. The loch contains salmon, sea trout, brown trout, rainbow trout, Arctic char, pike and, no doubt, one or two other things, lurking within its 300-foot depths.

Loch Awe fishes best from the boat and trout are caught all over the loch, particularly in the shallows, close to the margins. Fish average 8–10oz, but very much larger specimens are taken, usually by trolling: 1866, 39lb 8oz; 1973, 15lb 3oz; 1980, 19lb 8oz – and rainbow trout of over 10lb. Before fishing, obtain a copy of Loch Awe Improvement Association's angling guidelines from John Brown, Secretary, LAIA, Hayfield, Kilchrenan, Loch Awe, Argyll PA35 1HE.

INVERAWE FISHERIES 50/024316

Permission: Inverawe Fisheries, Inverawe Barn, Taynuilt, Argyll.
Tel: Taynuilt (08662) 262

There are three trout ponds here, managed as a commercial fishery, and stocked with rainbow trout. Their average weight is 1lb 8oz and fishing is from the bank only. An average day should produce up to five trout and this fishery has a reputation for producing very big fish indeed, with trout of up to 12lb being sometimes caught. Best flies to use here are Dunkeld, Black Pennell and reservoir lures. Easily accessible and set in pleasant surroundings, Inverawe offers good sport and good-quality trout. Open from April until October.

LOCH NANT 50/008240

Permission: Kilchrenan Trading Post, Kilchrenan, by Taynuilt, Argyll.
Tel: Kilchrenan (08663) 232

Loch Nant is 1½ miles long by 1 mile wide and may be approached from the north of Kilchrenan. Access to the loch is on foot only – cars are not allowed – so be prepared for a bit of a hike. There is a locked gate by the roadside and a good track leads out from here to the loch, which lies due west. Trout average 12oz and an average day should produce a basket of three or four fish. The shoreline of Loch Nant wanders round dozens of bays and points and the largest of these is in the north-east corner. This is the best fishing area, where the burn enters from the Soir Lochs. Standard pattern loch flies are fine.

CAM LOCH 55/905095
EUN LOCH 55/917091
LOCHAN DALACH 55/916103
LOCHAN A'BHRUIC 55/920105
LOCH EIREACHAIN 55/927095

Permission: David Murray, The Ford Hotel, Ford, Argyll.
Tel: Ford (054581) 273
The Sports Shop, 31 Lochnell Street, Lochgilphead.
Tel: Lochgilphead (0546) 2390

These small forest lochs all lie to the north of Loch Awe (above) and fishing is from the bank only – or at least used to be. Apart from Cam Loch, all the others seem to have disappeared within the commercial forestry plantations now surrounding them and David Murray tells me that they are almost impossible to find, there being no tracks. This is very sad and perhaps the Forestry Commission should investigate the matter and restore access as soon as possible.

LOCH AVICH 55/935145

Permission: Loch Awe Forest District Office, Whitegates, Lochgilphead, Argyll.
Tel: Lochgilphead (0546) 2518
Permits and boat hire from: W. Flemming.
Tel: Lochavich (08664) 230
Mrs M A Stewart, No. 31 Dalavich.
Tel: Lochavich (08664) 211
Norman Clark.
Tel: Lochavich (08664) 209
Facilities for disabled anglers: Contact above

Loch Avich lies to the west of Loch Awe, into which it drains. At the eastern end, near the island, the loch drops to nearly 200 feet deep. Trout rise and are caught from all round the shore line, but boat fishing generally brings the best results. Avich is some 3½ miles long by ½ mile wide, and can be a very windy loch. It is stocked with both brown trout and rainbow trout and fish average 12oz. Baskets of up to 20 fish are not uncommon and all the standard patterns of loch flies produce results. During 1991 a brown trout of 4lb was caught, and several fish of over 2lb were taken.

THE EDERLINE LOCHS 55/785905

Permission: The Ederline Estate Office, Ford, Argyll.
Tel: Ford (054681) 215

The Ederline Lochs are managed by the Ederline Estate and lie to the south of Ford village. There are over 30 lochs on the estate, some stocked and all containing good trout. The nearest of the hill lochs involves a walk of about 3 miles but excellent baskets are taken of 8–10-oz wild brown trout. Catches of 20–30 fish are unremarkable and from time to time a fish of 2–3lb is landed. But the real joy of these lochs is the beauty of the surroundings and their remote setting. This is a wild area, where the angler can lose himself and his worries at least for a while, and the Ederline Estate waters are highly recommended. Some of the lochs have boats but most are fished from the bank and all the usual flies produce results. For peace and quiet – and a good walk – contact Ford 215.

LOCH COILLE BHARR 55/785905

Permission: Mr and Mrs MacVicar, Gartnagrenach, Achnamara, Lochgilphead, Argyll.
Tel: Lochgilphead (0546) 85210

This is a Forestry Commission loch, controlled by the Lochgilphead and District Angling Club. It lies 7 miles to the west of Lochgilphead via the B841–B8025 road to Tayvallich. The loch is just under 1¼ miles long by 200 yards wide and there are two boats available for visitors. Bank fishing is not allowed. Standard loch fly patterns work well and the loch fishes best in a good south-west wind. Although fish are caught over most of the loch, the small bay, just before the south end, is a favourite area. Drift by, about 15 yards out, and as you pass the small headland dividing the bay from the end of the loch, look out for fireworks. The average weight here has dropped in recent years and is now 12oz.

LOCH BARNLUASGAN 55/793913

Permission: Mr and Mrs MacVicar, Gartnagrenach, Achnamara, Lochgilphead, Argyll.
Tel: Lochgilphead (0546) 85210

This is a Forestry Commission loch, controlled by the Lochgilphead and District Angling Club. It lies adjacent to the B841 to the west of Lochgilphead. Fishing is from the boat only, of which one is available for visitors. No bank fishing. Trout average 8–10oz and fight well. An average basket should account for up to six fish and all the standard loch fly patterns do well.

LOCH LINNHE 55/798910

Permission: Mr and Mrs MacVicar, Gartnagrenach, Achnamara, Lochgilphead, Argyll.
Tel: Lochgilphead (0546) 85210

A Forestry Commission loch, as above, and a short walk from the main road. Linnhe is about 800 yards long by 300 yards wide. Boat fishing only and no outboard motors, but there is plenty of sport on this attractive loch with trout averaging 12oz. The best drift is down the west shoreline, but you will catch fish all over using standard pattern loch flies. A very pleasant, secluded little loch and well worth a visit.

LOCH LOSGUNN 55/791898
LOCH BUIE (Seafield) 55/789890

Permission: Mr and Mrs MacVicar, Gartnagrenach, Achnamara, Lochgilphead, Argyll.
Tel: Lochgilphead (0546) 85210

As above, and lying within the Knapdale Forest, these two small lochs can be fished on the one permit. Fishing is from the bank only and standard loch fly patterns do fine. Trout average 8–10oz and good baskets are taken. Lovely setting and well worth seeking out.

CAM LOCH 55/824877
LOCH CLACHAIG 55/813870
GLEANN LOCH 55/815880
THE DUBH LOCH 55/810878
LOCH AN FAOILINN 55/815887
LOCH AN ADD 55/805888
LOCH NA BRIC 55/804829

Permission: H. MacArthur, The Sports Shop, 31 Lochnell Street, Lochgilphead, Argyll.
Tel: Lochgilphead (0546) 2390
D. MacDougall, Secretary, Lochgilphead and District Angling Club, 23 High Bank Park, Lochgilphead, Argyll.

All these lochs are managed and controlled by the Lochgilphead and District Angling Club and the club restricts visitor access. Fishing is therefore strictly private but a certain number of day tickets may be available, depending upon circumstances. The lochs are a fair walk from the road and are approached via the B841, 1 mile or so west of Fairnbaan. Loch an Add and Loch na Bric are in the Knapdale Forest, while Loch an Faolinn, the Dubh Loch and narrow Gleann are on the

34 Ready, waiting, and well worth a cast

western edge of the forest. All the lochs contain brown trout and the club restricts visitors to bank fishing only. Use standard pattern loch flies – if you manage to obtain permission.

BLACKMILL LOCH 55/950958

Permission: Loch Awe Forest District, Forest District Office, Whitegates, Lochgilphead, Argyll.
Tel: Lochgilphead (0546) 2518
R. Hardie, No. 1 Nursery Cottages, Minard.
Tel: Minard (05466) 86630

Blackmill Loch offers brown trout fishing from the south bank and there is a boat available for visitors. The loch is surrounded by forest and therefore relatively sheltered during high winds.

LOCH BEALACH GHERRAN 55/949949
LOCH GLASHAN 55/915930

Permission: Loch Awe Forest District, Forest District Office, Whitegates, Lochgilphead, Argyll.
Tel: Lochgilphead (0546) 2518
R. Hardie, No. 1 Nursery Cottages, Minard.
Tel: Minard (05466) 86630

Two small, sheltered forest lochs in the heart of the Minard Forest. Fly-fishing for stocked brown trout which average 8–10oz. A boat is available.

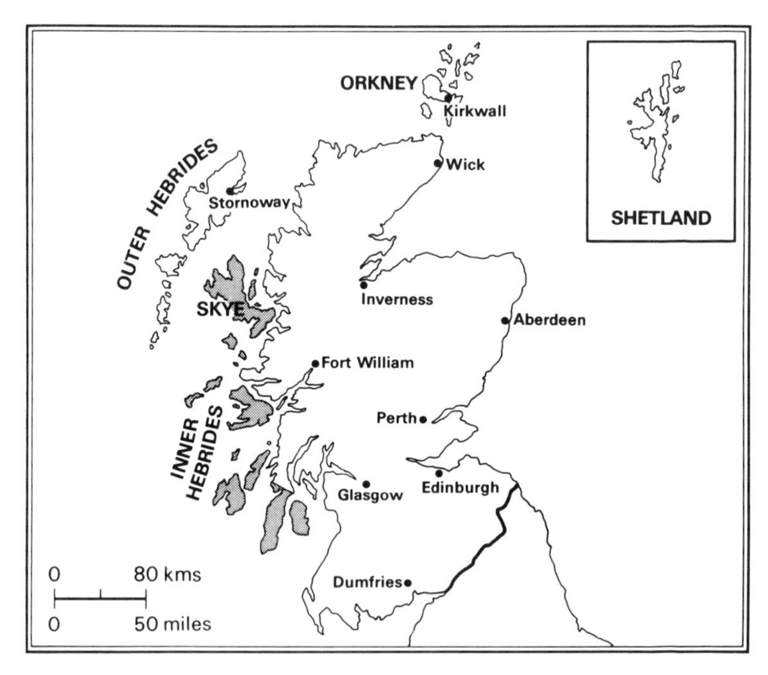

45 Inner Hebrides

11 Inner Hebrides

The Inner Hebrides offer visiting anglers some of the most exciting game fishing in Scotland, amidst some of the country's most dramatic scenery. Skye is a popular and romantic island much visited and soon to be even more so because of the construction of a new bridge which will join the island to mainland Scotland. Most people imagine that the well-loved 'Skye Boat Song', describing Bonnie Prince Charlie's escape, is about a boat trip from the Scottish mainland to Skye. In fact, it is about his flight from the Outer Hebrides, from Benbecula, 'Over the sea to Skye', the other way, west to east. The fugitive Prince had little time to stand and stare, and even less time to fish. Had he been able to do so he would have found dozens of delightful lochs, full of hard-fighting, wild brown trout. All the islands offer good sport, with the possible exception of Arran, which has little to offer the brown trout angler – but super sea-trout fishing. Mull and Islay have really first-class sport and the smaller islands all have a wonderful sense of peace and quiet that is utterly captivating. The islands of the Inner Hebrides will provide you with a perfect fishing and family holiday. There are also many interesting and delightful local malt whiskies to sample – great for dulling the pain of a lost fish, and for brightening the perception of the pleasure of days to come.

ISLE OF SKYE

LOCH CONNAN 23/388430

Permission: Ullinish Lodge Hotel, Struan, Isle of Skye.
Tel: Struan (04742) 214

North of the B885 Struan–Portree road, Connan is a circular loch of about 500 yards across. The hotel has a boat available and guests have priority. Trout average 12oz and catches vary from a few fish to baskets of 20 trout totalling 20lb. Success all depends upon the weather and your skill – or luck. Take standard pattern loch flies along and try, for it is an excellent little loch. Trout of over 2lb are also sometimes caught.

LOCH DUAGRICH 23/400400

Permission: Ullinish Lodge Hotel, Struan, Isle of Skye.
Tel: Struan (04742) 214

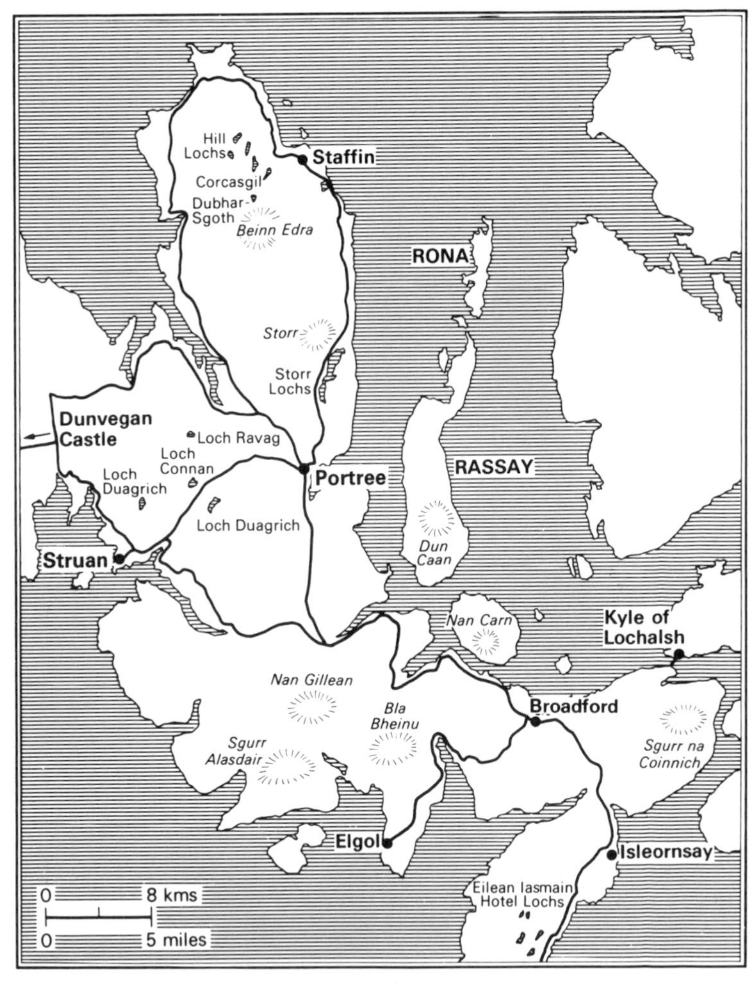

46 Skye

Boat and bank fish. Duagrich is ¾ mile long by 400 yards wide and is approached via a track up Glen Bracadale, in a distance of 2 miles. Trout average 8oz and catches of 20–30 fish are frequent. Standard pattern loch flies work well and this loch is in a most dramatic setting.

LOCH RAVAG 23/380450

Permission: Ullinish Lodge Hotel, Struan, Isle of Skye.
Tel: Struan (04742) 214

Ravag lies to the north of Loch Connan (above) and may be approached via the minor road which runs eastwards from the A863 near Caroy (309429), or from the B885. Weed was a problem but the loch has been improved in recent years. There is a good stock of wild trout in Ravag, waiting for your first, well-presented cast.

LOCH CORCASGIL 23/452643
LOCH DUBHAR-SGOTH 23/456640

Permission: Neil Cameron, Secretary, Portree Angling Association, 'Hillcroft', Treaslane, by Portree, Isle of Skye IV51 9NX.

Loch Corcasgil lies to the south of craggy Quiraing (543m) and is a walk of 2 miles from the Portree–Staffin road. The loch is at the foot of Beinn Edra (611m), and is 400 yards long by 100 yards wide. Trout average 12oz–1lb and there are also *ferox*. Fishing is from the bank and the water is deep near the edge so wading is not really necessary. Trout tend to move close inshore during the evenings, and on good days baskets of 10 fish may be taken. Loch Dubhar-Sgoth is to the south and the trout are smaller but fight just as well, and you can expect a basket of four to six fish averaging 8–10oz. These lochs are not fished very often owing to the long walk involved, but don't be put off: it is worth every step of the way and the scenery is quite superb.

THE STORR LOCHS 23/500505

Permission: Neil Cameron, Secretary, Portree Angling Association, 'Hillcroft', Treaslane, by Portree, Isle of Skye IV51 9NX.
Facilities for disabled anglers: As above

The Storr Lochs are the best trout waters on Skye and lie to the north of Portree, east of the A855. They cover an area 2½ miles long by up to ½ mile wide and are carefully managed by the Portree Angling Association. The Storr (719m) and the Old Man dominate the western horizon and this is one of the most scenic lochs in Scotland. Both boat and bank fishing are available and the average weight of fish is about 1lb 8oz. Neil Cameron caught the largest trout during 1991, a magnificent fish weighing 7lb 1oz. There have also been, during 1991, fish of 7lb, 6lb 7oz, 6lb 5oz and at least six others which weighed over 5lb. The record for the loch is 12lb. Baskets of 10–15 fish are not uncommon and the loch fishes well throughout its whole length. Particularly good fishing areas are round the island and headland at 507520 in the north, the Armishader bays on the east shore, and round the small island at 493491 at the south end. Best flies include Black Pennell, Woodcock & Yellow, Grouse & Claret, Teal & Green, Black

35 Old man country, the Storr Lochs, Skye

Zulu, Blue Zulu and Butchers. Highly recommended. If you only have time to fish one place on Skye, head for the Storr Lochs.

THE HILL LOCHS OF NORTH SKYE

LOCH MEALT 23/505650
LOCH CLEAT 23/447673
LOCHLEUM NA LUIRGINN 23/447676
LOCH CLEAP 23/467663
LOCH FADA 23/458697
LOCH HASCO 23/455701
LOCH LANGAIG 23/462708

Permission: Neil Cameron, Secretary, Portree Angling Association, 'Hillcroft', Treaslane, by Portree, Isle of Skye IV51 9NX.

The Portree Angling Association looks after fourteen North Skye hill lochs and in recent years has begun stocking selected waters with native trout reared by the Association. Some of these lochs, such as Mealt, which also contains excellent Arctic char, are easily accessible, while others, such as Fada, will exercise your legs and lungs mightily. They all offer the visiting angler great sport amidst utterly outstanding scenery which has to be seen to be believed.

DUNTULM LOCH 23/416742

Permission: Neil Cameron, Secretary, Portree Angling Association,

'Hillcroft', Treaslane, by Portree, Isle of Skye IV51 9NX.
Facilities for disabled anglers: As above

This little loch lies near the Duntulm Hotel and has been stocked with excellent trout of up to 2lb. It is easily accessible and ideal for disabled anglers.

LOCH AN IASGAICH 32/673142

Permission: Fearann Eilean Iasmain Hotel, An t-Eilean, Sgitheanach, Skye.
Tel: Isle of Ornsay (04713) 266

This is a small loch in the south of Skye, near to Drumfearn. Leave the Broadford–Isle Ornsay road by the telephone kiosk. The loch is a short walk into the hills and contains brown trout which average 8oz. Bank fishing only and you can expect excellent baskets of hard-fighting little trout. Lovely views of Cullin Hills to the north-east.

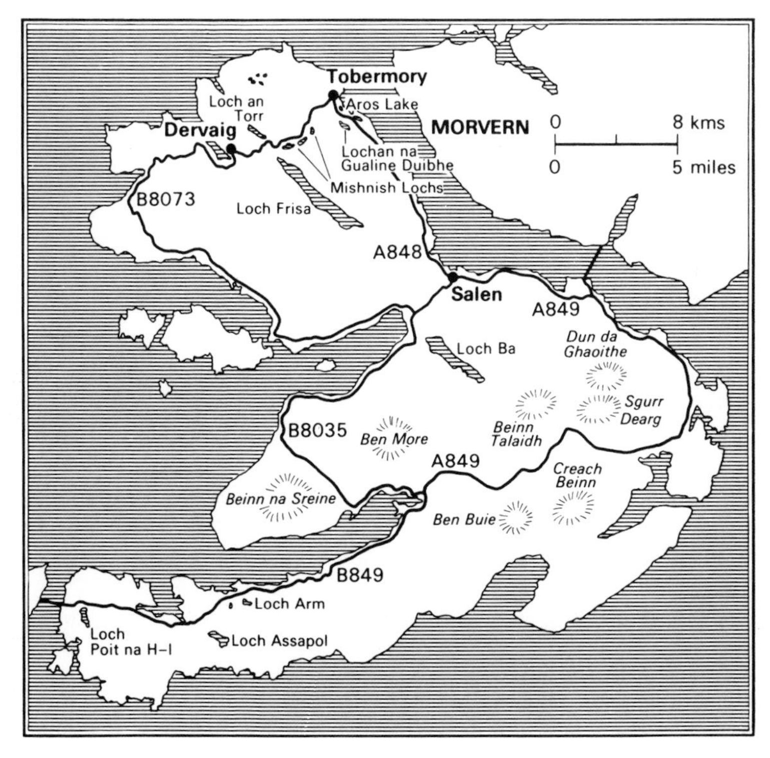

47 Mull

LOCH DUBH 32/676207

Permission: Fearann Eilean Iasmain Hotel, An t-Eilean, Sgitheanach, Skye.
Tel: Isle of Ornsay (04713) 266

There are three small interlinked lochs here to the west of the A581, past the junction to Skulamus. They contain trout which average 8oz and the occasional sea trout. Good baskets of small fish and marvellous scenery. Easily accessible from the road. Use small dark flies and spend an hour or so enjoying yourself.

LOCH BARAVAIG 32/685098

Permission: Fearann Eilean Iasmain Hotel, An t-Eilean, Sgitheanach, Skye.
Tel: Isle of Ornsay (04713) 266

Approach from the A851 by the small roadside loch south of the village. You must ask permission before crossing the farmland to the loch and the walk is an easy 20 minutes. This is the best of the south Skye lochs, with good natural feeding for trout. The fish average 10–12oz and fight hard. Fishing is from the bank only and the loch is occasionally stocked. A really delightful place to fish.

ISLE OF MULL

LOCH POIT NA H-I 48/325230

Permission: James Campbell, Fidden Farm, Fionnphort, Mull.
Tel: Fionnphort (06817) 427

This is a small, triangular loch near Fionnphort and the ferry to Iona. It is shallow and contains brown trout and the occasional sea trout. The average weight of trout is 8oz and baskets of eight to ten fish are taken frequently. However, trout of up to and over 1lb are sometimes taken on Poit na h-I and both boat and bank fishing are available. The best fishing is in the vicinity of the small island, and where the water leaves the loch on its short journey to the sea at An Caolas. Standard loch fly patterns work well.

LOCH ASSAPOL 48/405205

Permission: James McKeand, Scoor House, Bunessan, Mull.
Tel: Fionnphort (06817) 297

Assapol is 1½ miles south-east of Bunessan and is the largest loch on the Ross of Mull. Beautiful, remote and peaceful, Assapol is about ¾ mile long by 500 yards wide and contains salmon, sea trout and brown trout.

Brown trout average 8oz, sea trout up to 2lb and salmon 5lb. Sample catches include 17 sea trout for two rods, during a week's fishing in May, with the best fish weighing 4lb 8oz; and three rods over two weeks in August took 78 sea trout averaging 1lb, with a best fish of 3lb 8oz. The best brown trout in recent years weighed 7lb 8oz, the best sea trout 4lb 8oz and the heaviest salmon 10lb. Brown trout fishing is best in May and then again towards the end of the season, when larger fish are taken. The arrival of sea trout and salmon in Assapol depends entirely upon high tides, to bring them up into the loch; and in recent years, like most other west coast sea-trout fisheries, Assapol has seen a great decline in stocks. But given the right conditions and water levels, good sport may still be had and this is always an exciting loch to fish. Best flies include Peter Ross, Invicta and Greenwell's Glory. James McKeand is a very enthusiastic angler and will show visitors the best places to fish – and the best places for the bucket-and-spade brigade. He also has self-catering and guesthouse facilities available for visitors.

LOCH ARM 48/419217

Permission: James McKeand, Scoor House, Bunessan, Mull.
Tel: Fionnphort (06817) 297

This is a small hill loch to the east of Bunessan and is approached from the A849 by following up the Bun an Leiob. The walk to Loch Arm takes about 40 minutes – depending upon how often you stop to marvel at the panoramic view. The average size of trout here is 8oz and baskets of eight to ten fish may be expected. The best fish caught in recent years weighed 2lb. Use size 14–16 flies – Mallard & Claret, Invicta and Black Pennell to start off with, and enjoy splendid fishing in a splendid setting.

LOCH AN TORR 47/450530

Permission: W. R. Fairbairns, Cuin Lodge, Dervaig, Mull.
Tel: Dervaig (06884) 275

Loch an Torr is on the north side of the B8073 Tobermory–Dervaig road and is easily accessible. The loch is in a pleasant setting with a forest to the west and mountains to the south. Both boat and bank fishing are allowed, but outboard motors are not permitted. Loch an Torr contains brown trout, some rainbow trout and the occasional sea trout. Brown trout of up to 4lb have been caught and sea trout of 5lb. The whole area of the loch fishes well and standard patterns of loch flies will suffice.

THE MISHNISH LOCHS

LOCH CARNAIN AN AMIS 47/470523
LOCH MEADHOIN 47/480526
LOCH PEALLACH 47/485530

Permission: Tobermory Angling Association, c/o A. Brown & Son, 21 Main Street, Tobermory, Mull.
Tel: Tobermory (0688) 2020

The Mishnish Lochs are three interconnected lochs adjacent to the B8073 Tobermory–Dervaig road. They are easily accessible and their differing characteristics make for interesting fishing. Boat and bank fishing are available, but outboard motors are not allowed. The club insists upon there being no more than two anglers per boat, and the minimum age for hiring a boat is 16. The lochs cover an area nearly 2 miles long by 300 yards wide.

Peallach holds the largest fish but it tends to be weedy and a good fish is hard to control. The loch varies in depth between 2 and 10 feet and trout of up to 4lb have been caught there. The best drifts on Meadhoin are round the margins, but they also can be a bit weedy. Loch Amis is the deepest of the three lochs, and produces good baskets of smaller fish.

The Tobermory Angling Association stocks the lochs every two years with 5-inch fish which grow quickly because of the abundant natural food supply in the Mishnish Lochs. A basket of 15 fish weighing 12lb 8oz has been taken and the best flies to use include Soldier Palmer, Silver Butcher, Teal & Green, Peter Ross, Dunkeld, Wickham's Fancy, Ke-He, Black Pennell, Black Zulu and Blue Zulu.

LOCH FRISA 47/480490

Permission: W. R. Fairbairns, Cuin Lodge, Dervaig, Mull.
Tel: Dervaig (06884) 275

This is the largest freshwater loch on Mull and is nearly 5 miles long by ½ mile wide. Frisa is a deep loch which drops to 200 feet near the middle. High winds can make this a dangerous water so do listen to local advice if you are warned to stay off the loch. Otherwise, Frisa is a very beautiful loch and is full of hard-fighting trout of 8-12oz which are of a Loch Leven strain, pink-fleshed and well-shaped. There are occasional sea trout and salmon to be caught as well, depending upon water levels in the outlet burn. Boats are available from the Forestry Commission at Salen and Glenbellart House Hotel. Large baskets are frequently taken and the best flies to use are Dunkeld, Black Zulu, Peter Ross, Soldier Palmer, Mallard & Claret, Connemara Black and Black Pennell. Fish the shallows, close to the edge and remember the warning about the weather.

LOCHAN NA GUALINE DUIBHE 47/527524

Permission: Tobermory Angling Association, c/o A. Brown & Son, 21 Main Street, Tobermory, Mull.
Tel: Tobermory (0688) 2020

This loch lies 3 miles south of Tobermory and is easily accessible from the main road. Bank fishing only, in a pleasant woodland setting. The loch has been stocked by the club and the average weight of trout is about 8oz. It can be dour and average baskets amount to two or three fish. Fishes best during the early months of the season. Use standard loch pattern flies.

AROS LAKE 47/520538

Permission: Tobermory Angling Association, c/o A. Brown & Son, 21 Main Street, Tobermory, Mull.
Tel: Tobermory (0688) 2020

One mile south from Tobermory, Aros contains both brown and rainbow trout. Fishing is from the bank only and since the loch is surrounded by trees, access is limited to clearings from which to cast. There are rearing cages in the loch and some trout escape. The largest rainbow taken weighed 9lb 8oz and each season produces several trout of between 3 and 5lb. An average day should produce five fish weighing about 3lb. Reservoir-type lures seem to be necessary.

ISLE OF ISLAY

LOCH GORM 60/230660

Permission: Brian Wiles, Islay House, Bridgend, Islay.
Tel: Bowmore (049681) 293

Loch Gorm is the largest loch on Islay and both boat and bank fishing are available. Bank fishing is good. If it is too windy to use the boat, as it often is, concentrate on the dozens of little bays. Eilean Nan Uan in the western bay is a particularly good bank-fishing area, as is the vicinity of the feeder burns in the north-east bay. Gorm trout average 1lb and fight hard, and fish of over 2lb are sometimes caught. When using the boat, be cautious, since there are hidden shallows and sudden underwater boulders. Take a supply of spare sheer pins for the outboard, just in case. An excellent loch where standard pattern loch flies will bring results.

ARDNAVE LOCH 60/285728

Permission: Brian Wiles, Islay House, Bridgend, Islay.
Tel: Bowmore (049681) 293

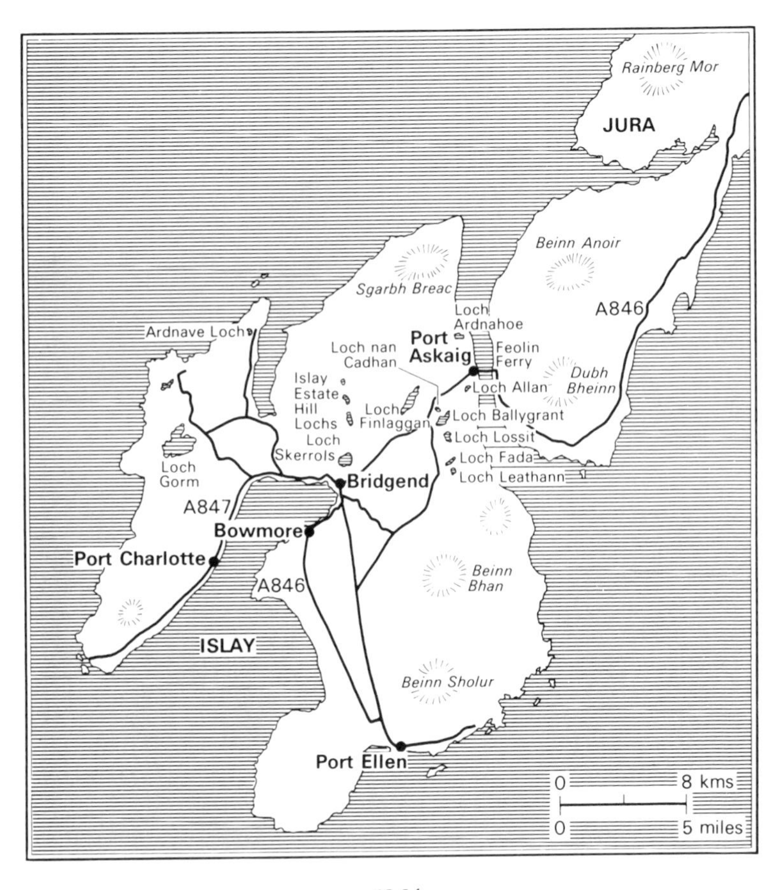

48 Islay

Ardnave is approached from the B8017 from Bridgend and is a small loch where boat and bank fishing are allowed. The trout average 1lb but do not give themselves up easily, and you will have to work hard for your fish. An average basket is two or three fish and expect trout of up to 3lb. Great fighters, which rise to standard loch fly patterns. A lovely, challenging loch to fish.

LOCH SKERROLS 60/340638

Permission: Brian Wiles, Islay House, Bridgend, Islay.
Tel: Bowmore (049681) 293

Loch Skerrols is in a woodland setting to the north of Bridgend. Boats are available but bank fishing is not allowed. This loch provides excellent sport and is very popular, so you are advised to book in advance. The trout average 8oz and baskets of up to 20 fish are often taken. An average day is likely to account for eight to ten fish, with the occasional trout of up to 1lb 8oz. Best fishing area is at the north end of the loch and favourite flies include Black Pennell, Coch-y-Bondhu and Soldier Palmer. Good fishing in attractive surroundings.

LOCH FINLAGGAN 60/385674

Permission: Brian Wiles, Islay House, Bridgend, Islay.
Tel: Bowmore (049681) 293

Finlaggan is a long, narrow loch between Port Askaig and Bridgend and is approached via the road to Finlaggan Farm, from the north end of the loch. There are two boats available and bank fishing is also allowed. A lovely loch, complete with island and ruined castle, the ancient parliament building of Clan Macdonald. The south end of the loch fishes best and trout average 8oz with baskets of 12 fish being taken frequently. Fish of 1lb are sometimes caught and standard loch fly patterns will do. Only one salmon has ever been caught on Finlaggan and it was landed by the famous Scottish comedian Harry Lauder.

LOCH ARDNAHOE 60/420715

Permission: Brian Wiles, Islay House, Bridgend, Islay.
Tel: Bowmore (049681) 293

This is a deep loch to the north of Port Askaig covering an area of 500 yards by 350 yards. Fishing is best in the shallow water close to the shore and both boat and bank fishing will produce good results. The fish average 8–12oz and six trout is normal for a day. There are some heavier fish and trout of 1lb are occasionally taken. Black Pennell, Cinnamon & Gold Blae & Black are good flies to try. Magnificent views over to Jura and a lovely loch to fish.

THE ISLAY ESTATE HILL LOCHS

LOCH SIBHINN 60/326654
LOCH CAM 60/345667
LOCH LEATHAN 60/344680
LOCH A'BHEALAICH AIRD 60/330702
LOCH A'CHUNIE BHRIC 60/324690
LOCH A'CHLAIDHEIMH 60/343691

LOCH LEINIBH

60/344698

Permission: Brian Wiles, Islay House, Bridgend, Islay.
Tel: Bowmore (049681) 293

The Islay Estate has good fishing on a number of hill lochs. Most involve a good tramp to reach but you will be more than rewarded by superb scenery and wildlife along the way. The lochs noted above are some of the most productive, containing good stocks of small trout, with the odd much larger fish sometimes taken. These lochs offer all that is best in hill-loch fishing in an outstanding setting.

LOCH BALLYGRANT

60/405662

Permission: The Port Askaig Shop, Port Askaig, Islay, Argyll.
Tel: Port Askaig (049684) 245

This loch lies close to the Port Askaig–Bridgend road and is in a woodland setting. The main part of the loch is circular and about 500 yards across. A narrow bay extends to the north-east and this can give good sport. Two boats are available, as well as bank fishing, but best results come from the boats. A favourite area to fish is in the vicinity of the island in the north-west corner, and trout average 8–10oz, with the occasional 1-lb fish. Baskets of 15–20 trout are taken, particularly in May and June, which are the best months. Use Black Pennell, Grouse & Claret and Zulus.

LOCH LOSSIT

60/407652

Permission: The Port Askaig Shop, Port Askaig, Islay, Argyll.
Tel: Port Askaig (049684) 245

Both boat and bank fishing are available on this small loch and good results come from either method. May and June are the best months and trout average 8–12oz. The best areas to fish are round the three small islands, and down the eastern shore. Standard loch fly patterns work well.

LOCH NAN CADHAN

60/403668

Permission: The Port Askaig Shop, Port Askaig, Islay, Argyll.
Tel: Port Askaig (049684) 245

This small loch lies to the north of Loch Ballygrant (above) and the trout average 8–12oz. It is easily accessible, adjacent to the Port Askaig–Bridgend road. The finger-like bays at the south end of the loch are the best fishing areas and standard loch fly patterns will do. Good baskets are often taken and you may expect up to 10 fish for your day out.

LOCH FADA 60/410638

Permission: The Port Askaig Shop, Port Askaig, Islay, Argyll.
Tel: Port Askaig (049684) 245

The name Fada means 'long' and this loch lies to the south of Ballygrant and the A846 Port Askaig–Bridgend road. Reaching it requires a 15-minute walk over the moor and the loch is ½ mile long by 100 yards wide. Weed can be a problem, but baskets of eight to ten trout averaging 8–12oz are often taken. Fish are caught all round the loch and the best cast to start with should include Black Pennell, Grouse & Claret and Silver Butcher.

LOCH LEATHANN 60/410634

Permission: The Port Askaig Shop, Port Askaig, Islay, Argyll.
Tel: Port Askaig (049684) 245

Reaching Loch Leathann, 'the broad loch', involves a longish walk over the moor but it is well worth the effort. Approach from the same point as for Fada. Fish average 12oz–1lb, with the odd trout of up to 3lb. Both boat and bank fishing are available and thigh waders would be useful. The loch has a reputation for being dour but Leathann trout are of excellent quality. The best area is the bay in the north-east corner, and standard loch fly patterns should produce results.

LOCH ALLAN 60/425678

Permission: The Port Askaig Shop, Port Askaig, Islay, Argyll.
Tel: Port Askaig (049684) 245

This loch is to the south of Port Askaig and a boat is available for anglers. Bank fishing is allowed, but is not very productive. Trout average 8–12oz and standard loch fly patterns work well. Baskets of up to eight fish may be expected and the best area to fish is where feeder burns enter the loch in the south-west and north-west corners. Easily accessible and an attractive water to fish.

ISLE OF JURA

THE FISHING LOCH 61/882887

Permission: Charles Fletcher, Ardlussa Estate, Isle of Jura, Argyll.
Tel: Jura (049682) 323

Primarily a sea-trout loch, lying at the head of the Lussa River, this is in a wonderful setting, and, given the right water and weather conditions, can give spectacular sport. The estate also offers really first-

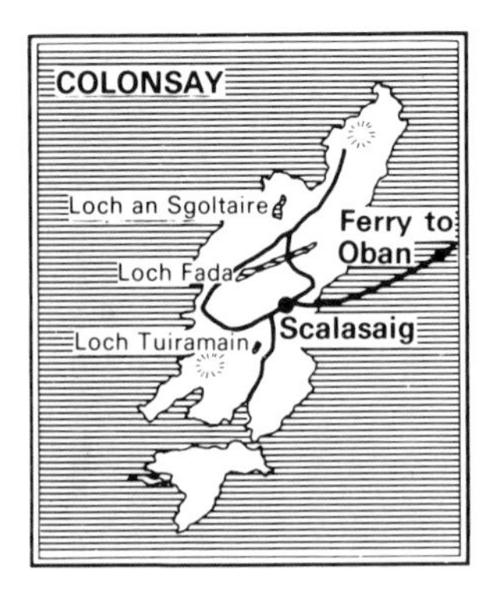

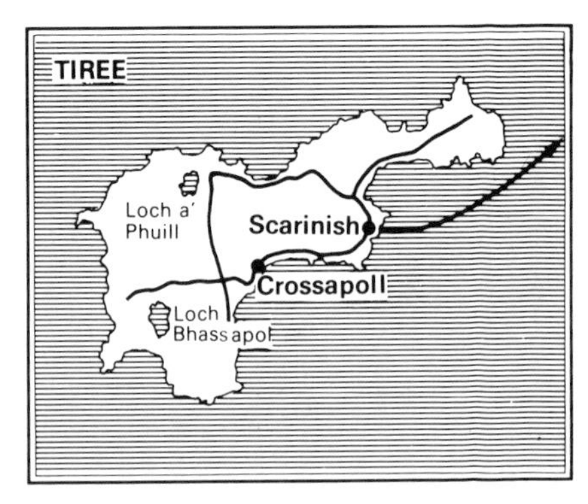

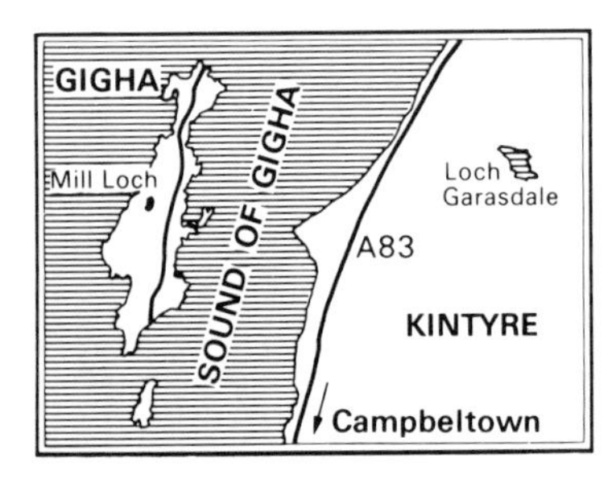

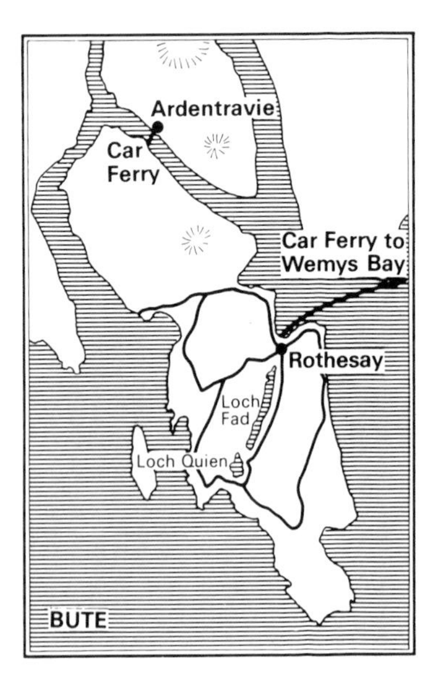

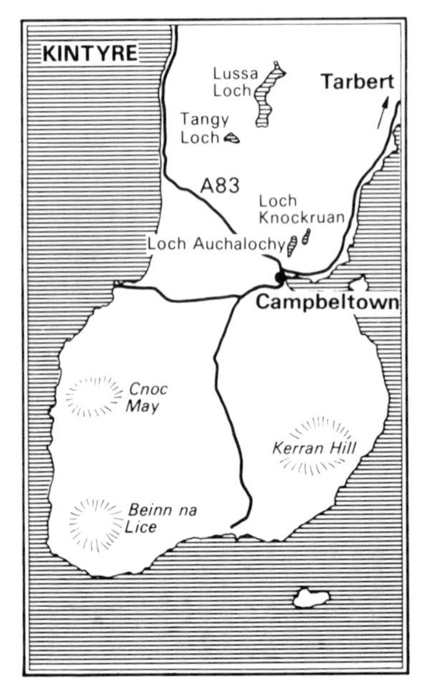

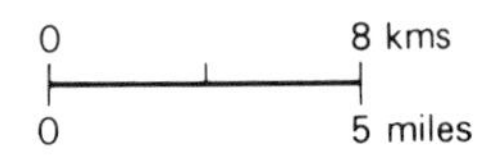

49 Kintyre and Islands

class, self-catering cottages, comfortably furnished and beautifully situated. Ideal for a family fishing holiday.

NORTH JURA HILL LOCHS

LOCH A'GHEOIDH 61/661953
LOCH DOIRE NA H-ACHLAISE 61/655957
LOCH A'BHURRA 61/669960
LOCH NAN EILEAN 61/662967
LOCH NA CONAIRE 61/677969
LOCH NA SGORRA 61/677976

Permission: Charles Fletcher, Ardlussa Estate, Isle of Jura, Argyll.
Tel: Jura (049682) 323

All these loch lie to the north of Ardlussa, to the west of the rough track that ends at Kinuachdrach – where George Orwell wrote his masterpiece 1984. These delightful little lochs are masterpieces in their own right, and all contain stocks of small, hard-fighting wild brown trout. There are few more lovely places to walk and fish, and nan Eilean, in particular, must be one of the most beautiful lochans in all of Scotland.

ISLE OF GIGHA

THE MILL LOCH 62/645505

Permission: Gigha Hotel, Gigha, Argyll.
Tel: Gigha (05835) 254

The Mill Loch on the Island of Gigha, off the west coast of Mull of Kintyre, is a delightful water on a splendid, peaceful island. The loch is stocked every April with rainbow trout which average 1lb–1lb 8oz. Fishing is from the boat only and the growth rate of these trout is excellent. The best fish caught during 1991 weighed 5lb 3oz. The loch is also stocked each year with 30–40 salmon and thė best salmon caught last season weighed 21lb. Use standard pattern loch flies, and crossed fingers. Just the place to escape from everyday cares. A comfortable hotel with a good trout loch close by – sounds about right.

ISLE OF COLONSAY

LOCH FADA 61/385957
LOCH AN SGOLTAIRE 61/387975
LOCH TUIRAMAIN 61/392953

Permission: Isle of Colonsay Hotel, Colonsay, Argyll.
Tel: Colonsay (09512) 316

The Island of Colonsay is absolutely wonderful, peaceful and perfect, offering complete escape amidst spectacular scenery. There is a wide choice of accommodation, ranging from a first-class hotel to comfortable, well-equipped self-catering cottages. The Colonsay Fly Fishing Association has been formed with a view to protecting Colonsay loch fishing for the pleasure and comfort of future generations. In recent years the fishing has been abused, and the association is determined to bring malpractice to an immediate end. Fishing is restricted to members of the association and membership cards are available for a small charge at the Colonsay Hotel and at the shop at Scalasaig. Funds so generated will be used to preserve natural stocks of fish with a view to maintaining this asset for everyone. Loch Sgoltaire is only available on application to the hotel, but membership of the association gives the right to fish on Fada and Tuiramain. Sgoltaire is the best loch, where fish average 1lb. Fishing is from the bank and the west shore produces the best results. Fada is a long, narrow water, divided into three distinct areas and an average basket from Fada would be four trout weighing up to 5lb. Fada has a boat, and fishing from the boat brings the best results. Loch Tuiramain trout average 12oz and a good day should bring three or four fish. Use standard loch fly patterns. There is something for every member of the family on this lovely island and it is well worth considering for an 'away-from-it-all' holiday.

LOCH CHOLLA 61/380919
LOCH BREAC 61/358910
DUBH LOCH 61/371947

Permission: Isle of Colonsay Hotel, Colonsay, Argyll.
Tel: Colonsay (09512) 316

Have a cast, but don't expect much, because they are thought to be devoid of stock. Nevertheless...

ISLE OF TIREE

LOCH BHASSAPOL 46/973470

Permission: The Factor, Argyll Estates Office, Heyipol, Scarinish, Isle of Tiree, Argyll.
Tel: Scarinish (08792) 516

Loch Bhassapol, on the warm, romantic, Atlantic-washed island of Tiree, is a first-class trout loch. It is strictly private and fishing is syndicated. However, from time to time days are available, and visitors should inquire at the Estate Office for further information. The loch contains brown trout and the occasional sea trout. The average weight of fish is 1lb and a reasonable basket might produce up to six. The south end of the loch is the best area to fish, and along this shore the water is not deep and wading is easy. Trout of up to 3lb 8oz have been taken and in recent years two rods had 26 fish in three hours' fishing. In spite of these dramatic records, Bhassapol fish do not give themselves up easily and are very selective about what they grab. Evening fishing is best and the flies to use include Grouse & Claret, Greenwell's Glory, Silver Butcher and Wickham's Fancy. Dry fly also works well. Try a Light Blue Dun. A perfect loch.

LOCH A'PHUILL 46/956420

Permission: The Factor, Argyll Estates Office, Heyipol, Scarinish, Isle of Tiree, Argyll.
Tel: Scarinish (08792) 516

This loch is syndicated and fishing is strictly private. Inquire at the Estate Office for the possibility of a day let. The loch contains brown trout and the occasional sea trout and the average weight of fish is 1lb. A good basket would be three or four trout, with the odd fish of up to 3lb. Dry fly does not work as effectively here as it does on Bhassapol, but other standard loch fly patterns all produce good results. The most productive area is along the shallow west bank, about 150 yards out from the shore. If water levels are low, then bank fishing this area can be just as productive as fishing from the boat.

ISLE OF BUTE

LOCH QUIEN 63/065595

Permission: The Bute Estate Office, Rothesay, Isle of Bute.
Tel: Rothesay (0700) 502627

Loch Quien is easily accessible and is to the west of the A845 from Rothesay. It is 1000 yards long by 500 yards wide and is stocked with rainbow trout. The average weight is 1lb and the best fishing area is in the vicinity of Quien Hill near to the small island. Bank fishing only. Standard loch fly patterns work well. This is a pleasant loch which produces good results throughout the season.

LOCH FAD 63/075610

Permission: At the loch.
Tel: Rothesay (0700) 504871

Fad is ¾ mile long by 350 yards wide and is easily accessible. Boat and bank fishing are allowed and the loch is being used as a fish farm from which it is being developed into a major new fishery. Rothesay

Seafoods stock and release fish from their fish farm into Fad and the present average weight of trout is 8oz–1lb, with larger fish of up to 4lb being landed regularly. Use standard pattern loch flies.

MULL OF KINTYRE

TANGY LOCH 68/692280

Permission: A. P. MacGrory, Main Street, Campbeltown, Kintyre, Argyll.
Tel: Campbeltown (0586) 52132

This is a small water on the west coast of Kintyre and is approached via the A83. The loch is a walk of about half an hour east of Tangy Farm and both boat and bank fishing are available. Tangy trout average 12oz and an average basket should produce four to six fish. The best fishing area is in the vicinity of the island at the eastern end of the loch, and along the north shore. Fish Tangy early in the season because weed can be a problem later on. The best cast is Black Pennell, Grouse & Claret and Kingfisher Butcher. Good sport in attractive surroundings.

LUSSA LOCH 68/710300

Permission: A. P. MacGrory, Main Street, Campbeltown, Kintyre, Argyll.
Tel: Campbeltown (0586) 52132

Lussa Loch is 2 miles long by ½ mile wide and is in a pleasantly wooded situation. It is easily accessible and both boat and bank fishing are available. Fishing is managed by the Kintyre Angling Club and visitors will find that members are very helpful and welcoming. Trout on Lussa average 8–12oz and a reasonable day should produce a basket of up to six fish. Best flies include Blae & Black, Grouse & Claret and Coch-y-Bondhu.

LOCH AUCHALOCHY 68/726226

Permission: A. P. MacGrory, Main Street, Campbeltown, Kintyre, Argyll.
Tel: Campbeltown (0586) 52132

This loch is to the north of Campbeltown and is an easy half-hour's walk from the road. It fishes best early in the season and the average weight of trout is 8–12oz. Expect up to six fish for the day. The most favoured areas to fish are in the shallows at the north end of the loch and both boat and bank fishing are available. From time to time Auchalochy produces trout of up to 2lb 8oz and the flies that tempt them are Cinnamon & Gold, Peter Ross and Wickham's Fancy.

LOCH GARASDALE 68/765510

Permission: A. P. MacGrory, Main Street, Campbeltown, Kintyre, Argyll.
Tel: Campbeltown (0586) 52132

This is a scattered loch, ½ mile long by 700 yards wide, to the east of Ballochroy on the A83 Tarbert–Campbeltown road. Two boats are available and the loch contains brown trout averaging 8–10oz. In spate conditions sea trout run up Ballochroy Burn. An average basket might contain six fish and standard loch fly patterns work well. The best fishing areas are at the south of the loch where the feeder burns enter, and down the east shore.

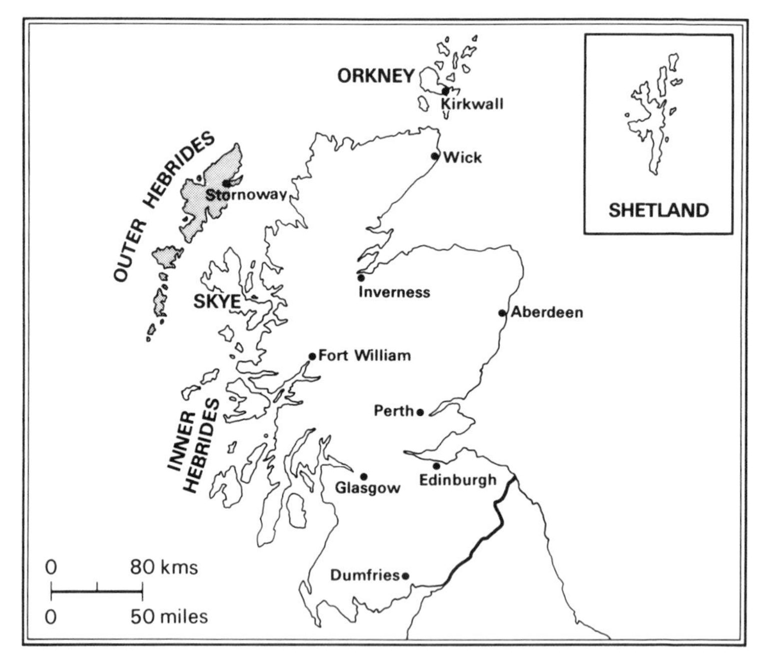

50 Outer Hebrides

12 Outer Hebrides

I once started to try to count all the lochs and lochans of the Outer Hebrides. When I got to about 2000 I gave up and decided just to be grateful. It is not possible, in this book, to describe all the trout fishing available. Look at a map and you will see what I mean. Benbecula and North Uist seem to be mostly water and all the Hebridean lochs contain wild brown trout which range from three to the pound up to fine fish of 5lb and more. I hope that the lochs I have described will help you to begin to explore this angling paradise. No doubt, you will soon discover your own favourites. Wherever you fish you will be enchanted by the magical beauty of these lovely 'islands on the edge of the world'. Time seems to pass more slowly in the Hebrides. On some crofts crops are still harvested by hand sickle and the smell of peat fires lingers in the soft air. In spring and early summer the machair lands of South Uist burst into a riot of colour that lays a magic carpet of wild flowers extending miles along the west coast. Climb Hecla on South Uist and marvel at the view: northwards to the mountains of Harris; southwards, Heaval and Barra; eastwards, the Cullin on Skye; westwards, a distant glimpse of sad St Kilda. There are few more wonderful places for a fishing holiday. Once you have visited them, you will return, as I do, again and again – always finding new pleasure.

ISLE OF LEWIS

LOCH LANGAVAT 8/215440

Permission: Sportsworld, 1-3 Francis Street, Stornoway.
Tel: Stornoway (0851) 705464

Loch Langavat lies to the north of Carloway on the A858. Turn left just past the village. Langavat is ½ mile in length. There are two long bays at the south end, guarded by a small island, and a further bay running northwards. It is an easy walk from the road and trout of up to 4lb have been caught here with baskets of three fish weighing 5lb. The average weight is 12oz. Not a loch for beginners but if you do hook a trout you will remember its strength and quality for a long time. Fish the peninsula which separates the two finger-like bays at the south end. A good north-east wind seems to 'move' the fish and large, dark patterns of fly work best.

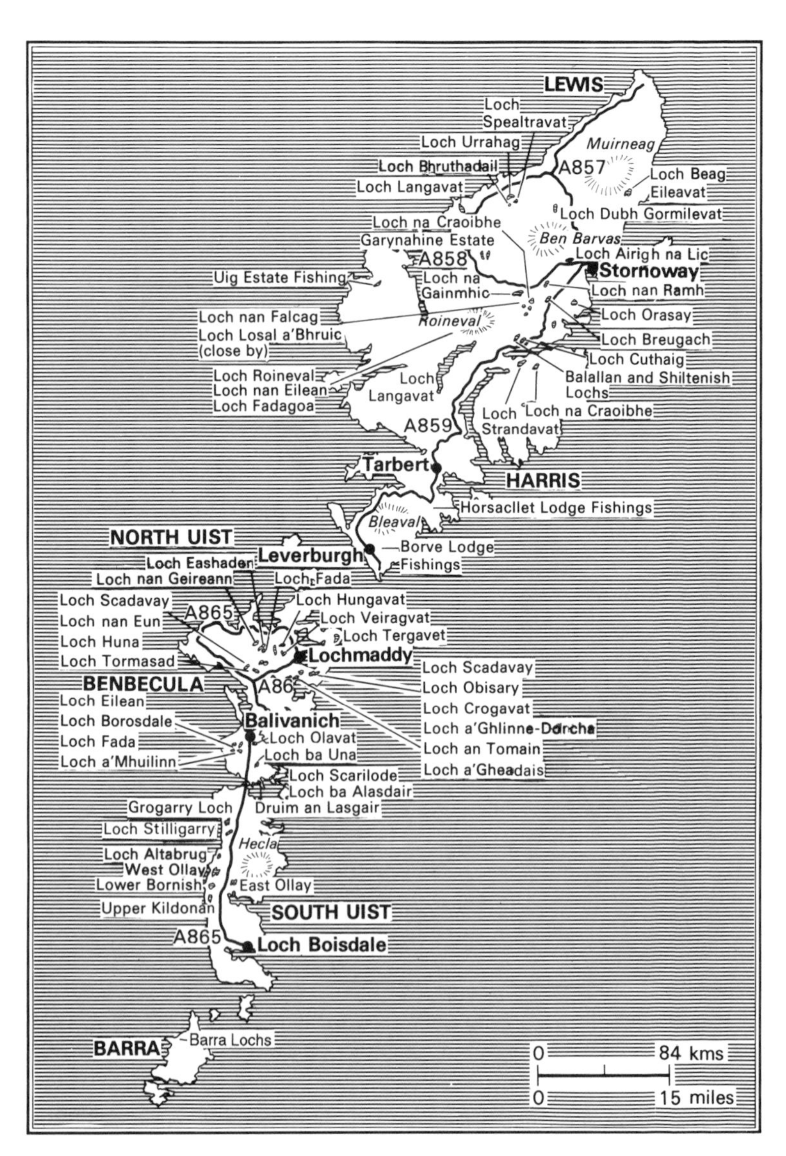

51 Outer Hebrides

THE PENTLAND ROAD LOCHS

LOCH CEANN ALLAVAT 8/276390
LOCH AIRIGH SEIBH 8/260386
LOCH AN TUIM 8/255358
LOCH ALMAISTEAN 8/220396
LOCH BORADALE 8/214414

Permission: Sportsworld, 1-3 Francis Street, Stornoway.
Tel: Stornoway (0851) 705464

The Pentland Road runs across Lewis from Carloway in the west to near Stornoway in the east. The moor to the north, in the vicinity of Beinn Bragar (261m), Beinn Rahacliet (248m) and Beinn Choinnich (210m), is scattered with trout lochs and deserted, ruined shielings. Eastwards from Pentland Road lie a further astonishing array of good fishing waters. The principal lochs are noted above and all contain trout which vary in size from modest 6-oz fish to the trout of up to 2lb produced by Loch Ceann Allavat. Most of these remote waters are rarely fished so information is sparse. Certainly, you could stumble into a fish for the glass case here, so always be prepared for that violent, heart-stopping tug.

LOCH VATANDIP 8/350336

Permission: Sportsworld, 1-3 Francis Street, Stornoway.
Tel: Stornoway (0851) 705464

This excellent little loch lies 5 miles from Stornoway on the A858, at the eastern end of Pentland Road. The loch covers 56 acres and two boats are available for hire, from Sportsworld in Stornoway. Vatandip fishes best early in the season, April and May being the most productive months. Trout average 6–12oz but much larger fish are caught. In March 1991 a trout of 2lb 12oz was taken on a size 10 Black Ke-He and trout of up to 1lb 8oz were also caught. This is an easily accessible loch, ideal for an evening's sport. Book in advance.

LOCH NA GAINMHICH 8/285295

Permission: Sportsworld, 1-3 Francis Street, Stornoway.
Tel: Stornoway (0851) 705464

This loch is 1 mile long by 400 yards wide and is a 15-minute walk from the A858 south of Lochganvich. Inquire in the village about boats since one may be available from time to time. The best areas to fish are round the north-east and north-west shores. The southern bay is also good and most of the larger trout are caught here. Fish average 8–12oz, with the odd one of over 1lb. They fight very well and an average day should produce four to six fish. Most popular flies include Blue Zulu, Teal & Green and Black Pennell. Several other small lochs lying to the south all contain trout of about 8oz and offer great sport if things are quiet on Gainmhich.

LOCH NAN RAMH — 8/327300

Permission: Sportsworld, 1-3 Francis Street, Stornoway.
Tel: Stornoway (0851) 705464

Loch nan Ramh is a small loch 6 miles from Stornoway by the side of the A858. Trout average 12oz and a day's fishing might account for three or four fish. The most productive area is along the roadside bank. Pay particular attention to the area round the large rock. Flies should include Teal & Green, Mallard & Claret, Silver Butcher and Invicta. Bank fishing only and waders are really required if you are to cover the water properly. But take care as there are areas down the roadside bank where the mud is soft and dangerous. Recent sample catches have been: two trout at 1lb 14oz; two at 1lb 10oz; one at 1lb 12oz. This loch fishes very well in the late evening and the fish are great fighters.

EAST ARINISH WATERS

LOCH AIRIGH AN SGAIRBH — 8/408310
LOCH MOR A'CHROTAICH — 8/410305

Permission: Sportsworld, 1-3 Francis Street, Stornoway.
Tel: Stornoway (0851) 705464

These lochs lie east of the A859 Stornoway–Balallan road and involve an easy walk over the moor. An Sgairbh is known locally as Pipers Loch and a'Chrotaich as the Frying Pan. Trout average 10oz. On an Sgairbh, concentrate on the west shore, by the small island; on a'Chrotaich, the north-west shore produces best results.

LOCH URRAHAG — 8/325480
LOCH BHRUTHADAIL — 8/316460
LOCH SPEALTRAVAT — 8/313454

Permission: Sportsworld, 1-3 Francis Street, Stornoway.
Tel: Stornoway (0851) 705464

These lochs are situated near Bragar on the A858. The end of Urrahag touches the road 2 miles from the Lower Barvas junction. The two main lochs are separated by a causeway, the southern section being known as Bhruthadail. Spealtravat is joined to them by a short stream and this series of lochs is over 2 miles long. Urrahag is the most productive and the trout average 8oz, with the occasional fish of up to 1lb. There are similar-sized trout in the other lochs and the water tends to be rather coloured, but they fight well and an average basket should produce six to ten fish. An inflatable boat would be an advantage here since much larger trout are often seen rising, but far out of reach from the bank. Who says that trout are stupid? Standard loch fly patterns work well.

LOCH DUBH GORMILEVAT 8/365435

Permission: Sportsworld, 1-3 Francis Street, Stornoway.
Tel: Stornoway (0851) 705464

To the west of the A857 Stornoway–Lower Barvas road, Gormilevat is a ¾-mile walk over the moor. Park the car near to where the Barvas River comes down the hill and then turns north to follow the road. Walk out from here. The trout in this loch are of excellent quality and average 2lb. Fish of 4–5lb are also sometimes taken. Bank fishing only and take care round the outlet in the north-east corner: there is a dangerous bog there. Best flies are large, dark patterns, or reservoir-type lures; and fish them deep, because trout seldom rise to surface flies. Recent catches have included fish of 3lb, 2lb 12oz and a fine basket of three trout totalling 6lb 12oz. Not a beginner's loch but it is hard to resist the challenge.

WEST ARINISH WATERS

LOCH NAN SGIATH 8/362303
LOCH FAOILEAG 8/358298

Permission: Sportsworld, 1-3 Francis Street, Stornoway.
Tel: Stornoway (0851) 705464

An easy walk to the west of the roadside Loch Breugach (below) brings you to these two delightful waters. Park at the north end of Breugach and walk out past the ruined croft. You will come to a small, triangular lochan where you should stop for an experimental cast. Although it is very weedy, trout of up to 2lb have been taken here. Midway between Breugach and Sgiath, as you bear south-west, there is another small, dour loch – also worth a throw – where a fish of up to 2lb may be your reward. Trout in Sgiath and Faoileag are of excellent quality, average 10–12oz and fight well.

LOCH BREUGACH 8/375300

Permission: Sportsworld, 1-3 Francis Street, Stornoway.
Tel: Stornoway (0851) 705464

This loch is on the A859 Stornoway–Balallan road and is easily accessible. The Stornoway Angling Club manages the loch and has carried out improvements, although the loch has a reputation for being dour. However, the 1991 season produced some excellent results, including a fish of 2lb 12oz in May and one of 3lb 4oz in July. Other sample catches during the season were: ten trout from 8oz to 1lb 4oz; three trout for 4lb 12oz; and seven trout from 8oz up to 1lb. There are two boats available and bank fishing is also allowed. The best bank-fishing areas are the two points on the north shore. Dark flies work well and the average weight of fish in the loch is 12oz.

LOCH ORASY 8/390280
LOCH CROGAVAT 8/375272
LOCH OICHEAN 8/388271
LOCH BEINN NA GAINMHEICH 8/379280
LOCH AIRIGH NA T-SAGAIRT 8/380285

Permission: Sportsworld, 1-3 Francis Street, Stornoway.
Tel: Stornoway (0851) 705464

Orasy is a beautiful loch to the south of the A859 Stornoway–Balallan road. It is easily accessible from the B897 which runs down the east bank, and this makes it a very popular venue. Evening fishing produces the best results and trout average 12oz. Orasy also contains Arctic char. The northern half of the loch round the west shore, and among the scattered islands, are the best fishing areas and trout of up to 2lb 8oz have been caught. Even larger fish may be encountered on Loch Crogavat, which is joined to Orasy by a small stream in the south-west corner. Trout of up to 5lb have been caught here. Best flies to use include Peter Ross, Teal & Red and Butchers. Orasy's other satellite waters also hold some excellent fish and are all worthy of your close attention.

LOCH AIRIGH NA LIC 8/400343

Permission: Sportsworld, 1-3 Francis Street, Stornoway.
Tel: Stornoway (0851) 705464

This loch is just outside Stornoway and contains brown trout and the occasional sea trout. Brown trout average 8oz and a reasonable day should produce up to six fish. The best area is at the east end of the loch and flies to use are Silver Butcher, Kingfisher Butcher, Dunkeld and

Peter Ross. The loch is rather spoiled by the proximity of the town rubbish dump. Fish it for sea trout, but walk out into the hills for better sport with brown trout.

LOCH NAN LEAC 8/430485
LOCH NA FAING 8/424487

Permission: Sportsworld, 1-3 Francis Street, Stornoway.
Tel: Stornoway (0851) 705464

Drive north-west from Stornoway along the A857 Barvas road and park at 389453, by the bridge over the Cliastul Burn. Nan Leac and na Faing are a 3-mile hike north across the featureless moor. You must take a compass and map, otherwise, should the mist descend, you could spend days walking round and round in ever-decreasing, fishless circles. Both lochs contain trout which average 1lb, with heavier fish of up to 3lb occasionally taken. On nan Leac, the most productive area is along the south-east shore, by the remains of the old crofts. On na Faing, fish the south-west shore, round to the single island and the ruined crofts on the outlet burn. Bank fishing only.

COLL MOOR LOCHS

LOCHAN A'SGEIL 8/434435
LOCH AN TUIM 8/425435
LOCH FADA CAOL 8/437444
LOCH AN TOBAIR 8/435456
LOCH NA FOLA 8/444454
LOCH NAN LEAC 8/446458
LOCH AN FHEOIR 8/452460

Permission: Sportsworld, 1-3 Francis Street, Stornoway.
Tel: Stornoway (0851) 705464

Follow the B895 north from Stornoway to the little community of Coll. Just before the church turn left, past the school, to Lighthill. A peat road leads west, out onto the moor. Follow it, clutching your compass and map. Lochan a'Sgeil has the largest trout and fish of up to 4lb have been caught, but this loch has a reputation for being dour. The other waters are kinder, with a good stock of 6–8-oz trout and the odd fish of up to 1lb. Pay particular attention to an Tobair because it contains very silvery fish, some of which may be up to 2lb in weight. These lochs provide an excellent day out, fishing and walking, amidst super scenery.

LOCHS OF TOLSTA

LOCH MOR A'GHOBA	8/485472
LOCH IONADAGRO	8/513466
SOUTH BEAG SGEIREACH	8/500468
LOCH SGEIREACH MOR	8/490455
LOCH NAN GEADH	8/484464
SOUTH A'CHITEAR	8/480468

Permission: Sportsworld, 1-3 Francis Street, Stornoway.
Tel: Stornoway (0851) 705464

These lochs lie to the west of the B895 North Tolsta road and getting to them will exercise your lungs, legs and map-reading skills.

All the Lochs of Tolsta contain trout in the 6–8-oz class. South Beag Sgeireach (unnamed on the map), however, can produce trout of up to 3lb, although they do not give themselves up easily, but it is well worth trying. Similarly, South a'Chitear has also produced trout of up to and over 3lb.

LANGAVAT WATERS

LOCH LANGAVAT	8/525545
LOCH BEAG EILEAVAT	8/512540
LOCH MOR EILEAVAT	8/514535
LOCH VATALEOIS	8/520538
LOCH SGEIREACH NA CREIGE BRIST	8/545535
LOCH EILLAGVAL	8/528523
NORTH EILLAGVAL	8/525528

Permission: Sportsworld, 1-3 Francis Street, Stornoway.
Tel: Stornoway (0851) 705464

The starting-point for the Langavat Waters is north of New Tolsta, at the end of the B895 from Stornoway. There are dozens of lochs out on the moor and the principal ones have been listed above. All the Langavat Waters contain wild brown trout which average 6–8oz and are rarely fished. Consequently, for the angler who is prepared to walk for more than an hour over the moors, there could be the odd surprise. For instance, Creige Brist has produced fish of up to 5lb; narrow North Eillagval (unnamed on the map) has trout of up to 3lb and Loch Beag Eileavat has fish which average 12oz – and the odd fish of up to 2lb as well, particularly in the east section of the loch. Park at 541501, drag on the climbing boots and have a good day. You will not meet another soul.

THE GARYNAHINE ESTATE FISHINGS

Permission: Garynahine Estate Office, Isle of Lewis,
Tel: (08502) 209

The Garynahine Estate lies to the west of Stornoway, on the A858 and has more than 30 excellent trout lochs available for guests and visitors. Contact the factor regarding availability and access. The estate also has salmon and sea-trout fishing on the famous Blackwater River and when rods are not taken up by guests they may be available to visitors on a day-let basis. The estate has changed hands recently (1991) so make inquiries before fishing.

LOCH ROINEVAL 13/235225
LOCH NAN EILEAN 13/233235
LOCH FADAGOA 13/245235

Permission: The Factor, Soval Estate, Balallan, Isle of Lewis.
Tel: Balallan (085183) 223
Edward Young, The Soval Angling Club, Stile Park, Willowgreen Road, Stornoway.
Tel: Stornoway (0851) 703248

These are three of the many lochs in the vicinity of Roineval (218m) and are approached from Balallan on the A859 Stornoway–Tarbert road. The lochs lie to the north of Roineval and are full of trout which vary in size from 8oz to 1lb. Baskets of 20–30 fish are taken frequently and no one loch is particularly better than another. This is a perfect area, and a day out in the hills here will be one to remember. Good sport in superb surroundings. Flies to use include Black Pennell, Teal & Green, March Brown and Greenwell's Glory. Well worth a visit. The Soval Angling Club looks after 10 of the lochs in the area and also issues visitor permits.

LOCH NA CRAOIBHE 13/300277
LOCH NAN FALCAG 13/300270
LOCH LOSAL A'BHRUIC 13/290275

Permission: Sportsworld, 1-3 Francis Street, Stornoway.
Tel: Stornoway (0851) 705464

Reaching these lochs involves a walk of about half an hour from Achmore, to the south of Stornoway, on the A858 Stornoway–Garynahine road. There are dozens of other waters nearby, all of which hold trout, and this is a most attractive and pleasant area to fish. The three named lochs are linked and their trout average between

12oz and 1lb. Loch na Craoibhe is the best loch and the east side is the place to fish; but the small bays can also hold good trout and should be carefully explored as well. An average basket on na Craoibhe will consist of six to eight trout and much greater numbers of fish will be caught on the other lochs. Standard loch fly patterns will do and at the end of the day it will be hard to leave.

LOCH LANGAVAT 14/155130-225220

Permission: Grimersta Estate, Grimersta Lodge, Callanish, Isle of Lewis.
Tel: Callanish (08502) 262
The Factor, The Soval Estate, Balallan, Isle of Lewis.
Tel: Balallan (085183) 223
Scaliscro Estate, Estate Office, Scaliscro, Uig, Isle of Lewis.
Tel: Timsgarry (085175) 325

Loch Langavat is the largest loch in the Hebrides and is 8 miles long by about ½ mile wide. It is situated amongst some of the finest scenery in all of Scotland and the loch contains salmon, sea trout and brown trout. Brown trout are caught all over the loch, but some places are more productive than others. A good area on the north-west shore is off the promontory (185197), near the junction with Loch Coirigerod. The fish here average 1lb 12oz, have pink flesh and fight like demons. Further up Langavat, Boathouse Bay (224208) is not so productive for trout although it is a good salmon lie, particularly during the early months of the season. Morsgail Bay, below Scalaval Sandig on the west bank, is also an excellent salmon lie, and at the end of the season produces good brown trout. Probably the best trout fishing on Langavat is in the vicinity of the Dyke, halfway along the loch on the east shore. It gets its name from an old dry-stone wall which used to run from Arivruach on the A859 out to the loch. This wall has long since disappeared but the line is a good route to follow out to the loch from that side. Where the Dyke meets the loch is a great place for brown trout and many large fish have been caught here, with trout of up to 4lb not unusual. To the south of the Dyke, there are a number of delightful bays known as Aline Bays, and these should be very carefully fished. The south end of Langavat will also provide good sport. However, watch out if you are on the wrong side of the River Langdale when it starts to rain heavily. It can become unfordable within a hour and if so, will present you with a daunting walk back to civilization. Loch Langavat is a perfect loch to fish and standard pattern loch flies will do fine.

GRIMERSTA ESTATE

LOCH NAM FIASGAN 13/218285

LOCH AN OIS GHUIRM 13/227278
LOCH CLEIT STEIRMEIS 225270

Permission: David Whitehouse, Fishery Manager, Grimersta Estate, Isle of Lewis.
Tel: Callanish (08502) 262

The Grimersta Estate has a wide range of first-class trout lochs many of which may be available to visiting anglers from time to time. It is always worth asking, and some of these lochs contain very good fish indeed. The lochs noted above are the most popular and are reached by a vigorous walk up the Allt na Muilne burn, between Garynahine and Grimersta. All hold good stocks of hard-fighting wild brown trout which average 8–12oz; but in some of the estate lochs trout of up to 7lb have been caught. Standard pattern loch flies may tempt them.

SCALISCRO ESTATE

LOCH AN FHIR MHAOIL 13/183260
LOCH MOHAL BEAG 13/175257
LOCH SUIRSTAVAT 13/150253
LOCH UAMASBROC 13/140284
LOCH NA CRAOBHAIG 13/14094
LOCH SPAGACH 13/144293
LOCH TUNGAVAT 13/160288
LOCH FHREUNADAIL 13/168317

Permission: Scaliscro Estate, Estate Office, Scaliscro, Uig, Isle of Lewis.
Tel: Timsgarry (085175) 325

The Scaliscro Estate has a wide variety of excellent fishing, including sport with salmon, sea trout and brown trout. And the best place to stay to enjoy all this area has to offer is at Scaliscro Lodge Hotel, on the shores of Little Loch Roag. Excellent food and super accommodation. The principal estate lochs are listed above and all contain good-quality wild brown trout. Spagach can produce fish of up to 2lb and the average weight in most of the other waters is 8–12oz. Wonderful sport in wonderful surroundings and highly recommended.

UIG ESTATE FISHINGS 13/056333

Permission: Kenny Mackay, The Factor, Uig Estate, Estate Office, Uig, by Stornoway, Isle of Lewis.
Tel: Timsgarry (085175) 250

Uig Lodge has the salmon and sea-trout fishings on the River Fhorsa system and this is strictly preserved for the proprietors and tenants of

Uig Lodge. However, there are numerous trout lochs and permission to fish them is readily obtained from the factor. The most interesting loch is Suainaval, which is reported to have a large *ferox* population.

LOCH STRANDAVAT 14/255195

Permission: Sportsworld, 1-3 Francis Street, Stornoway.
Tel: Stornoway (0851) 705464

This is a long, narrow loch adjacent to the A859 Stornoway road, south of Balallan. The setting is superb, with the hills of Harris to the south and Roineval to the west. Fishing is from the bank only. Wading is safe and easy and trout average 8oz, with the odd fish of up to 1lb. Best flies are Teal & Green, Silver Butcher and Black Pennell, and an average basket should account for eight to ten trout. Fish the narrows below Sullanan Ard.

LOCH CUTHAIG 14/275215
LOCH NA CROIBHE 14/285220

Permission: Sportsworld, 1-3 Francis Street, Stornoway.
Tel: Stornoway (0851) 705464

These lochs are to the north of Balallan on the road from Stornoway and are approached via a peat track which begins just past Balallan school. Loch na Croibhe is the smaller of the two and has an ill-deserved reputation for being dour. The trout average 12oz and tend to leave it to the last moment before taking the fly, so make sure you give them plenty of time to grab. The best area to fish is down the west shore. A recent basket included a trout of 1lb 8oz and trout of over 2lb have been caught. Loch Cuthaig, to the west of the peat track, has fish which average 8–10oz and a good day should produce about six nice fish. Flies to use on both lochs are Silver Butcher, Dunkeld, Teal & Green and Grouse & Claret.

LOCH KEOSE 14/366223
LOCH NA MUILNE 14/362225
LOCH NAM BREAC 14/368234

Permission: Sportsworld, 1-3 Francis Street, Stornoway.
Tel: Stornoway (0851) 705464
Western Isles Tourist Board, 4 South Beach Street, Stornoway, Isle of Lewis.
Tel: Stornoway (0851) 703088 Fax: (0851) 705244
Murdo Morrison, Handa Guest House, 18 Keose Glebe, Lochs, Isle of Lewis.
Tel: Balallan (085183) 334

Loch Keose is one of the most beautiful lochs on Lewis. It lies some 10 miles south of Stornoway and is best approached from the village of Keose Glebe, off the A859, just south of Soval Lodge. The loch has an area of 90 acres and is 3/4 mile long by 250 yards wide. There are two lovely islands upon which visitors are allowed to land. The smaller, northernmost island is a perfect place for a picnic. The loch has a large natural population of well-conditioned brown trout averaging 8oz which are fierce fighters. Boats and fishing tackle are available for hire at Handa Guest House – which is an excellent centre for launching a concentrated assault on Keose and the hundreds of other lochs nearby.

LOCH NA CRAOIBHE 14/300182

Permission: Sportsworld, 1-3 Francis Street, Stornoway.
Tel: Stornoway (0851) 705464
Western Isles Tourist Board, 4 South Beach Street, Stornoway, Isle of Lewis.
Tel: Stornoway (0851) 703088 Fax: (0851) 705244
Murdo Morrison, Handa Guest House, 18 Keose Glebe, Lochs, Isle of Lewis.
Tel: Balallan (085183) 334

This is an excellent loch in magnificent surroundings, approached from the B8060 Balallan–Kershader road. There is a 10-minute walk from the road to the loch and the trout average 12oz. The west and south shores fish best and a good cast to begin with would be Black Pennell, Teal & Black and Bloody Butcher. Fishing is from the bank only and trout of up to 2lb are caught. A good day should account for four to six trout. Re-seeding nearby seems to have improved the fishing on this loch and it fishes best early in the season.

HARRIS

BORVE LODGE ESTATE FISHINGS 18/031947

Permission: Tony Scherr, The Factor, Borve Lodge Estate, Scarista, Isle of Harris.
Tel: Scarista (085985) 202

Borve is at the southern end of Harris and the estate has a vast number of small lochs and lochans, all containing small brown trout eager and willing to jump straight out of the water and into your frying pan – with the odd larger fish from time to time, to catch you unawares. Many of these lochs will not have seen an angler for years and each new water is an exciting adventure into the unknown. Borve is in a supremely beautiful area, with marvellous beaches and glorious scenery.

HORSACLIET LODGE FISHINGS 14/141965

Permission: Neil Macdonald, 7 Diraclett, Isle of Harris.
Tel: Harris (0859) 2464

The Horsacliet Lodge Fishings are beautifully situated amongst the hills of South Harris and offer salmon, sea trout and brown trout fishing. Fishing is let with the lodge, but from time to time day lets may be available. The lodge may be booked through C. J. Lucas, Warnham Park, Horsham, West Sussex, and it makes a delightful centre for a family holiday. The best trout loch here is Loch Drinishader, which is just over 1 mile long by 250 yards wide. There are lovely bays and islands and both boat and bank fishing are available. The trout are pink-fleshed, prawn-fed and average 8oz, with the odd fish of up to 2lb 8oz. Flies to use include Blue Zulu, Black Pennell and Invicta. Contact Neil Macdonald for further information on casual lets.

NORTH UIST

LOCH SCADAVAY 18/880660
LOCH OBISARY 22/900620
LOCH CROGAVAT 22/924627
LOCH A'GHLINNE-DORCHA 22/915625
LOCH AN TOMAIN 22/915595

Permission: Lochmaddy Hotel, North Uist, Outer Hebrides.
Tel: Lochmaddy (08763) 331

These lochs all lie to the south of the A865 Lochmaddy–Benbecula road, alongside dozens of other unnamed lochs, all of which contain trout averaging 8–12oz. Be cautious, however, since there is always the possibility of much larger fish and it is generally during a concentration lapse that the big one grabs. Properly exploring Scadavy could take some time – the shoreline wanders round for a distance of some 50 miles – and this lovely loch is said to contain an island for every day of the year, many of which have their own small lochans. Turn left at the road junction before the sea and follow the B894 out towards Drim Sidinish, to Loch Obisary, the best trout loch in the area. Obisary is a brackish water where the trout are of outstanding quality, and the loch is wonderfully situated beside the graceful slopes of Eaval (347m), the highest mountain on North Uist. Head for the east bay at 903613, behind the island of Eilean Leathann, for this is the best fishing area; also, explore the south end, and perhaps park the boat and walk over to have a cast in Loch Dun an t-Siamain. In the other lochs, watch out for sea trout; they run the tiny burns to the lochs from June onwards, so be prepared. This area is another world of peace and tranquillity and the fishing it contains would take years to properly explore. Take along the usual standard pattern loch flies.

LOCH EASHADER 18/805727

Permission: North Uist Angling Club, North Uist Estate Office, Lochmaddy, North Uist.
Tel: Lochmaddy (08763) 329

This is one of the best trout lochs on North Uist and is easily accessible from the A865. A good track leads from the main road to the loch, where the average weight of fish is 12oz, although much larger trout are taken. The loch is easily fished from the shore, where wading is safe and comfortable. The north-east shore fishes very well and it is possible to wade out 5 or 6 yards from the bank. Fish down the bay, past the remains of the old wall. The other good fishing area is from the headland on the south shore, below the whins. All the standard loch fly patterns work well and dry fly can also produce good results. Highly recommended for a super day out and the ideal place for a family picnic.

LOCH NAN GEIREANN 18/845725
LOCH NA CEARDAICH 18/853725

Permission: North Uist Angling Club, North Uist Estate Office, Lochmaddy, North Uist.
Tel: Lochmaddy (08763) 329
The Lochmaddy Hotel, Lochmaddy, North Uist, Outer Hebrides.
Tel: Lochmaddy (08763) 331
Department of Agriculture and Fisheries, Area Office, Balivanich, Benbecula, Outer Hebrides.
Tel: Balivanich (0870) 2346
D. J. Macdonald, 8 Clachan Sands, North Uist.
Tel: Lochmaddy (08763) 227

Nan Geireann is a large loch 2 miles long by 1/2 mile wide and it lies just to the south of the A865 at the top of North Uist. Na Ceardaich is a tiny off-shoot from the main loch, on the east side. The shoreline of Nan Geireann wanders in and out of bays and promontories over a distance of nearly 6 miles and the loch contains salmon, sea trout and brown trout. Brown trout average 8–12oz and the best area is in the large bay close to the road and enclosed by Aird Reamhar; salmon tend to lie further down the loch in the large bay on the west shore, close in; sea trout are generally encountered near to the site of the chambered cairn on the east bank. Use standard pattern loch flies.

LOCH SCADAVAY 18/855695
LOCH NAN EUN 18/845675
LOCH HUNA 18/814665
LOCH TORMASAD 18/820650

Permission: North Uist Angling Club, North Uist Estate Office, Lochmaddy, North Uist.
Tel: Lochmaddy (08763) 329
The Lochmaddy Hotel, Lochmaddy, North Uist, Outer Hebrides.
Tel: Lochmaddy (08763) 331
Department of Agriculture and Fisheries, Area Office, Balivanich, Benbecula, Outer Hebrides.
Tel: Balivanich (0870) 2346
D. J. Macdonald, 8 Clachan Sands, North Uist.
Tel: Lochmaddy (08763) 227

These lochs all lie to the north of the A867 Lochmaddy–Benbecula road and cover several square miles. They present an endless panorama of perfect bays, headlands and island-dotted lochs and lochans. The brown trout average 8oz and a day out here will be very rewarding – or perhaps several days, since there is so much water to cover. There is a regrettable and ugly fish farm on Loch a'Bharpa, where fishing is not permitted.

LOCH HUNGAVAT 18/872727
LOCH VEIRAGVAT 18/880072

Permission: Department of Agriculture and Fisheries, Area Office, Balivanich, Benbecula, Outer Hebrides.
Tel: Balivanich (0870) 2346
D. J. Macdonald, 8 Clachan Sands, Lochmaddy, North Uist.
Tel: Lochmaddy (08763) 227

These lochs are to the north of Lochmaddy, a short walk west of the A865. Good baskets of 8–10-oz trout are caught and fish rise well to all the standard pattern loch flies. Fishing is from the bank only but trout are taken from all round the shores, so fish anywhere with confidence. Golden eagle country – look north.

LOCH FADA 18/870710

Permission: Department of Agriculture and Fisheries, Area Office, Balivanich, Benbecula, Outer Hebrides.
Tel: Balivanich (0870) 2346
D. J. Macdonald, 8 Clachan Sands, Lochmaddy, North Uist.
Tel: Lochmaddy (08763) 227

The Lochmaddy Hotel, Lochmaddy, North Uist.
Tel: Lochmaddy (08763) 331

Loch Fada is 1½ miles north from Lochmaddy and visitors should park at Blashaval on the A865. Boats are moored at the end of the north-east arm of the loch (884711) and boat fishing produces the best results because the most productive fishing areas are round the many small islands scattered across Fada. Trout average 8–10oz and great sport may be had, particularly in June and July, which are the best months for all the Uist lochs. A very pleasant loch to fish and standard loch fly patterns will do fine.

LOCH TERGAVAT 18/925735
LOCH NA CRICHE 18/923730

Permission: Department of Agriculture and Fisheries, Area Office, Balivanich, Benbecula.
Tel: Balivanich (0870) 2346
D. J. Macdonald, 8 Clachan Sands, Lochmaddy, North Uist.
Tel: Lochmaddy (08763) 227

Loch Tergavat is the larger of these two lochs and contains good trout. There is a boat available on the loch, which is joined to Loch na Criche by a small stream. Approach via the A865 from Lochmaddy and turn right to Lochportain. About 2 miles from the junction, as the road begins to head due south, you will see the lochs on your left. Trout average 12oz and standard loch fly patterns will tempt them. A very attractive setting and a pleasant place to fish.

LOCH AN DUIN 18/890740
THE DEADMAN'S LOCH 18/892746
LOCH AN ARMUINN 18/902748

Permission: Department of Agriculture and Fisheries, Area Office, Balivanich, Benbecula.
Tel: Balivanich (0870) 2346
D. J. Macdonald, 8 Clachan Sands, Lochmaddy, North Uist.
Tel: Lochmaddy (08763) 227

Follow the Lochportain road from Lochmaddy, and Loch an Duin is on your immediate left. The boat is moored here and the loch stretches north in a long, narrow scattering of bays and points. Loch an Duin and Deadman's are joined and accessible by boat, but Loch an Armuinn must be fished from the bank. These lochs are very beautiful and remote and hold better than average trout. However, nothing is that simple, for they are also harder than average to catch. It is worth trying, though, since trout of 3–4lb are sometimes taken. Standard pattern loch flies work well. A splendid place to fish – with a good chance of seeing a golden eagle.

LOCH AN T-SAGAIRT 18/949725
LOCH NA COINTICH 18/964720
UPPER LOCH AULASARY 18/937724

Permission: Department of Agriculture and Fisheries, Area Office, Balivanich, Benbecula.
Tel: Balivanich (0870) 2346
D. J. Macdonald, 8 Clachan Sands, Lochmaddy, North Uist.
Tel: Lochmaddy (08763) 227

Loch an t-Sagairt is a roadside loch 3½ miles north of Lochmaddy, to the left of the road to Lochportain. Upper Loch Aulasary is to the west of t-Sagairt, and na Cointich is to the east of the road. All these lochs are fished from the bank and contain good numbers of 8–10-oz trout, with the odd heavier trout from time to time. The larger fish tend to feed deep and rarely rise to surface flies. A sinking line can often be used to good effect here. Again, a perfect place to fish, in marvellous surroundings.

BENBECULA

LOCH EILEAN IAIN 22/786535
LOCH BOROSDALE 22/783528
LOCH FADA 22/793530
LOCH A'MHUILINN 22/785523

Permission: Department of Agriculture and Fisheries, Area Office, Balivanich, Benbecula, Outer Hebrides.
Tel: Balivanich (0870) 2346

These lochs lie to the south of Balivanich and contain trout which average 8–10oz, with the exception of a'Mhuilinn, which holds very much larger fish. A'Mhuilinn is a narrow water and easy to cover from the bank. Wading is safe from either shore and the angler quickly gets the 'feel' of the water. Trout of over 2lb may be caught with standard pattern loch flies. Approach these lochs from the B892 at Aird.

LOCH DUN MHURCHAIDH 22/795547

Permission: Department of Agriculture and Fisheries, Area Office, Balivanich, Benbecula, Outer Hebrides.
Tel: Balivanich (0870) 2346

Also known locally as the Caravan Loch, Dun Mhurchaidh is the most frustrating loch on Benbecula, for it contains really excellent trout but is very dour. It is a shallow water and, all too often, as you stalk the banks huge trout may be glimpsed heading off for the middle, having been disturbed by your approach. The loch is reputed to hold fish of over 5lb and is always worth a visit. June evenings, with a good wind to disguise evil intent, are the best time to attack.

DRUIM AN LASGAIR 22/895495

Permission: Department of Agriculture and Fisheries, Area Office, Balivanich, Benbecula, Outer Hebrides.
Tel: Balivanich (0870) 2346

This is a small loch at the end of a farm road and anglers should request permission from the farmer before using the road. Turn left from the A865 and onto the B891, just north of Greagorry. This loch is easily fished from the bank and the best areas are along the west and north-east shores. The loch becomes weedy the further down you go, and best results come from the top end. Standard pattern loch flies will do and trout average 12oz–1lb. Ideal for a few after-dinner casts.

LOCH OLAVAT 22/818528

Permission: South Uist Angling Club, Colin Campbell Sports, Balivanich, Benbecula, Outer Hebrides.
Tel: Balivanich (0870) 2236
John Kennedy, Bornish Post Office and General Stores, Bornish, South Uist, Outer Hebrides.
Tel: Bornish (08785) 366

Loch Olavat is a roadside loch south of Gramsdale. The northern end of the loch touches the A865. The loch is 1 mile long by ½ mile wide and the best fishing areas are near the islands and along the north bank and east shores. Loch Olavat holds good stocks of 8–10-oz trout, and a few larger fish. Standard pattern loch flies work well.

EAST LOCH OLAVAT 22/797513
WEST LOCH OLAVAT 22/805504

Permission: South Uist Angling Club, Colin Campbell Sports, Balivanich, Benbecula, Outer Hebrides.
Tel: Balivanich (0870) 2236
John Kennedy, Bornish Post Office and General Stores, Bornish, South

Uist, Outer Hebrides.
Tel: Bornish (08785) 366

It may be confusing, but it is worth making sure that you are on the correct Olavat, because West Olavat is the best of the Benbecula trout lochs. However, I prefer East Olavat, perhaps because it is more scenic and less public, and it also contains excellent, hard-fighting trout. Both waters are great fun and always worth a visit.

LOCH BA UNA 22/818525

Permission: South Uist Angling Club, Colin Campbell Sports, Balivanich, Benbecula, Outer Hebrides.
Tel: Balivanich (0870) 2236
John Kennedy, Bornish Post Office and General Stores, Bornish, South Uist, Outer Hebrides.
Tel: Bornish (08785) 366

Ba Una can be reached via a peat track and it is possible to drive to the lochside. This track is to the east of the A865, 1½ miles south from the garage at Gramsdale. This is a delightful little loch where trout average 8oz and rise readily to standard pattern loch flies. Trout of over 1lb are sometimes caught as well and wading is easy. The best areas to fish are along the north and east shores. The east shore is backed by a steep bank, but there are rocky points and patches of shingle from which you may cast. Baskets of eight to ten trout are often taken and this is the ideal loch for beginners, and for a family fishing picnic.

LOCH SCARILODE 22/847523

Permission: South Uist Angling Club, Colin Campbell Sports, Balivanich, Benbecula, Outer Hebrides.
Tel: Balivanich (0870) 2236
John Kennedy, Bornish Post Office and General Stores, Bornish, South Uist, Outer Hebrides.
Tel: Bornish (08785) 366

Follow the same route as for Ba Una, along the peat track south from Gramsdale. In recent years this track has been extended past Ba Una and it possible, with care, to drive another mile further east. Park the car at the end of the track and walk eastwards. A half-hour's walk should bring you to Scarilode, one of my favourite Benbecula lochs, surrounded by steep hills, rowan-clad and utterly captivating. This is not a large loch but it is deep and difficult to fish. The angler has to do a fair bit of clambering and scrambling to get to the best places, and the area where the track comes down to the water's edge is a good place to start. Left and right of this bay can also be very good. At the far end of the loch, near to where the feeder burn enters, there is a natural rock ledge under the water. This is a good casting platform – but don't go too far though. The best area is from the headland by the bay on the right-hand side of the loch. A promontory juts out into the water and it is possible to wade a short distance to the left of it. Again, be careful, for the water deepens quickly. Scarilode trout average 12oz, and some heavier fish are caught from time to time. They fight furiously, are pink-fleshed and very attractively marked. Standard pattern loch flies will do. I highly recommend this lovely little loch to you, one of the most beautiful that I have ever seen.

LOCH BA ALASDAIR 22/857495

Permission: South Uist Angling Club, Colin Campbell Sports, Balivanich, Benbecula, Outer Hebrides.
Tel: Balivanich (0870) 2236
John Kennedy, Bornish Post Office and General Stores, Bornish, South Uist, Outer Hebrides.
Tel: Bornish (08785) 366

Ba Alasdair is a large, scattered loch to the east of the B891 Sheiling–Craigastrome road. The loch can't be seen from the road but if you park (at 862490) and walk over the small hills to your left, you will come to the loch within about 10 minutes. The first part of Ba Alasdair is brackish, and an excellent sea-trout fishery. Above the main loch, and joined to it by a tiny stream, is Loch Druim na Lice, a perfect trout loch. Cross Ba Alasdair at the narrows at the southern end and climb up past the frying-pan-shaped lochan halfway up the hill. Stop for a cast, and for a cast in the little loch to the left. They might surprise you. Over the next rise is Druim na Lice, also known locally as Bluebell Loch. This super water contains large stocks of bright little fish which average 8oz and fight very well indeed. The hillside slopes sharply to the water's edge at the southern end, but there are several bays where it is possible to wade – and swim on hot summer days. There is a small island at the narrows, and, with care, it is possible to wade over and scramble through the undergrowth to the far end. From there it is just possible to manage a few casts towards the far bank, and fish always take. The north end of the loch is easier to fish and also offers great sport. Work round the north shore and on your way back south you will come upon one of the most attractive little bays in the world. Surmounted by a grand promontory, heather and rowan-clad, it is a perfect spot. Climb down to the rock ledge to fish, or don't bother – just sit and watch – it is utterly beautiful.

SOUTH UIST

CASLUB LOCH 22/82515

Permission: South Uist Angling Club, Colin Campbell Sports, Balivanich, Benbecula, Outer Hebrides.
Tel: Balivanich (0870) 2236
John Kennedy, Bornish Post Office and General Stores, Bornish, South Uist, Outer Hebrides.
Tel: Bornish (08785) 366

After crossing O'Regan's Bridge, the causeway between Benbecula and South Uist, take the second road on the left to Lochcarnan. Just past Holmar, by the cattle grid, you will see the east end of Caslub. A boat is moored here and Caslub should always be fished from the boat. Wading is very dangerous. The water is brackish and trout average 1lb with good numbers of 2-lb fish also taken, when conditions are right. There are other, huge trout in this loch, but they are very hard to catch. Concentrate round the islands, and when the tide is on the turn fish the narrows where the loch empties into Sheilavaig. On its day, fabulous sport, but more often than not, very dour.

UPPER LOCH KILDONAN 22/735280

Permission: Lochboisdale Hotel, Lochboisdale, South Uist, Outer Hebrides.
Tel: Lochboisdale (08784) 332

Upper Kildonan is 3/4 mile long by 1/3 mile wide and lies to the west of the A865 at Kildonan. Trout average 12oz and both boat and bank fishing are available, although bank fishing is not as productive as fishing from the boat. Good baskets come from this excellent machair loch, including 21 fish at 17lb, and trout of over 2lb are sometimes taken. There are several islands in the north end of the loch and this is the best place to fish. Use Black Pennell, Peter Ross, Black Zulu and Blue Zulu.

LOCH BORNISH 22/734294

Permission: Lochboisdale Hotel, Lochboisdale, South Uist, Outer Hebrides.
Tel: Lochboisdale (08784) 332

This is one of the best of the South Uist machair lochs, lying to the west of the A865. Follow the minor road out to Bornish church and park there. There is a gate in the left-hand wall, and a path leads to where the boats are moored. Trout on Bornish average 12oz and fish of over 2lb are not uncommon. The east end of the loch is the most productive area, and trout rise and are taken anywhere here. Soldier Palmer, Black Pennell and Silver Butcher are good flies to start with.

WEST LOCH OLLAY 22/740327

Permission: Lochboisdale Hotel, Lochboisdale, South Uist, Outer Hebrides.
Tel: Lochboisdale (08784) 332

This is an island-dotted, shallow, machair loch to the west of the A865, 3/4 mile long by 1/2 mile wide. West Ollay has the reputation of being dour, but it also contains some stunningly beautiful large trout. They average 12oz, but fish of over 3lb are often taken and the best flies to use to tempt them are standard patterns – and crossed fingers. Don't be put off by the weed. Fish carefully round the margins. Good fish lie there, waiting to grab.

MID LOCH OLLAY 22/755315

Permission: Lochboisdale Hotel, Lochboisdale, South Uist, Outer Hebrides.
Tel: Lochboisdale (08784) 332

Easily accessible, adjacent to the A865, with boats moored on the south shore. Mid Ollay is full of small fish which average 8oz, but it also can produce trout of over 1lb and the best place to look for them is at the

36 Quasimodo with East Loch Ollay salmon

west end of the loch, past the islands. Arrange your drift close to the shore – trout lie very close in – and use standard pattern loch flies. Expect good baskets of hard-fighting little trout.

EAST LOCH OLLAY 22/765313

Permission: Lochboisdale Hotel, Lochboisdale, South Uist, Outer Hebrides.
Tel: Lochboisdale (08784) 332

East Loch Ollay is adjacent to the A865 and linked to Mid and West Ollay by a small stream that passes under the road. Consequently, East Ollay can produce some really large trout, wandering through the system from the machair. Trout of over 5lb have been caught, in the autumn, but East Ollay trout are more modest in size, generally averaging 8oz, with the odd fish of over 1lb. East Ollay also contains salmon and has improved mightily in recent years – which is warranted by the fact that even I had an 8-lb salmon there, bank fishing, in 1989.

LOCH CEANN A'BHAIGH 22/766303

Permission: Lochboisdale Hotel, Lochboisdale, South Uist, Outer Hebrides.
Tel: Lochboisdale (08784) 332

Park by the telephone box (at 766298) and make for the east end of the loch – the most productive end. Fish average 12oz with the odd one of up to 2lb. In the autumn, there is also the chance of salmon and sea trout. Be ready.

MILL LOCH 22/747270

Permission: Lochboisdale Hotel, Lochboisdale, South Uist, Outer Hebrides.
Tel: Lochboisdale (08784) 332

Park at 744272, near the small island with the Dun. Mill Loch is a loch for all seasons, giving excellent sport with wild brown trout of 1lb–1lb 8oz throughout the season, and great sport with salmon and sea trout in the autumn. Another plus is the fact that Beinn a'Mhuilinn and Sheaval provide welcome shelter from high winds, which are not unknown in these parts, although the loch fishes best in good wind from the north and north-west.

LOCH DUN NA CILLE 31/745190

Permission: Lochboisdale Hotel, Lochboisdale, South Uist, Outer Hebrides.
Tel: Lochboisdale (08784) 332

This is a large loch to the south of Kilpheder. Park at the end of the loch, on the B888. The most productive areas are along the south-west shore, by the islands, and down the north-west shore. Na Cille has a reputation for being dour – and for producing trout of up to 3lb and more.

LOCH ALTABRUG 22/745346

Permission: Lochboisdale Hotel, Lochboisdale, South Uist, Outer Hebrides.
Tel: Lochboisdale (08784) 332

Pay particular attention to direction details, because finding the mooring bay on Altabrug can be difficult. Follow the road to Stonybridge, from the A865, onto the machair, and turn east. At the end of the road, park, facing the loch. You should see the boat. Altabrug is a fascinating loch, divided into a western, shallow, machair section, and eastwards, through the narrows, traditional peaty water. The machair section contains the best trout, and you should concentrate your efforts at the west end, by the rushes, and round the little island. However, the other end can also produce excellent sport, with trout of up to 2lb being taken. Watch out for underwater obstructions in the east end and row with caution. All the standard pattern loch flies produce excellent results.

LOCH STILLIGARRY 22/765380

Permission: Lochboisdale Hotel, Lochboisdale, South Uist, Outer Hebrides.
Tel: Lochboisdale (08784) 332

If I could fish only one South Uist loch, it would have to be Stilligarry. This is a classic, magnificent, beautiful water, surrounded by gentle machair fields, home for corncrake and an astonishing array of wildflowers. And really superb wild brown trout, which can reach over 4lb. In recent years the loch has had problems, happily now resolved, but in spite of any difficulties, to visit South Uist and not fish Stilligarry would be an unforgivable crime. The best fishing area is at the west end, and from the north-west shore. Drift across the loch and expect action at any point. Best flies are Black Pennell, Grouse & Claret and Peter Ross. Highly recommended.

GROGARRY LOCH 22/762395

Permission: Lochboisdale Hotel, Lochboisdale, South Uist, Outer Hebrides.
Tel: Lochboisdale (08784) 332

Leave the A865 at its junction with the B890 and travel west onto the machair. Grogarry is to the south of this track, ½ mile long by 300 yards wide, the premier machair loch on South Uist. Trout average 12oz and fish of over 3lb are not uncommon. There are excellent boats, and boat fishing brings the best results. Like all the machair lochs, Grogarry is heavily weeded in parts, but good fish use these weed banks both for shelter and for feeding, and trout may be caught almost anywhere on this fine loch. An utterly lovely place to fish, with stunning views eastwards to the South Uist mountains. Black Pennell, Greenwell's Glory and Silver Butcher all produce results.

EAST LOCH BEE 22/785425

Permission: Lochboisdale Hotel, Lochboisdale, South Uist, Outer Hebrides.
Tel: Lochboisdale (08784) 332

East Loch Bee is considered by many South Uist anglers to be the finest loch on the island – and by others, to be the most difficult. Without doubt, the quality of its trout is outstanding, and it produces some really magnificent fish. Trout of over 4lb have been taken and each season brings a good number of fish of 2–3lb. This a very shallow, large water, brackish, with a sandy bottom over a wide area. Boats are moored at 774433, close to the road, and the loch is easily accessible. Best places to fish are from the main island, southwards, and in the vicinity of the inlet from Loch Bee, adjacent to the causeway. The Shell Loch, joined to East Bee (but difficult to get the boat through to) can also provide first-class sport.

BARRA

LOCH TANGUSDALE 31/647997
LOCH AN DOIRLINN 31/643003
LOCHAN NAM FAOILEANN 31/710014
LOCH AN DUIN 31/703033
LOCHAN CADHA MOR 31/663000

Permission: D. Macneil, Clachan Beag Hotel, Castlebay, Barra, Outer Hebrides.
Tel: Castlebay (08714) 279

Barra is the ideal place to take the family if they do not fish. While the members of your tribe enjoy the beauty of this lovely island, with its unspoiled, wonderful beaches and warm climate, you may attend to man's proper function in life – the removal of trout from their natural habitat – with a clear conscience. Lochan nam Faoileann contains small fish which average three to the pound, while Loch an Duin, easily accessible and the local water supply, has larger trout and the occasional sea trout. Visit Cadha Mor for the glorious views and a good hill walk, and expect to catch bright little 8-oz trout. However, the real gem of Barra is Loch Tangusdale, also known as Loch St Clair, and this superb loch contains trout which average 2lb. They may be caught either from the boat or from the bank, and they fight like fish of twice their size. The loch has a dramatic little ruined castle on an island at the south end, and fish may be taken from almost anywhere in the loch. West from St Clair, towards the Atlantic, is Doirlinn, which offers barely a couple of casts, because of weed. Try it. Fish of up to 5lb lie waiting. Barra is marvellous and highly recommended.

Alphabetical Index of Lochs